Praise for

*Coming Back to Life*

Here is a blueprint for our present time—an honest and openhearted appraisal of our globally destructive and abusive behavior, and the work required to transform, to shift into a life-sustaining culture. Joanna Macy and Molly Brown outline the simple and essential choices we need to make, and give us the tools to make this shift. A vitally necessary book.

—Llewellyn Vaughan-Lee Ph.D., Sufi teacher and author,
*Spiritual Ecology, the Cry of the Earth*

The Dalai Lama nailed it: a timeless manual for Earth healers, *Coming Back to Life* inspires actionable hope. The new edition reminded me again how to replace despair with constructive optimism; blame with imagination, innovation and collaboration. As a former middle-school teacher, I say "Hooray!" for the new chapter designed to aid mentors and teachers on whom it will fall to guide those likely to suffer the worst consequences of the Great Unraveling: Generations X through Z and beyond. The meditations at the close of the book are both balm and goad. From their unique and clear-eyed analysis of our present crises and their causes, through exercises to catalyze the Great Turning, Macy and Brown's book models the changes it aims to facilitate in our hearts and minds. A heart-lifting read.

—Ellen LaConte, author, *Life Rules* and *Afton: A Love Story*

In a time of catastrophic climate change, Joanna Macy and Molly Brown offer a treasure-trove of principles, practices, poems, and prayers that must become as natural to us as breathing. Only this quality of spiritual nourishment can sustain us in our planetary hospice condition. These tools not only fortify us for the long haul, but intimately join us with the Earth, our bodies, and one another, thereby enabling us to experience an exuberant aliveness.

—Carolyn Baker, Ph.D., author,
*Collapsing Consciously* and *Love In the Age of Ecological Apocalypse*

Joanna Macy's and Molly Young Brown's new book is a spectacular and accessible blueprint for conflict resolution, environmental sustainability and a planet we all hope to embrace collectively and enjoy. The measures recommended in this book are ones that every individual and community can get behind. *Coming Back to Life* is a perfect title for a marvelous book.

—Michael Charles Tobias, president, Dancing Star Foundation

We live in truly perilous times. If you want to face what is happening with an open heart and mind, if you want to use your suffering to awaken to greater aliveness and compassion, this book is for you. *Coming Back to Life* doesn't just teach that our suffering can be the birthplace for a greater capacity for healing. It shows you how. It's a brilliant guidebook to the power you have at your core to let your light shine its brightest even in the presence of fear and planetary anguish. If you want true wisdom for tough times, if you want to connect with your joy even in the midst of sadness, if you want to see new life arise out of despair, *Coming Back to Life* has my highest possible recommendation.

—John Robbins, author, *Diet For A New America* and co-founder and president, The Food Revolution Network

A must for all who want to mobilize humanity in service of all beings. These concepts, exercises, and meditations have proven to work across generations, religions, ethnicities and races.

—Rabbi Mordechai Liebling, Director of Social Justice Organizing at the Reconstructionist Rabbinical College

Modern civilisation has brought the planet and untold numbers of species, including our own, to the brink of existence. To honestly witness this with our hearts, minds, and spirits wide open and remain able to react, adapt, and, when necessary, resist, often seems impossible. *Coming Back to Life*, the wisdom, clarity and urgency of Joanna Macy's lifelong body of incredible work shines brighter and more important than ever before. Our very lives now depend on being present in order to stay sane amidst this suicidal culture, and Macy shows us the way.

—Dahr Jamail, journalist and author

*Coming Back to Life* is the aptly-titled compendium of what has been learned over many years and can be shared with us all from the successful Work That Reconnects workshops that Joanna Macy and associates have offered to thousands of people from all walks of life. The book ranges from the purpose of such work and its role in what's called the "Great Turning" to the most specific details of how to conduct a successful workshop of this kind. It's a fine example of something the progressive world often lacks: a way to pass on what's been learned in one successful project or another so that this work can grow.

—Michael Nagler, president,
Metta Center for Nonviolence

*Coming Back to Life* is for me a treasured core text and I am among the many who are delighted with this upgrade. It distils a further sixteen years of experience, names more clearly the context we face and broadens the reach of this work with important new chapters. Thank you Joanna and Molly.

—Chris Johnstone, co-author, *Active Hope*

The earlier edition of *Coming Back to Life* has been a roadmap to me and to others at the Gandhi Institute for years, especially for strengthening our systemic thinking in relation to social injustice and for increasing our capacity to practice mourning in community settings. This new edition is a gift, like a visit from an old friend during a rough time. I feel so grateful to Joanna and to Molly for choosing to return to and refresh this work — a more timely, practical book is unimaginable. I pray that it strengthens our collective ability to lovingly take action on behalf of our descendants.

—Kit Miller, Director,
MK Gandhi Institute for Nonviolence

Every generation needs its sacred texts, its scriptures. Our journey through the damaged landscape and perilous time on this precious Earth requires a new kind of soul guide. *Coming Back to Life* gives voice to our generations' psalms, praises, and lamentations, our call for justice. It provides practices and meditations so we can make sense of who we are. This book is our wisdom text.

—Carolyn Raffensperger, executive director,
Science and Environmental Health Network, and
co-founder, Women's Congress for Future Generations

Reading this blessed treasure of a book is a healing experience. It names and honors the overwhelming emotions, paradoxes, complexities and desires that swirl deep in us as we face the reality of this time. And with gentle assurance it offers us actions that reconnect us to our deepest sources of well-being, energy and love, no matter the external realities. I am forever grateful that this book returns to our world at this time.

—Margaret Wheatley, author, *Leadership and the New Science,*
*Perseverance* and *So Far From Home*

If you ever feel pain or guilt for events in the world, dismay at useless cruelty, rage at environmental damage and waste, or powerlessness because you do not know what to do, this is the book for you. In *Coming Back to Life* Joanna Macy and Molly Young Brown show how these feelings need not be suppressed. Far from being an agonizing companion, they can be a friend and an aid at reconnecting with your heart and taking useful action.

—Piero Ferrucci, author, *Your Inner Will*

*Coming Back to Life* opens our eyes to both the difficulties and the possibilities — while inspiring our hearts and minds with practices that allow us to become wise activists in a very complex world.

—Lynne Iser, founder, Elder-Activists.org

Joanna Macy and Molly Brown in their expansive new book *Coming Back to Life* help us understand the urgency of and the steps to take for this necessary journey. This book is as challenging as it is breath-taking. Macy and Brown remind us over and over the importance of not just facing but claiming suffering, our own, other's and the planet's. Not to despair but to live out and embody our spiritual being in mutuality with each other and the world. They offer practical exercises to help us on our way. Rays of joy leap from the pages but without a guarantee that we will prevail. I found myself continually feeling grateful for this book and the wonderful beings who bring up the necessary challenge of reconnecting and coming back to life

—John Powell, director, Haas Institute for a
Fair and Inclusive Society, UC Berkeley

This legacy edition reflects forty years of highly refined, time-tested experiential group work that has now spread around the globe. Built on the wisdom and principles of Macy's life work, the volume offers a bounty of resources for teachers and facilitators engaged in social transformation. New chapters include insights and progress from expanding the work to children, young people, and activists of color. Macy and Brown provide clear analysis and guidance for cultivating a profound shift in perception critical to a viable future. They express great urgency about what must be done, yet their methods are grounded, powerful, and proven as a path of action. The creative strength of the work lies in its confidence in the human imagination as a basis for hope. This work is wisdom work, an inspired project for healing the wounded parts of the earth and the human psyche. It is filled through and through with the huge hearts and passionate dedication of all those who have been touched by this compelling vision and most visionary teacher.

—Stephanie Kaza, author, *Mindfully Green*

Joanna Macy is one of the great teachers of our age. It is cause for great celebration that an updated guide to her Work That Reconnects has now appeared in the form of a new edition of the classic she wrote with Molly Young Brown. As the world spirals ever deeper into disconnect, as we witness the natural world plundered and unravelling into horror, it becomes ever more difficult to muster the psycho-spiritual resources necessary to face the reality unflinching and compassionate, to swim against the current of egoism and denial and to represent life, speak for life, come back to life. The testimony and practices contained in this volume offer us priceless and practical resources for transforming despair into creative action and answer the questions: "how are we to live at such a time? How are we to represent the 4 billion years of living ancestry on whose shoulders we stand and whose future lies in our trembling hands?"

—John Seed, founder, Rainforest Information Center, Australia

Whenever I am leading group processes to feel both the urgency and revolutionary patience of this extraordinary moment on Earth, I turn to this book. The exercises poetically deposit just right amount of theory in the explanations, and for more depth, one can just flip through the chapters. First introduced to *Coming Back to Life* and the Work That Reconnects in the context of a 2014 leaders of color cohort with Joanna Macy and Patricia St. Onge, the words and energy of this book illustrate the interconnectedness of social justice, environmental, and liberation theology movements for wholeness.

—Sarah Thompson, executive director,
Christian Peacemakers Teams

Where there is bewilderment, Joanna Macy brings wisdom. Where there are division and discord, she speaks for the Other. Where there is despair, she joins hands to dance. Humankind is about to make a Great Turning in one direction or another. If we find a way to turn toward a deeper, fuller humanity, one of the reasons will be the fiercely compassionate genius of Joanna Macy. [This] book is a great gift to the reeling world.

—Kathleen Dean Moore, author of *Wild Comfort*
and co-editor of Moral Ground

THE UPDATED GUIDE TO
*THE WORK THAT RECONNECTS*

# COMING
# BACK TO
# LIFE

## JOANNA MACY
## MOLLY BROWN

FOREWORD BY MATTHEW FOX

new society
PUBLISHERS

Cover design by Diane McIntosh.
Cover Art: iStock — Nature Mandala : srdjan111

Printed in Canada. Seventh printing February 2021.

New Society Publishers acknowledges the financial support of the Government of
Canada through the Canada Book Fund (CBF) for our publishing activities.
Paperback ISBN: 978-0-86571-775-6
eISBN: 978-1-55092-580-7

Inquiries regarding requests to reprint all or part of *Coming Back to Life* should be addressed to New Society Publishers at the address below.

To order directly from the publishers, please call toll-free (North America)
1-800-567-6772, or order online at www.newsociety.com

Any other inquiries can be directed by mail to:
New Society Publishers
P.O. Box 189, Gabriola Island, BC V0R 1X0, Canada
(250) 247-9737

New Society Publishers' mission is to publish books that contribute in fundamental ways
to building an ecologically sustainable and just society, and to do so with the least possible impact on the environment, in a manner that models this vision. We are committed to
doing this not just through education, but through action. The interior pages of our bound
books are printed on Forest Stewardship Council®-registered acid-free paper that is **100%
post-consumer recycled** (100% old growth forest-free), processed chlorine-free, and
printed with vegetable-based, low-VOC inks, with covers produced using FSC®-registered
stock. New Society also works to reduce its carbon footprint, and purchases carbon offsets
based on an annual audit to ensure a carbon neutral footprint. For further information, or to
browse our full list of books and purchase securely, visit our website at: www.newsociety.com

LIBRARY AND ARCHIVES CANADA CATALOGUING IN PUBLICATION
Macy, Joanna, 1929-, author
      Coming back to life : the updated guide to the work that reconnects
/ Joanna Macy, Molly Brown ; foreword by Matthew Fox.
Revision of: Coming back to life : practices to reconnect our lives, our
      world / Joanna Macy, Molly Young Brown ; foreword by Matthew
      Fox. — Gabriola Island, B.C. : New Society Publishers, 1998.
Includes bibliographical references and index.
Issued in print and electronic formats.
ISBN 978-0-86571-775-6 (pbk.).—ISBN 978-1-55092-580-7 (ebook)
      1. Self-actualization (Psychology). 2. Human ecology--Religious
aspects. 3. Nature—Effect of human beings on. 4. Conservation of
natural resources. 5. Environmental policy—Citizen participation.
6. Environmental protection—Citizen participation. I. Brown, Molly
Young, author II. Title.
BF637.S4M22 2014                  158.1                  C2014-905770-9
                                                         C2014-905771-7

*In grateful memory of*

**Francis Macy**
(1927-2009)
who loved and named this work
and is ever at our side
as it continues to flower.

# Contents

# Permissions

The authors thank the following publishers and authors for permission to reprint material copyrighted or controlled by them.

Anita Barrows for "Psalm" from *We Are The Hunger*, unpublished manuscript 1998. Reprinted by permission of the author.

Doug Hitt. Untitled and unpublished poem, 2008. Used with permission.

Robinson Jeffers. "The Tower Beyond Tragedy" from Tim Hunt, ed. *The Collected Poetry of Robinson Jeffers, Vol. 1 1920–1928*. Stanford, 1988. ©1995 by the Board of Trustees of the Leland Stanford Junior University.

Bill Johnston. "I Take to Myself." Reprinted with permission of the author.

Aries Jordan. "Honoring my Pain." Quoted with permission of author. Published on her website: journey2womanhood.tumblr.com/page/3

Molly Lockwood. For unpublished poem in Chapter 11.

Alberto Ríos. "Who Has Need, I Stand with You." *Orion Magazine* (online), May/June 2010. © Alberto Ríos. Used with permission.

Susa Silvermarie. "A Thousand Years of Healing." Published with permission, susasilvermarie.com

The authors have made every effort to find the photographer of the Elm Dance in Chapter 6, but have been unsuccessful. If you have any information about this photo, please contact the publisher at the address below:

New Society Publishers
P.O. Box 189, Gabriola Island, BC V0R 1X0, Canada
(250) 247-9737

## Message from the Dalai Lama

ALTHOUGH IT IS INCREASINGLY EVIDENT how interdependent we are in virtually every aspect of our lives, this seems to make little difference to the way we think about ourselves in relation to our fellow-beings and our environment. We live at a time when human actions have developed a creative and destructive power that has become global in scope. And yet we fail to cultivate a corresponding sense of responsibility. Most of us are concerned only about people and property that are directly related to us. We naturally try to protect our family and friends from danger. Similarly, most people will struggle to defend their homes and land against destruction, whether the threat comes from enemies or natural disasters such as fire or flooding.

We take the existence of clean air and water, the continued growth of crops and availability of raw materials, for granted. We know that these resources are finite, but because we only think of our own demands, we behave as if they are not. Our limited and self-centered attitudes fulfill neither the needs of the time, nor the potential of which we are capable.

Today, while many individuals grapple with misery and alienation, we are faced with global problems such as poverty, overpopulation and the destruction of the environment. These are problems that we have to address together. No single community or nation can expect to solve them on its own. This indicates how small and interdependent our world has become. In ancient times, each village was more or less self-sufficient and independent. There was neither the need nor the expectation of cooperation with others outside the village. You survived by doing everything yourself. The situation now has completely changed. It is no longer appropriate to think only in terms of even my nation or my country, let alone my village. If we are to overcome the problems we face, we need what I have called a sense of universal responsibility rooted in love and kindness for our human brothers and sisters.

In our present state of affairs, the very survival of humankind depends on people developing concern for the whole of humanity, not just their own community or nation. The reality of our situation impels us to act and think more clearly. Narrow-mindedness and self-centered thinking may have served us well in the past, but today will only lead to disaster. We can overcome such attitudes through the combination of education and training. This book by Joanna Macy and Molly Young Brown contains a wealth of advice drawn from their own experience for putting such training into effect, both on a personal and on a public level. It gives me great pleasure to express my admiration for such work and to encourage readers not only to give their approval, but to act upon it for the benefit of all sentient beings and this earth that is our only home.

HIS HOLINESS TENZIN GYATSO
The Fourteenth Dalai Lama of Tibet

September 7, 1998

# Foreword

by Matthew Fox

A NEW MILLENNIUM, a time of planetary destruction but also planetary communication, the loss of legitimacy among our religious institutions, youth alienation, species disappearance — all these realities of our time require a book like this book and deep thinkers and activists like Joanna Macy and Molly Young Brown. This is a source book in the true sense of that word *source*. It returns us to our source, our spiritual roots, so that our action will come from non-action; our action will be from our freedom and our self-awareness and not from our acting out or projecting.

Joanna Macy, the root teacher of the Work That Reconnects, represents the best of her generation's (and my) efforts to replace the dualistic, secularist and anti-mystical biases of the modern era with compassion and loving action. Though descending from an impressive line of Calvinist preachers, Macy's deepest spiritual gift is her application of Buddhism's principles that acknowledge the deep suffering of the world and resolve to assist a Great Turning beyond that suffering. Like the mystics of old, she invites us into the despair and darkness and fear that grips all of us, dispelling the notion that denial, numbing or escape are valid options. She challenges us to analysis as well as action, and she gifts us with exercises that will strengthen our minds and hearts for the struggle ahead. Molly Brown's contribution, from years of coaching and teaching with tools of psychosynthesis, ecopsychology and the Work that Reconnects, is also welcome and substantive in rendering the book useful as well as challenging.

In many ways this book can be called a manual for mystics and prophets as we enter the 21st century. It is deep in its ecumenism and employment of interfaith and inter-spirituality practices, drawing not only on the rich Buddhist spiritual practices but also on exercises from other traditions and from the authors' imaginative experience in leading workshops in healing of despair all over the world.

It has been my privilege to be present at several of those workshops, often co-leading with Joanna, and I have always gone away deepened and strengthened by her gifts of spiritual leadership. I recall our work together on an ecojustice workshop in Munich, on bringing the virtues of darkness and awareness of suffering to the Findhorn people in northern Scotland, and our doing "Cosmic Christ and Buddha Nature" workshops in Santa Barbara, California and at the University of Creation Spirituality in Oakland, California. All these experiences rise to the surface on reading this book, and blessings of strength and spirit fill my consciousness on recalling them. That is what is so special about Joanna Macy's work — not just her passionate commitment (this may be a hint of the healthy zeal she inherited from her Calvinist predecessors) and not just her strong analytic mind — but especially her awareness that learning takes place not just in the head but in the heart and indeed with the benefit of all the chakras. With Macy, her process experiences are just as valuable as her theory. Praxis and theory come together in this book as it does for other liberation theologians the world over.

This book, deriving from four decades of inner work and of work in the field, emanating from the wisdom of our ancestors East and West and coming from the heart, mind and experience of a spiritual visionary and a committed activist for eco- and social justice, is a blessing for our times.

To write a book entitled *Coming Back to Life* implies that death is around us and has overtaken us. How can there be a return to life without an acknowledgment of death? This seems to be the case, namely that ours has become a culture overwhelmed with death — some of it real and much of it brought on ourselves by ourselves. When one sees the young lost, cigarette corporations targeting thirteen-year-olds to render them addicts, corporations growing rich on exploiting women and child labor in Asian factories with substandard working conditions, sexual exploitation on a grand scale, climate warming and its denial, the tragedy of Fukushima, one becomes more and more aware of the presence of death. Moral death. Spiritual death. Even physical death.

And so, in times like ours, one rejoices to see this book by two persons who have committed their hearts, work and considerable passion to the theme of resurrection, of ways out of death. How do we go about coming back to life, i.e. spirit, in these troubled days? Macy and Brown offer us both theory and practice on how to do this. This is a spirit book. This is spirit work. It heals and it gives us hope, thereby empowering us on the way to a healing life. Meister Eckhart, the great Dominican mystic and prophet of the Middle Ages who was condemned by the papacy because he supported peasants, women and other outcasts, once wrote that "a healing life is a good life." A healing book is a good book.

This book is a wisdom book because it operates from the perspective of cosmology and spirituality which are integral to wisdom traditions the world over. It does not settle for knowledge alone. In addition, because so many of its stories and teachings have come from or been tested by thousands of persons around the world in workshops of healing, that too assures the wisdom of the collective. Indeed, the wisdom of the community is strongly felt on these pages. Furthermore, the attention given to future generations not yet born adds to the role of wisdom in leading us to spiritual awareness and action — as does the passion for the more-than-human beings with whom we are called to share community.

This work is a healing work; it comes from healing women, priests in their own right, midwives of grace. It holds the promise to awaken healing in society and its institutions, in religion and in the hearts and minds of all workers for justice and ecojustice. Joanna Macy is one of those authentic voices in our time who is a prophet speaking out on behalf of the poor and those without a voice, the young, the dispossessed, the ecologically threatened. But she does not stop there. She also passes on this prophetic voice to others — she draws it out, she coaxes us not to be afraid and not to be in denial. She encourages us, that is, she builds our courage up to find our prophetic voice and to contribute as teams and as communities to the healing work our times and pain require. We are grateful for her voice and for our own. And we all welcome this book that is sure to unite many voices, hands and hearts. May it fulfill its promise! May we all fulfill our promise.

Matthew Fox is author of 31 books including *Original Blessing, The Coming of the Cosmic Christ, A Spirituality Named Compassion, Occupy Spirituality, Hildegard of Bingen: A Saint for Our Times* and *Meister Eckhart: A Mystic Warrior for Our Times.*

# Preface

by Joanna Macy

THIS IS A GUIDEBOOK. It maps ways into our innate vitality and determination to take part in the self-healing of our world. It presents a form of group work that has grown steadily since the 1970s, helping hundreds of thousands of men and women around the globe find solidarity and courage to act, despite rapidly worsening social and ecological conditions.

This work can be done alone and has reached into countless individual lives. It is most effectively done in groups, for its methods are interactive and their power synergistic. Workshops vary in length from one day to a full lunar cycle; but even in briefer time frames, such as in classrooms or churches, the practices can yield remarkable openings to the truth of our common condition. They can bring us into fresh relationship with our world, and not only arouse our passion to protect life, but also steady us in a mutual belonging more real than our fears and even our hopes.

I know that the Work That Reconnects belongs to us all; that makes me all the more grateful for the ways the events and preoccupations of my own life, as mother, scholar, activist, provided soil for its roots to grow and spread. The spiritual and philosophical nutrients in that soil included, from my Protestant preacher forebears, the life of Jesus and the words of the Hebrew prophets. For the last 50 years, that ancestral legacy has been worked over and illumined by the Buddha Dharma, for which I thank kind and noble teachers in Asia and a wide-awake graduate school in the US. While I was there, systems theory set my mind on fire. Its convergences with Buddhist teachings generated insights that prepared me for the impact of Deep Ecology and shaped the Work That Reconnects from its beginning.

My life flows into this body of work in practical, strategic ways as well. Five-plus decades of activism let me harvest lessons from the movements I took part in. When I worked for a fair housing ordinance in the nation's capital, and then became a speech writer for the Urban League, the civil rights movement expanded my life in widening circles. The Movement for a New Society, which changed our family life with its macroanalysis seminars, has left fingerprints all over the Work That Reconnects. The anti-nuclear power movement, taking me to and over the gates of Seabrook and Three Mile Island power stations, as well as into Chernobyl-poisoned towns, served as impetus and cradle of our Deep Time work. Yet another stream flowing into the Work That Reconnects comes from the Sarvodaya Shramadana Movement in Sri Lanka, and the years that produced my book about its Gandhian and Buddhist-inspired village organizing strategies. To me the two most enduring of Sarvodaya's lessons have been: work from the bottom up, and trust the intelligence of the people.

Each person, as he or she undertakes the Work that Reconnects, has such resources to offer. My coauthor Molly Brown draws from her childhood in Los Alamos, home of the Los Alamos National Laboratory, as well as her training and practice in psychosynthesis, her intuitive grasp of systems theory and her current work to defend Mount Shasta from corporate plunder. Other colleagues bring in their backgrounds and skills as artists, naturalists, ministers, teachers, farmers. May you who read this book find that the Work That Reconnects appeals to your own experiences and strengths.

From the first public workshop in 1978, it has been the aim and the genius of the Work That Reconnects to help people open their eyes, rather than tell them what they see and what they should think. Our aim has been to *unblock the feedback loops*, so people can trust their own experience and speak the truth of what they see and feel and know is happening to their world. This essential function of the Work That Reconnects — good medicine at any time — has been of enormous value when corporate-controlled government tightens its grip on the public mind.

In our work together on this new edition, Molly and I stopped and looked back over the years since *Coming Back to Life* first appeared. In the short time span since the US Supreme Court put George W. Bush in the White House, the changes have been swift, deep and dramatic, giving free rein to economic forces that despoil the Earth and impoverish her people. Now with greater need than ever for public monitoring and outcry, we have become a truth-deprived and fearful populace.

As these developments darken our future, our trust is in the mind's ability to discern and to choose. Despite all the very real as well as fabricated fears, despite the pace of destruction and the fog of distraction, it is still possible to turn back to the wellsprings of life. We can find, in the love that grounds us in the living Earth, clarity, courage and self-respect to free ourselves from bondage to a sick and death-dealing economy.

After 36 years, it is still the Work That Reconnects, but it's got a finer edge — like Manjushri's sword, ready to slice through the confusions and delusions that entangle the mind. I like to picture its sharp tools cutting us free from all we do not need and do not want. I think of how its practices reveal what we *do* want — and how it's right there in front of us, waiting for us to reach for it, together.

# Preface

by Molly Young Brown

I FIRST MET JOANNA MACY IN 1987 at a gathering of Interhelp, an organization founded by Joanna's colleagues who wanted to help themselves and others respond to threats to their common survival. Our next connection was at a workshop with Joanna in the winter of 1991, where I learned of her vision of *nuclear guardianship*. I was especially drawn to Joanna's work because of my childhood in the Atomic City of Los Alamos, New Mexico; I felt a kind of karmic connection to the problem of radioactive materials and began to work with the Nuclear Guardianship Project that Joanna had inaugurated. When I enrolled at Starr King School for the Ministry at the Graduate Theological Union in Berkeley the following fall, I signed up for Joanna's class in Deep Ecology, which brought me more fully into the worlds of systems thinking, Deep Ecology and engaged Buddhism and helped me understand their common threads.

Soon Joanna and I were working together: editing (with Wendy Oser, Fran Macy and others) three pithy issues of the *Nuclear Guardianship Forum*, and teaching a year-long class in applied living systems thinking at the California Institute of Integral Studies. I began offering talks and workshops in this work through my connections in the psychosynthesis world, continuing to this day.

When Joanna asked me to coauthor the first edition of this book with her, I jumped at the chance to bring together my love of writing, my love of this work and my love for this woman. In his Foreword, Matthew Fox wrote of Joanna's prophetic voice, and her ability to pass it on to others. Writing these books with Joanna has helped me develop my own prophetic voice and build my courage to write and speak and act on behalf of Earth, something I have sought to do all my life.

I would like to share a little of my life story, to make clearer what has called me to this work. Being raised in Los Alamos, New Mexico gave me an intensive experience in what historian Hannah Arendt called "the banality of evil." It has taken me a good part of my adult life to fully grasp how deeply flawed were the assumptions of the scientific/military culture that predominated there — and how good and loving people could perpetrate such harm.

Los Alamos is nestled in the forested mountains of Northern New Mexico, so my childhood playground was nature. From an early age, I camped, picnicked and played outside, establishing a strong relationship with trees, mountains, creeks and critters. I was also subtly shaped by the Native American and Hispanic cultures in the region. But my family was part of a scientific community (although neither of my parents were scientists themselves), so I learned to worship the God of Science along with the Christian God. I remember going to Family Days Open House at the Lab, the rare opportunity to go behind the security fences and see a little of what people did there. The apparatus, the cloud chambers, the accelerators, the glove boxes and the tissues studied under microscopes enchanted me. I wanted to be a Scientist when I grew up. I wanted that access to the mysterious inner workings of the world.

I also learned that there was a correct way of thinking: *logical*, *rational*, backed by scientific data and framed within measurable parameters. If something couldn't be measured and replicated in the lab, it probably didn't exist. Even then, one would have to defend one's understandings and hypotheses against the rigorous (and often hostile) critique of other scientists. I learned that feelings and fantasy had little place in scientific thinking, and that I had best keep those kinds of things out of discussions. Feelings and dreams were fine for girls' slumber party chatter, but had no place in The Real World.

Nearly 50 years later, on a solo vision quest at the beginning of 1996, I saw more clearly than ever before how this "mere purposive rationality" (to use Gregory Bateson's term) distorted people's innate morality at Los Alamos — and led them to enable grievous harm to the world. I was finally able to break through my own denial about my community of origin and see how profoundly this distortion affected me as I grew up there. During the vision quest, I felt sick to my stomach and remembered how often I had stomachaches as a child, how I spent much time in the school nurse's office, especially during kindergarten and first grade. As I focused on sensations of discomfort and pain, so similar to what I had felt as a child, I found myself asking, "What is the secret? What is this deeply hidden trauma from which I have defended myself all my life?" And suddenly I knew.

My family moved to Los Alamos a few months after the bombing of Hiroshima and Nagasaki in 1945. I believe now that I knew, as a small child can, that something wrong was going on. I doubtless heard radio news and conversations about bombs and Hiroshima and Nagasaki. I must have known on some level that people in Los Alamos had something to do with what had happened there. I came to know that the town existed solely for the Lab to carry on atomic research, primarily focused on nuclear weapons, and instinctively I must have known that this work was wrong. Even so-called Atoms for Peace, highly touted in Los Alamos in the 1950s, was an elaborate self-justification for the main work of the Laboratory: designing weapons of mass destruction. The good that came from the Lab's work could have come anyway. It didn't justify the bad. As a child I *knew* all this at a deep unconscious level.

Yet from everyone around me, all the important people in my life, from the entire community, I heard only rationalizations, justifications and deceptions. We were special people doing important and special work, protected from the rest of the world by fences and guard gates. Even while I felt proud of the title Atomic City, I felt pain and confusion in my heart about its implications. Although I may never have consciously thought about this deep contradiction, I carried it in my body, primarily in my digestive system. I couldn't stomach it. But neither could I, as a dependent child, speak of it. How could I let myself know that nice, good people that I loved and admired were engaged in destructive work, when they themselves could not acknowledge it? How could I challenge the myth of my whole community?

I can play the tapes of rational justification in my head, and they still have the power to confuse me. "We had to invent the bomb before the Nazis did" and then, after Germany was defeated, "we had to stop the Japanese." We have all heard justifications for the bombing of Hiroshima and Nagasaki, and yet we know the deep anguish most of us feel for the massive suffering engendered by that so-called justified act. In Los Alamos, however, such emotions were taboo. Emotions might call into question behavior so elaborately rationalized by thought.

Los Alamos is not alone in this practice of covering up and denying its wrongdoing, and inventing elaborate so-called rational justifications for it. The whole structure of corporate capitalism participates in this kind of self-deception, as we ignore and cover up the enormous harm done to the environment, to our fellow creatures and to oppressed peoples around the world and within our own country — for the profit of a very few and the convenience of some. Too many law-abiding, church-going, family-loving moral people enjoy their sport-utility vehicles, their vacation cruises and their GMO-laced foods with little or no thought to the true costs of those short-lived pleasures.

Living within a society that denies the pain it causes engenders deep conflict within us, but the taboos against speaking of it, or even seeing it, are subtle, strong and complex. Being nice — even being *intelligent* — means going along with the communal deception, like the mutually shared trance of an alcoholic family. Yet we do ourselves and the larger world real damage when we go along with the taboos and deny the truth of our inner knowing, as I did for so long.

I believe we can cut through denial and take a good hard look at the dysfunctional economic system that has captured humanity and is destroying our life-support system. This is not who we really are: self-centered, arrogant, greedy, contemptuous of other humans and life-forms. No! We have been hijacked by an insane, alien culture of our own foolish making. Let's reclaim our true humanity: loving, generous, caring, connected and joyful, heroic, persevering, willing to endure suffering as part of life, heart-centered, creative and wise.

The Work That Reconnects as presented in this book can help us reclaim our true humanity. I am profoundly grateful to be part of the Great Turning to a Life-Sustaining Society, in the company of my beloved friend Joanna.

# 1

## To Choose Life

*How shall I begin my song*
*in the blue night that is settling?*
*In the great night my heart will go out,*
*toward me the darkness comes rattling.*
*In the great night, my heart will go out.*

— Papago Medicine Woman Chant

*I call heaven and earth to record this day to your*
*account, that I have set before you life and death, blessing*
*and cursing: therefore choose life, that both you*
*and your seed shall live.*

— Deut. 30.19

WE LIVE IN AN EXTRAORDINARY MOMENT ON EARTH. We possess more technical prowess and knowledge than our ancestors could have dreamt of. Our telescopes let us see through time to the beginnings of the universe; our microscopes pry open the codes at the core of organic life; our satellites reveal global weather patterns and hidden behaviors of remote nations. And our electronic surveillance capacity leaves no aspect of anyone's life safe from corporate and governmental scrutiny. Who, even a century ago, could have imagined such immensity of information and power?

At the same time we witness destruction of life in dimensions that confronted no previous generation in recorded history. Certainly our ancestors knew wars, plagues and famine, but today it is not just a forest here and some farmlands and fisheries there. Today entire species are dying, and whole cultures, and ecosystems on a global scale, even to the oxygen-producing plankton of our seas.

Scientists may try to tell us what is at stake when we burn rainforests and fossil fuels, dump toxic wastes in air, soil, sea and use chemicals that devour our planet's protective ozone shield. But their warnings are hard to heed. For ours is an Industrial Growth Society.[i] Our political economy requires ever-increasing extraction and consumption of resources. To the Industrial Growth Society, the Earth is supply house and sewer. The planet's body is not only dug up and turned into goods to sell, it is also a *sink* for the often toxic products of our industries. If we sense that the tempo is accelerating, we are right — for the logic of the Industrial Growth Society is exponential, demanding not only *growth*, but rising rates of growth and market share. The logic of ever-expanding need for resources and markets is generating what is increasingly recognized as a global corporate empire, secured by military threats, interventions and occupations.

The Industrial Growth Society generates great suffering worldwide. Buddhist social thinkers see that what is at work here are institutionalized forms of the three mutually reinforcing *poisons* at the root of all

> Just as a continually growing cancer eventually destroys its life-support systems by destroying its host, a continuously expanding global economy is slowly destroying its host — the Earth's ecosystem.
>
> — Lester Brown
> *State of the World, 1998*

---

[i.] We are indebted to Norwegian eco-philosopher Sigmund Kwaloy for this term. We use it as a more inclusive term than capitalism, because it also applies to state-controlled industrial economies premised on growth.

human suffering: greed, aggression and delusion. Consumerism can be seen as institutionalized greed, the military-industrial complex as institutionalized aggression and state- and corporate-controlled media as institutionalized delusion. It follows that we are confronting in the Industrial Growth Society universal errors to which all humans are prone, rather than evil or satanic forces. It also follows that once these errors become institutionalized as political, economic and legal agents in their own right, they attain a degree of autonomy extending beyond the control and the conscious choices of any individuals involved. This understanding can motivate us not to condemn so much as to work to free ourselves and others who are in bondage to these institutionalized poisons.

In any case, we are wreaking unparalleled destruction on the life of our planet. What will be left for those who come after? What is in store for the future ones? Too busy running to think about that, we try to close our minds to nightmare scenarios of struggle over what's left in a wasted, contaminated world.

We've come so far. The life that is in us has survived so many millennia of trials and evolved through so many challenges, and there is so much promise still to unfold — yet we can lose it all as the web of living systems unravels. Yahweh's words through Moses now bear a literal truth: "I have set before you life and death; therefore, choose life."

## We Can Still Opt for a Life-Sustaining World

We *can* choose life. Even as we face global climate disruption, world-encompassing nuclear contamination, hydro-fracking, mountaintop removal mining, tar sands extraction, deep sea drilling and the genetic engineering of our food supply, we can still choose life. We can still act for the sake of a livable world.

It is crucial that we know this: *we can meet our needs without destroying our life-support system.* We have the scientific knowledge and the technical means to do that. We have the savvy and the resources to grow sufficient quantities of real, unaltered food. We know how to protect clean air and water. We can generate the energy we require through solar power, wind, tides, algae and fungi. We have birth control methods to slow the growth of, and eventually reduce, human population. We have the technical and social mechanisms to dismantle weapons, deflect wars and give everyone a voice in democratic self-governance. We can exercise our moral imagination to bring our lifestyles and consumption into harmony with the living systems of Earth. All we need is the collective will.

To choose life means to build a life-sustaining society. "A sustainable society is one that satisfies its needs without jeopardizing the prospects of future generations,"[1] according to Lester Brown of Earth Policy Institute. In contrast to the Industrial Growth Society, a Life-Sustaining Society operates within the carrying capacity of its life-support system, regional and planetary, both in the resources it consumes and the wastes it produces.

To choose life in this planet-time is a mighty adventure. As people everywhere are discovering, this adventure ignites more courage and solidarity than any military campaign. From high school students restoring streams for salmon spawning, to inner-city neighbors creating community gardens on vacant lots, from First Nations peoples blocking oil production and pipelines on their ancestral lands to village women bringing solar and water-purifying technologies to their communities — numberless people are organizing, learning, taking action.

This multifaceted human activity on behalf of life may not make today's headlines or newscasts, but to our progeny it will matter more than anything else we do. For, if there is to be a livable world for those who come after us, it will be because we have managed to make the transition from the Industrial Growth Society to a Life-Sustaining Society. When people of the future look back at this historical moment, they will see more clearly than we can now, how revolutionary our actions were. Perhaps they'll call it the time of the Great Turning.

They will recognize it as epochal. While the agricultural revolution took centuries and the industrial revolution took generations, this ecological revolution has to happen within a matter of years. It also has to be conscious — involving not only the political economy, but the habits, values and understandings that foster it.

## Choosing Our Story

By *story* is meant our version of reality, the lens through which we see and understand what is happening now in our world. Often our story is largely unconscious and unquestioned, and we assume it to be the only reality.

In the industrialized world today, the most commonly held stories seem to boil down to three. We have found it helpful in workshops to present these three stories as all happening right now; in that sense, they are all "true." We can choose the one we want to get behind, the one that seems to hold the widest and most useful perspective.

1. **Business As Usual** is the story of the Industrial Growth Society. We hear it from politicians, business schools, corporations and corporate-controlled media. Here the defining assumption is that there is little need to change the way we live. The central plot is about getting ahead. Economic recessions and extreme weather conditions are just temporary difficulties from which we will surely recover, and even profit.

2. **The Great Unraveling** is the story we tend to hear from environmental scientists, independent journalists and activists. It draws attention to the disasters that Business As Usual has caused and continues to create. It is an account backed by evidence of the ongoing derangement and collapse of biological, ecological, economic and social systems.

> All together, we are changing from a society whose organizing principle is the pyramid or hierarchy to one whose image is a circle. Humans are linked, not ranked. Humans and the environment are linked, not ranked.
>
> — Gloria Steinem

3. **The Great Turning** is the story we hear from those who see the Great Unraveling and don't want it to have the last word. It involves the emergence of new and creative human responses that enable the transition from the Industrial Growth Society to a Life-Sustaining Society. The central plot is about joining together to act for the sake of life on Earth.

## The Great Turning [ii]

Let us borrow the perspective of future generations and, in that larger context of time, look at how this Great Turning is gaining momentum today, through the choices of countless individuals and groups. We can see that it is happening simultaneously in three areas or dimensions that are mutually reinforcing. These are:

1. Actions to slow the damage to Earth and its beings
2. Analysis and transformation of the foundations of our common life
3. A fundamental shift in worldview and values

Many of us are engaged in all three, each of which is necessary to the creation of a life-sustaining society. People working quietly behind the scenes in any of these three dimensions may not consider themselves activists, but we do. We consider anyone acting for a purpose larger than personal gain or advantage to be an activist.

### 1. Holding Actions in Defense of Life

Perhaps the most visible dimension of the Great Turning consists of the countless actions to slow down the destruction being wrought by the Industrial Growth Society. These take political, legislative and legal forms, as well as direct action. We call them *holding actions* because they attempt to hold the line, to buy time for systemic changes to take place. Holding actions can take various forms:

+ Documenting the deleterious effects of the Industrial Growth Society on ecosystems as well as on animal and human health and rights

---

[ii.] This term, the Great Turning, is a cultural meme that appeared in the 1980s and 1990s to convey the revolutionary nature of the changes seen as necessary for the survival of life on Earth. Craig Shindler and Gary Lapid used it as the title of their 1989 book (Craig Schindler and Gary Lapid., *The Great Turning: Personal Peace, Global Victory*. Bear & Co, 1989) advocating a turn away from war and toward peace. The term arose again spontaneously from role-plays in the Work That Reconnects, as people spoke for future beings in Deep Time practices.

- Blowing the whistle and exposing illegal and unconstitutional corporate and governmental practices
- Circulating petitions, writing letters to the editor and to officials, writing articles, blogs and books, lobbying legislators
- Giving talks, showing films, tabling in public places, organizing study/action groups
- Vigils, marches and other demonstrations of protest
- Bringing legal actions against corporations and government agencies
- Divestment campaigns
- Boycotting and picketing institutions and businesses to protest unfair and dangerous practices
- Maintaining a long-term protest camp, such as climate camps in the UK
- Blockading construction of ecologically destructive and military installations
- Civil disobedience, including trespassing and symbolic sabotage on government or corporate property, tax resistance, refusing to move when ordered to do so
- Providing sanctuary to people in danger of unfair arrest
- Fasting and hunger strikes
- Providing shelter, food, clinics and legal assistance for people especially victimized by the Industrial Growth Society

Practices, policies and institutions targeted by these holding actions include:

- Extraction, transport and refining of fossil fuels
- Nuclear power, nuclear bomb production and testing
- Hydro-fracking
- Uranium and other heavy metal mining
- Mountaintop removal mining
- Deforestation
- Genetic modification
- Dredge fishing, drift nets and factory ships
- Privatization of water (extraction and bottling)
- Chemically-based agriculture and factory farming

+ Animal abuse
+ Secret international trade agreements (e.g. Transpacific Trade Partnership, Transatlantic Trade and Investment Partnership)
+ Decimation of civil liberties and Constitutional rights, including reproductive rights, along with mass surveillance by corporations and government
+ Military invasions and occupations
+ Torture and rendition
+ Drone warfare
+ Arms industry and trade
+ Abuses of First Nations sovereignty
+ Mass incarceration, solitary confinement, forced feeding and the prison industrial system
+ Extended detention and deportation of undocumented people, including children
+ Human trafficking and slavery
+ Homelessness, hunger and joblessness
+ Profit-based health care and Big Pharma, including their campaign against herbalists and midwives
+ Assaults on state-funded social and medical supports such as Social Security and Medicare in the US
+ Corporate financing of political campaigns
+ Predatory financial capitalism in all its forms: credit card debt, student loan debt, subprime mortgages, hedge funds and derivatives

> Climate change is global-scale violence, against places and species as well as against human beings. Once we call it by name, we can start having a real conversation about our priorities and values.
>
> — Rebecca Solnit

This first dimension of the Great Turning is wearing. It is heroic work. When we're in the spotlight, it can bring respect and applause from the many who see what's at stake. We can also get stressed out of our minds by nonstop crises, battles lost, constant searches for funding and escalating threats and violence against activists.

Protests and civil disobedience become ever more dangerous as law enforcement officers — and the laws themselves — treat activists as terrorists, repressing dissent, abusing demonstrators and punishing whistle-blowers. Shock tactics, arbitrary arrests and police brutality are condoned, even encouraged. As the corporate empire is exposed and threatened, the violence of its response becomes more naked and indifferent to public opinion.

So we often take a lot of punishment for this kind of activism, and may need to step back to take a breather. Let's not feel guilty in doing so, for in truth we are not abandoning the cause. We are choosing to continue the work of the Great Turning in another form — the way the head goose, when she's tired, repositions herself to fly in the wind stream of the others, and another flyer takes her place.

Holding actions are essential because they buy time and save some lives, ecosystems, species and cultures, as well as some of the gene pool, for the life-sustaining society to come. By themselves, however, holding actions cannot bring that society about. For that, we require systems and structures more appropriate to our collective needs.

## 2. Transforming the Foundations of Our Common Life

The second dimension of the Great Turning is also essential in order to free ourselves and our planet from the damage inflicted by the Industrial Growth Society. It has two aspects:

1. Understanding the dynamics of corporate capitalism, including the structures of law and governance that support it
2. Generating structures based on the inherent authority and rights of We the People to govern ourselves and to protect the grounds of our common life

What are the assumptions and agreements that create obscene wealth for a few, while impoverishing the rest of humanity? What indentures us to an insatiable economy that uses our larger body, Earth, as supply house and sewer? What are the structures of law that make it illegal for local communities to define their own future and protect themselves from corporate harm?

> We are in an era of profound change that urgently requires new ways of thinking instead of more business as usual; capitalism, in its current form, has no place in the world around us.
>
> — Klaus Schwab, founder
> World Economic Forum

This is not a pretty picture. It takes courage and confidence in our own intelligence to look at it clearly; the rewards are great when we do. As citizens are discovering in a plethora of websites, blogs and publications, we can demystify the workings of the Industrial Growth Society. For all its apparent might, we also see its fragility — how dependent it is on our obedience and on deception, secrecy, surveillance and force.

In this second dimension of the Great Turning, we are not only studying the structural causes of the global crisis; we are also learning old and new ways to better serve the common good. These two efforts go hand in hand. They use the same mental muscles, the same kind of knowledge, the same itch for practicality. In countless localities, like green shoots pushing up through the rubble, social and economic arrangements are sprouting to free us from injustice and ruin. They may be hard to see at first, because they are seldom featured in the media. Not waiting for our national or state politicos to catch up with us, we are banding together, taking action in our own communities. Paul Hawken, in describing this upwelling of grass roots initiatives, called these actions "the largest social movement in human history." In the early 20th century, the Wobblies (as Industrial Workers of the World were known) struggled to "build the new within the shell of the old." The actions that burgeon from our hands and minds may appear marginal, but they hold the seeds for the future.

Some examples of the second dimension of the Great Turning include:

+ Study circles and symposia to explore and understand the workings of the global economy
+ Retrieval and creation of laws to protect the commons from privatization and industrial harm, formulating and claiming

Community Rights, the Rights of Nature, the Rights of Future Generations

+ Establishment of the Precautionary Principle[iii] as the legal basis for health and environmental policy
+ Cultural recognition and legal definition of the rights of LGBTQ (lesbian, gay, bisexual, transgender, queer) persons
+ People's Tribunals and Truth & Reconciliation Commissions
+ Restorative justice and conflict resolution to replace litigation and punishment
+ Holistic measures of wealth and prosperity, e.g. the Genuine Progress Indicator (GPI), Index of Sustainable Economic Welfare (ISEW), Social Progress Indicator (SPI), Gross National Happiness (GNH) to replace the dangerously misleading index called the Gross Domestic Product (GDP)
+ Renewable, localized, non-polluting energy generation such as wind, solar and tidal technologies
+ Land trusts serving the needs of local ecosystems and future generations
+ Intentional sustainable communities, such as cohousing and ecovillages
+ Permaculture courses; family and community gardens; farmers' markets, local food clubs; Community Supported Agriculture
+ Municipal composting, recycling and zero-waste programs
+ Citizen restoration projects reclaiming streams, watersheds, wetlands and arable land

---

*iii.* "When an activity raises threats of harm to human health or the environment, precautionary measures should be taken even if some cause and effect relationships are not fully established scientifically. In this context the proponent of an activity, rather than the public, should bear the burden of proof. The process of applying the precautionary principle must be open, informed and democratic and must include potentially affected parties. It must also involve an examination of the full range of alternatives, including no action." "The Wingspread Consensus Statement on the Precautionary Principle." Wingspread Conference on the Precautionary Principle, January 26, 1998. [online]. [cited June 8, 2014]. sehn. org/wing.html.

+ Holistic health and wellness programs; locally grown herbal medicines
+ Local currencies, Time Banks, tool sharing and skill banks that cycle resources within the community
+ Cooperative forms of ownership, including food co-ops, worker-owned enterprises, credit unions and state banks
+ Citizen radiation monitoring networks such as SafeCast, measuring nuclear contamination from Fukushima in the absence of government monitoring and reporting
+ The Occupy movement, demonstrating radical democracy in the center of town, occupying public spaces, providing free food, health care, education and talks; exploring consensus decision-making

The broadside below from the Community Rights movement in the United States, circa 2014, illustrates the originality and practicality of campaigns in the second dimension of the Great Turning.[2]

## Community Rights: First Steps in Dismantling Corporate Rule

Since 2000, the Community Rights movement has been spreading across the United States, one city, town, and county at a time. Communities are passing new-paradigm laws that:

1) strip corporations of all of their so-called constitutional "rights";
2) ban a variety of corporate activities that are legal but harmful to people and environment;
3) declare the inherent right of a community to govern itself.

These new-paradigm laws challenge existing legal structures that forbid communities to pass laws protecting their own health and welfare. Thus, each of these local ordinances is in itself an act of municipal civil disobedience.

### Imagine if ...

### We Change the Ground Rules

• No more playing by corporate rules.
• No more battling one corporate harm at a time.
• We no longer allow corporations to operate when they harm people and nature. ☛

### We Learn Our History

- Why has it been illegal for communities to pass laws that protect us from corporate harms?
- What can we learn from the American revolutionaries, the Abolitionists, the Suffragists, the Populists?

### We Define Ourselves and Our Responsibilities

- We are not merely consumers and workers. We are We the People. We are the sovereign people. We are guardians of life for present and future generations.
- Corporations are not "good corporate citizens". They are merely private property — legal fictions — business structures — and we will define them as such in order to protect the health and welfare of our communities.
- To do this, we will reclaim our language and our thought-forms from corporate culture.

### We Govern Ourselves

- Corporations have become a cancer on the body politic. They have to be removed from all political participation. No corporate money in politics. No lobbying. No corporate-sponsored "educating" of citizens.
- We the People have the inherent right of self-governance.

### We Meet Our Common Needs Democratically

- We don't need Safeway Corp to feed us. We can feed ourselves from local sources.
- We don't need Fox Corp and MSNBC Corp to tell us the news or Disney Corp to entertain us. We can inform one another and entertain ourselves within our communities and through citizen-controlled media.
- We the People can reclaim our self-governing authority to restrict the creation of business institutions to those that do not harm communities, people, and nature.

### We Define Rather Than Regulate

- Most regulations are written by the industries being regulated, letting "the fox guard the hen house."
- Let's start defining what we need and banning what we don't.

### 3. Shift in Perception and Values

It is hard to undertake the holding actions or initiatives described above unless we are nurtured by deeply held values and ways of seeing ourselves and the world. The actions we take — and structures we build — mirror how we relate to Earth and each other. They require a shift in our perception of reality — and that shift is happening now, both as cognitive revolution and spiritual awakening. This is the third dimension of the Great Turning.

> The deep imagination is also our primary resource for recognizing the emerging future, for "seeing" the visionary possibilities of what we can create right now — individually and collectively... It is our essential resource for all genuine human creativity.
>
> — Bill Plotkin

The insights and experiences that enable us to make this shift may arise from grief for our world that contradicts illusions of the separate and isolated self. Or they may arise from breakthroughs in science, such as quantum physics and systems theory. Or we may find ourselves inspired by the wisdom traditions of native peoples and mystical voices in the major religions; we hearken to their teachings as to some half-forgotten song that reminds us again that our world is a sacred whole in which we have a sacred mission.

Now, in our time, these three rivers — anguish for our world, scientific breakthroughs and ancestral teachings — flow together. From the confluence of these rivers we drink. We awaken to what we once knew: we are alive in a living Earth, the source of all we are and can achieve. Despite our conditioning by the industrial society of the last two centuries, we want to name, once again, this world as holy.

These insights and experiences are necessary to free us from the grip of the Industrial Growth Society. They offer us nobler goals and deeper pleasures. They help us redefine our wealth and our worth. The reorganization of our perceptions liberates us from illusions about what we need to own and what our place is in the order of things. Moving us beyond tired old notions of competitive individualism, we come home to each other and our mutual belonging in the living body of Earth.

> May a good vision catch me
>     May a benevolent vision take hold of me, and move me
> May a deep and full vision come over me
>     And burst open around me...
> May I awaken into the story that surrounds,
> May I awaken into the beautiful story.
>
> — David Abram

Some examples of cultivating new perceptions and values include:

+ Grassroots programs to raise awareness of racism in all its forms and transform attitudes, unconscious assumptions, habits and behaviors, e.g. "Unlearning Racism" and "White Awake"
+ First Nation peoples bringing their spiritual message to struggles against Tar Sands extraction and pipelines and the epidemic of open pit mining. The Idle No More movement includes public protests and fasts, enriched by traditional dances and prayers, and petitions to the United Nations.
+ First Nation leaders achieving a Permanent Forum for Indigenous Peoples at the United Nations.
+ Initiatives to promote understanding and celebration of the Rights of Mother Earth, the Rights of Nature and the Rights of Future Generations — and our responsibility to honor and protect those rights
+ Aboriginal teachings for the protection of sacred sites in Africa and Amazonia being put into writing for the development of an Earth jurisprudence.
+ Shamanic traditions, including sweat lodges and trance drumming motivating, guiding and sustaining activists.
+ Wilderness immersion experiences, including vision quests, helping participants to connect more deeply with wild nature, within and without
+ Creation spirituality in Christianity, Sufism in Islam and versions of the Kabalah in Judaism spreading their messages of the sanctity of all life.

+ Engaged Buddhism and similar currents in Hindu, Taoist, Shinto and other East Asian traditions coming forward to teach respect for Earth and the *interbeing* of all life-forms, as grounds for both spiritual practice and social action.
+ Ecopsychology expanding our understanding of mental health, including our needs for deep relationship to the natural world, and also of the psychological damage wrought by the Industrial Growth Society.
+ Ecofeminism, blending political critique with the women's movement, re-anchoring us in the natural world and refigures world and self in radically relational terms.
+ The environmental justice movement addressing the racism and colonialism evident in the disproportionate damage that the Industrial Growth Society inflicts on disadvantaged communities.
+ Music, visual arts, poetry and visionary novels, dance, theater and film increasingly expressing our interconnectedness, allowing more novelty to break through and enable us to trust more deeply.

Though we hardly have words for it, this cognitive, perceptual and spiritual revolution is occurring at a great rate of speed. These lines from the late California poet Robinson Jeffers capture the flavor of this awakening:

> ... I entered the life of the brown forest,
> And the great life of the ancient peaks, the patience of stone, I felt the
> changes in the veins
> In the throat of the mountain, a grain in many centuries, we have our own
> time, not yours; and, I was the stream
> Draining the mountain wood; and I the stag drinking; and I was the stars
> Boiling with light, wandering alone, each one the lord of his own summit;
> and I was the darkness
> Outside the stars, I included them, they were a part of me.

I was mankind
   also, a moving lichen
On the cheek of the round stone...
   ... how can I express the excellence I have found,
   that has no color but clearness;
No honey but ecstasy ...[3]

This shift in our sense of identity will be lifesaving in the socio-political and ecological traumas that lie before us. All honest forecasts are for very rough weather ahead. As distant markets and supplies dry up, financial institutions collapse and climate-induced disasters multiply, the shock waves washing over us could tumble us into fear and chaos.

The realizations we make in the third dimension of the Great Turning save us from succumbing to either panic or paralysis. They help us resist the temptation to stick our heads in the sand. They help us withstand the temptation to turn on each other, finding scapegoats on whom to vent our fear and rage. When we know and revere the wholeness of life, we can stay alert and steady. We know there is no individual salvation. We join hands to find the ways the world self-heals.

Though we can discern the Great Turning and take courage from its manifold activities, we have no assurance that it will unfold quickly enough. We cannot tell which will happen first: the tipping point beyond which we cannot stop the unraveling of the systems supporting complex life-forms — or the moment when the elements of a Life-Sustaining Society cohere and catch hold.

If the Great Turning should fail, it will not be for lack of technology or relevant data so much as for lack of political will. When we are distracted and fearful and the odds are running against us, it is easy to let the heart and mind go numb. The dangers now facing us are so pervasive and yet often so hard to see — and so painful to see when we manage to look at them — that this numbing touches us all. No one is unaffected by it. No one is immune to doubt, denial or distraction in relation to the severity of our situation, nor to doubt about our power to change it. Yet of all the dangers we face, from climate change to nuclear wars, none is so great as the deadening of our response.

That numbing of mind and heart is already upon us — in the diversions we create for ourselves as individuals and nations, in the fights we pick, the aims we pursue, the stuff we buy. So let us look at it. Let's see how it happens so we can awaken. The Work That Reconnects helps us open up our eyes, our minds and hearts. Then, reconnected with our deepest desire, we will choose life.

## 2

# The Greatest Danger —
# The Deadening of Heart and Mind

*It is the destruction of the world
in our own lives that drives us
half insane, and more than half.
To destroy that which we were given
in trust: how will we bear it?*

— Wendell Berry

*Our hope is that if we keep all the distractedness going, we
will not have to look at who we are, we will not have to feel
what we feel, we will not have to see what we see.*

— Judy Lief

THE GREAT TURNING ARISES in response to what we know and feel is happening to our world. It entails both the perception of danger and the means to act. As conscious, embodied beings endowed with multiple senses, we are geared to respond: instantly we leap from the path of an oncoming truck, dash to douse a fire, dive into a pool to save a child. This response-ability has been an essential feature of life throughout human evolution; it allows us to adapt to new challenges and generate new capacities. It enables whole groups and societies to survive, so long as their members have sufficient information and freedom to act. In systems terms, response to danger is a function of *feedback* — the information circuit that connects perception to action. Appropriate response depends on an unblocked feedback loop.

Now, however, perils facing life on Earth are so massive and unprecedented they are hard even to take in. The very danger signals that should rivet our attention, summon up the blood and bond us in collective action, tend to have the opposite effect. They make us want to pull down the blinds and busy ourselves with other things. Our desire for distraction supports billion dollar industries that tell us everything will be all right so long as we buy this car or that deodorant. We eat meat from factory-farmed animals and produce grown by agribusiness, ignoring the pesticides, hormones and genetic alterations they contain. We buy clothes without noticing where they are made, preferring not to think of the sweatshops they may have come from. We don't bother voting, or if we do, we vote for candidates we may not believe will address the real problems, hoping against all previous experience that they will suddenly awaken and act boldly to save us. Has our society become callous, nihilistic? Has it ceased to care what happens to life on Earth?

It can look that way. Reformers and revolutionaries decry public apathy. To rouse people, they deliver yet more terrifying information, as if people didn't already know that our world is in trouble. They preach about moral imperatives, as if people didn't already care. Their alarms and sermons tend to make people pull the shades down tighter, resisting what appears too overwhelming, too complicated, too out of their control.

So it's good to look at what this *apathy* is, to understand it with respect and compassion. *Apatheia* is a Greek word that means, literally, non-suffering. Given its etymology, apathy is the inability or refusal to experience pain. What is the pain we feel — and desperately try not to feel — in this planet-time? It is of another order altogether than what the ancient Greeks could have known; it pertains not just to privations of wealth, health, reputation or loved ones, but to losses so vast we can hardly comprehend them. It is pain for the world.

## What Is Pain for the World?

From news reports and life around us, we are bombarded with signals of distress — of job layoffs and homeless families, of nearby toxic wastes and distant famines, of more devastating hurricanes, floods and droughts, of ever-widening military offensives. These events stir fear, sorrow and anger within us, although we may never express such feelings to others. These deep responses arise by virtue of our connectivity with all life. To be conscious in our world today is to be aware of vast suffering and unprecedented peril.

Even the words — fear, anger, sorrow — are inadequate to convey the feelings we experience, for they connote emotions long familiar to our species. The feelings that assail us now cannot be equated with ancient dreads of mortality and "the heartache and the thousand natural shocks that flesh is heir to."[1] Their source lies less in concerns for the personal self than in apprehensions of collective suffering — of what is happening to our own and other species, to the legacy of our ancestors, to coming generations and to the living body of Earth.

What we are dealing with here is akin to the original meaning of compassion: "suffering with." It is the distress we feel on behalf of the larger whole of which we are a part. It is the pain of the world itself, experienced in each of us.

No one is exempt from that pain, any more than one could exist alone and self-sufficient in empty space. Feeling pain for the world is as natural to us as the food and air we draw upon to fashion who we are. It is inseparable from the currents of matter, energy and information that flow through us and sustain us as interconnected open systems. We are not closed off from the world, but integral components of it, like cells in a larger body. When that body is traumatized, we sense that trauma too. When it falters and sickens, we feel its pain, whether we pay attention to it or not.

That pain is the price of consciousness in a threatened and suffering world. It is not only natural; it is an absolutely necessary component of our collective healing. As in all organisms, pain has a purpose: it is a warning signal, designed to trigger remedial action.

The problem, therefore, lies not with our pain for the world, but in our repression of it. Our efforts to dodge or dull it surrender us to

> The truth that many people never understand
> until it is too late is that the more you try to
> avoid suffering, the more you suffer.
>
> — Thomas Merton

futility — or in systems terms, we cut the feedback loop and block effective response.

So let us explore two questions. First, what causes this repression, and then what that repression costs us and our world.

## What Deadens Heart and Mind?

What inhibits our experience of pain for our world, and the actions that it would summon? No external authority can stop us from feeling and sensing what's happening to our world nor force us to close our eyes to what's around us. So what stifles our responses, as individuals and as a society?

### Fear of Pain

Our culture conditions us to view pain as dysfunctional. There are pills for headache, backache, neuralgia and premenstrual tension — but no pills for this pain for our world. Not even a stiff drink nor a Prozac prescription really helps. To permit ourselves to suffer anguish for the world is not only painful, but frightening; we imagine it threatens our ability to cope with daily life. We are afraid that if we were to let ourselves fully experience these feelings, we might fall apart, lose control or be mired in pain permanently.

### Fear of Despair

A sense of some overarching meaning to our lives is as necessary as oxygen. We can face and endure tremendous hardships with heroic courage so long as we believe there is some purpose to our existence, some value to our actions. But the present planetary crises, if we dare to look at what they forebode, present vistas of such unprecedented loss as to threaten with absurdity all that we have believed in. So, fearing that our lives might be drained of meaning, we look away.

When we are brave enough to study the available data, they turn out to be more alarming than most of us had assumed. Many peace and environmental advocates carry a heavy burden of knowledge. It is compounded by feelings of frustration, as they fight an uphill battle to arouse the public. Yet they view their own frustration and despair as counterproductive to their efforts. They take little or no time to honor their feelings, much less mourn. In their role as mobilizers of the public will, they may feel they can't "let their hair down" and expose the extent of their own distress. The consequent and continual repression of feelings takes a toll on their energies that leaves them vulnerable to bitterness, depression, exhaustion and illness.

For people of religious faith, the prospect of losing hope is particularly challenging. "God won't let this happen," many think when faced with prospects of vast destruction and loss. Even to entertain such possibilities can seem to contradict our belief in a loving and powerful God, and in the goodness of creation itself. Are feelings of despair a sign of inadequate faith? Although every major religion calls us to open to the suffering we see around us, we tend to forget those summonses. Assuming, perhaps unconsciously, that our God is too fragile or too limited to encompass that pain, unsure whether God will meet us in the midst of such darkness, we hesitate to let ourselves experience it lest our faith be shattered or revealed as inadequate.

### Other Spiritual Traps

There are those of us on a spiritual path who consider feelings of distress for the world as obstacles to be transcended. Grief and anger over current social and ecological conditions are then seen as *attachments* and judged to be less valuable than experiences of tranquility.

Moreover, some spiritual seekers view the personal and the political in a sequential fashion, believing that they must achieve enlightenment or salvation before they can serve the world. "I'll find peace within myself first, then I'll see what I can do." Supposing world and self to be essentially separate, they imagine they can heal one in isolation from the other.

There is also the fear that attention to the world's suffering will only make it worse. That notion resembles a philosophical perspective called *subjective idealism*, which sees consciousness as more "real" than the phenomenal world. This can lead to a belief that contemplating the world's problems is negative thinking.

The understanding on which this book is based, however, is that we are inseparable from the world, and that the beauty and terror of our society co-arise with us. The crises facing us arise not from projections of our individual minds, so much as from our institutionalized ignorance, fear and greed.

### Fear of Not Fitting In

A sanguine confidence in the future has been a hallmark of the American self-image and a source of national pride. The successful person — commercials and political campaigns tell us — has an optimistic can-do attitude and unquestioning faith in Progress. In such a culture, feelings of anguish and despair for our world appear as a failure of character and competence. Sadness and regret are taken as a sign of weakness, while impassivity is seen as "cool." No one wants to be called emotional or soft or seen as a prophet of doom or a conspiracy theorist.

### Distrust of Our Own Intelligence

Many of us are reluctant to express our concerns for fear of getting embroiled in a debate requiring facts and figures beyond our command. The global economy encourages us to rely on so-called experts who tell us that there is no link between nuclear power plants and breast cancer, pesticide spraying and asthma, trade agreements and joblessness. It is easy to distrust our own judgment and intuitions, especially when others around us seem to agree with the way things are. This intellectual timidity, so useful to the powerholders, can override our own perceptions and judgments.

### Fear of Guilt

Few if any of us in the Industrial Growth Society are exempt from the suspicion that we are accomplices to far-reaching abuses. It is nearly impossible in today's global economy to feed, clothe and transport ourselves without unintended harm to the natural world and other people's well-being. Peter Marin wrote 40 years ago in an essay on moral pain:

> Many of us suffer a vague, inchoate sense of betrayal, of having somehow taken the wrong turning, of having somehow said yes or no at the wrong time and to the wrong things, of having somehow taken upon ourselves a general kind of guilt, having two coats while others have none, or just having too much while others have too little — yet proceeding, nonetheless, with our lives as they are.[2]

We also carry a sense of accountability for the massive acts of violence perpetrated in our name. Americans have a huge burden to bear in this respect: the decimation of our native peoples; the enslavement of Africans and the oppression of their descendants; the nuclear bombing of Hiroshima and Nagasaki; the Vietnam War; the military and economic devastation of Iraq, Afghanistan and beyond; suppression of liberation movements around the world; drone warfare and spiraling arms exports; CIA-abetted drug traffic; torture and detention without trial; mass surveillance of governments and citizens. The painful list goes on. We prefer to sweep it under the rug, because we hate feeling guilty because it undermines our self-respect. We have neither patience nor practices for dealing with collective guilt, but we can learn. South Africa, Germany and Guatemala among other nations have shown it is possible to acknowledge moral shame with strength and dignity — and that doing so is healing. Meanwhile, until we all learn what to do with our feelings of guilt, we are likely to lock them away — and in so doing, lock up our pain for the world.

### Fear of Distressing Loved Ones

Pain for the world is repressed not only out of embarrassment and guilt, but out of caring as well. We are reluctant to burden our loved ones; we would shield them from the distress we carry. For parents and grandparents this psychological dilemma is especially difficult and delicate. We don't want our children to be troubled or fearful as they face the already challenging tasks of learning and growing. Our deep desire to protect them from harm can make us try to protect them from knowing what's happening to their world. Our silence, however, may give our children the impression that we don't know what's happening — or worse, that we don't care.

### View of Self as Separate

It is hard to believe we feel pain for the world if we assume we're separate from it. The individualistic bias of Western culture supports that assumption. Feelings of fear, anger or despair about the world tend to be interpreted in terms of personal pathology. Our distress over the state of the world is seen as stemming from some neurosis, rooted perhaps in early trauma or unresolved issues with a parental figure that we're projecting on society at large. Thus we are tempted to discredit feelings that arise from solidarity with our fellow-beings. Conditioned to take seriously only those feelings that pertain to our individual needs and wants, we find it hard to believe that we can suffer on behalf of society itself, or on behalf of other life-forms, and that such suffering is real and valid and healthy.

> The world is not a problem to be solved; it is a living being to which we belong. The world is part of our own self and we are a part of its suffering wholeness. Until we go to the root of our image of separateness, there can be no healing. And the deepest part of our separateness from creation lies in our forgetfulness of its sacred nature, which is also our own sacred nature.
>
> — Llewellyn Vaughan-Lee

### Hijacked Attention

Almost everywhere we go, electronic devices exert an ongoing claim on our attention. Our vulnerability to interruption makes it difficult to reflect deeply or sustain meaningful conversation. Electronic communications — smart phones and texting, email, Facebook and Twitter — all have effects on the human mind that we have barely begun to understand. As David Orr has reflected:

If useful in real emergencies, the overall result is to homogenize the important with the trivial, making everything an emergency and an already frenetic civilization even more frenetic. As a result, we are drowning in unassimilated information, most of which fits no meaningful picture of the world. In our public affairs and in our private lives we are, I think, increasingly muddle-headed because we have mistaken volume and speed of information for substance and clarity.[3]

This distraction of the mind dulls our response to the fragments of news we receive, which begin to constitute a virtual reality with little more emotional impact than a video game. We drown in bits of information that engulf our self-awareness and dilute our connection to the real world around us. Not only is our attention hijacked, but our imagination as well, diminishing our capacity to envision what we might yet create.

### Fear of Powerlessness

"I don't think about that because there is nothing I can do about it." We have all heard this response to a discussion of a social or ecological problem. Logically, it is a non sequitur, confusing what can be thought and felt with what can be done. And it is a tragic one, for when forces are seen as so vast that they cannot be consciously contemplated or seriously discussed, we are doubly victimized — impeded in thought as well as action.

Resistance to painful information on the grounds that we cannot do anything about it springs less from powerlessness (as measured by our capacity to effect change) than from the fear of *feeling* powerless.

> It seems both outrageous and irresponsible that so few mental health clinicians connect the epidemics of mental distress in industrial societies with the devastating impact of our suicidal destruction of our own habitat and ecocidal elimination of whole species.
>
> — Linda Buzzel and Craig Chalquist

The predominant model of self in Western culture —"I am the master of my fate: I am the captain of my soul"[4] — discourages us from confronting issues for which we have no immediate solutions. We feel that we ought to be in charge of our existence and to have all the answers. And so we tend to shrink the sphere of our attention to those areas that we believe we can directly control. This becomes a self-fulfilling prophecy: the smaller our sphere of attention, the smaller our sphere of influence.

### Fear of Knowing — and Speaking

The plight of a child in an alcoholic family is more familiar to us now than in generations past. We know that such a child is often afraid to acknowledge even to herself the abuse and neglect suffered at the hands of an alcoholic parent — much less disclose it to anyone else. This happens for a number of reasons, such as:

1. Any complaint or mention of the problem is likely to incur the wrath of the parent, leading to more physical and verbal abuse.
2. Disclosure to outside authorities could result in the child's losing the only family and home she knows.
3. A child may be told she's crazy and imagining things, inducing her to doubt her own perceptions, or at least to keep very quiet about them.

A similar drama plays out on the national political stage. For example, there is a mountain of evidence regarding the 9-11 attacks that was excluded from the 9-11 Commission's report. It remains unaddressed by the US government, mainstream media and most of US civic institutions. Why do we avoid raising the questions and discussing the evidence publically, even with our own families and friends? Perhaps we are under similar pressures as the child in the alcoholic family:

1. We may fear retribution from the Powers That Be: being fired, blackballed, imprisoned or disappeared.
2. Like the child who clings to an abusive parent, we may cling to an image of our leaders as essentially well meaning, even if

incompetent. "Our government would never knowingly allow that to happen! How can you suggest such a thing?"
3. Perhaps more prevalent, especially for public figures, is the fear of risking reputation and public confidence by being seen as crazy as the oft-ridiculed conspiracy theorist.

The trouble is that the more we in the US avoid discussing 9-11 publically, the more taboo the subject becomes. And the more we live under a collective cloud of ignorance and denial on this matter, the more docile and obedient we become, abdicating our civic responsibility to take remedial measures.

### Mass Media

The corporate global economy, with the increasing pressures it exerts on individuals, families and communities and its spreading control of information channels makes it difficult for people to hear the world's cries of distress.

Most Americans get their news from corporate-controlled media. At the same time, right-wing interests and ideologues are buying up the major newspapers, radio and television stations across the country which people have looked to over the years for balanced reporting. Now too often, they find misinformation, outright deception and the fomenting of false fears in once-trusted media. Such manipulation of the news keeps people ignorant and confused about what's really going on.

> The world is babbled to pieces after the divorce of things from their names.
>
> — Wendell Berry

Moreover, corporate-controlled media serve largely as entertainment, soporific, and as a goad to consume. As the economy has globalized and corporations have sunk their teeth into every society they can reach across the world, the monoculture they purvey spins dreams of an unobtainable and irresponsible life style. The message of this monoculture is dramatized by Australian activist Benny Sable. At protests against clearcutting, uranium mining and other corporate depredations, he stands motionless, often high atop a pile of casks marked radioactive, in a black wetsuit painted with a skeleton and these words:

CONSUME
OBEY
BE SILENT
DIE

## Job and Time Pressures

The worldwide financial crisis forces people to scramble for jobs and makes them insecure in those jobs they manage to hang on to. Moonlighting, workers rush from one job to another to piece together a living wage. Most young families in North America, in order to pay the bills, need both parents to hold a job — or try to. The pace accelerates, taking its toll on every spare moment, every relationship. As employment benefits are cut, labor unions destroyed and social health and welfare programs decimated, the world narrows down to one's own and one's family's survival. There's little time or energy to learn about the fate of the world — or to let it sink in. If a free hour is left at the end of the day, it's easy just to zone out in front of the tube.

## Social Violence

These economic hardships tear the fabric of our society and breed violence. Jobless youth, inflamed by the brutality portrayed by the media, act out their hopelessness and sense of betrayal. We walk fearfully on our own city streets, put armed police in our schools, barricade ourselves behind locked doors or take refuge in gated enclaves. Demagogues direct our frustrations against other groups, blaming those most victimized. For the failures of corporate capitalism, we scapegoat each other.

Whether or not the violence of our society injures one physically, it colors our common life. It finds

> You can hold yourself back from the suffering of the world: this is something you are free to do... But perhaps precisely this holding back is the only suffering you might be able to avoid.
>
> — Franz Kafka

expression in everyday thoughts and acts, in verbal abuse and road rage as well as police brutality at home and military brutality abroad. We try to protect our heart with a defensive armor that closes it to the pain of our world.

## The Cost of Blocking Our Pain for the World

We may try to protect ourselves from feeling pain for the world, but that very effort costs us a great deal. We pay a high price in diminished awareness, understanding and authenticity.

### Impeded Cognitive Functioning

Repression takes a mammoth toll on our energy and dulls our perceptions of the world around us. It is not a local anesthetic. If we won't feel pain, we won't feel much else either — loves and losses are less intense, the sky less vivid, pleasures muted. As a doctor working with Vietnam veterans observed, "The mind pays for its deadening to the state of our world by giving up its capacity for joy and flexibility."[5]

Repression of our anguish for the world affects our thinking as well. It weakens our cognitive functioning. We cut ourselves off from information that contradicts our preferred assessment of the situation and that might arouse stressful feelings. Consequently, there's less of our natural intelligence available to us.

### Impeded Access to the Unconscious

To filter out the truth of one's situation is a form of self-deception. This subliminal censorship impedes access to the vast realm of the unconscious, that wellspring of intuition, creativity and foodstuff for genius, the part of us that knows we're embedded in life.

What we ban from consciousness does not disappear. On an individual level, we store repressed material in our bodies where it may manifest as illness. And on the collective level, as Carl Jung pointed out, the distress we would banish gets acted out on the stage of history.

### Impeded Instinct for Self-Preservation

The instinct for self-preservation, recognized as the most powerful drive in the biological realm, is essential to the preservation of our species and the ongoingness of life. In the ancient Hindu chakra system, this drive is identified with the base chakra or *muladhara*. It represents and feeds our instinctual nature, source of our claim on life itself.

To be afraid to look at and respond to that which threatens all life constitutes a blocking of the *muladhara*, cutting off primal intelligence and energies essential to survival. This chakra not only represents a last line of defense in the protection of life, but it also feeds the erotic currents of our days and years. Opening the base chakra — and thereby our full will to live — means opening ourselves to the repressed tears and rage of our pain for the world.

### Impeded Eros

To be cut off from this root chakra robs us of our birthright to deep ecstatic connections within the web of life. Without Eros, our lives become more desiccated and robotic, even as we dream up robots to serve us. This loss of Eros has led to a flourishing of pornography in which we pathetically try to revitalize our sexual natures in contrived and trivializing ways. The frustration of so basic an urge can lead to violence as well.

When the erotic drive is weak, we pay less respect to the aesthetic dimension of life. No longer seeing the arts as essential, we use them for embellishment and display of wealth, and we cut support and funding for art, music and drama in our schools and communities.

At the same time, we see a desperate pursuit of pleasure and short-term gratification in our culture today. There seems to be a new hedonism in the consumption of goods, entertainment, sex, alcohol. This hedonism derives from more than sheer appetite. Its frantic quality does not reflect a healthy lust for life so much as the contrary: the absence of — and yearning for — a truly erotic connection to life.

### Impeded Empathy

Eros nourishes our rootedness in the web of life, fostering empathy, that vital connection to those with whom we share this world. Without empathy, our natural capacity to sense and identify with the joy and suffering of others is crippled. Instead, we tend to project our repressed fears and anger onto other people. Carl Jung called this the projection of the Shadow. The 9-11 event made us afraid, and people in the US were given an enemy as an object for our fear: Muslim people of the world. This allowed us to feel justified in our military actions against Muslim countries and fosters fear of those in our midst. It is hard to feel empathy for those we fear and hate, precisely when empathy is most needed. Zhiwa Woodbury has captured the dismal situation this leads to:

> Unfortunately, it seems all too predictable that a freedom-loving, gun-toting, substance-abusing, individualist country like America will approach the end of life as we know it with a fair amount of anti-social pathology, transposing the breakdown of our life support system into a breakdown in the social order, with many responding to the existential threat with paranoia and hostility, deciding it's "every man for himself" or, alternatively, seeking security in like-minded militias and religious cults.[6]

## Impeded Imagination

Free play of the imagination requires trust in life and courage to walk where there is no path. It takes us beyond our perceptions of what is to what might be, opening us to new ways of seeing and new ways of being. The powers of mind are then liberated from the dead hand of habit. Imagination suggests alternatives to the dominant narratives of our time and can keep us from surrendering to conformity and mob mentality.

This crucial source of all creativity is blocked when we resist images, ideas or feelings that might trigger moral pain.

## Impeded Feedback

All open systems, be they organic or social, self-regulate by virtue of feedback — that is, by monitoring the results of their moment-by-moment behavior. Our sensory, cognitive and emotional responses can bring us information to guide our actions. If we consider that we are an integral part of our world, then we can see that closing our hearts and minds to its suffering blocks feedback essential to life.

Silencing our deepest responses to the condition of our world not only fosters a sense of futility, but also mires us in it. Each act of denial, conscious or unconscious, is an abdication of our power to respond. It relegates us to the role of victim, before we even see what we can and want to do.

## Coming Back to Life

Our pain for the world, including the fear, anger and sorrow we feel on behalf of life on Earth is not only pervasive. It is natural and healthy. It is dysfunctional only to the extent that it is misunderstood and repressed. We have seen in this chapter how that repression happens in today's culture and what it costs us.

We don't break free from denial and repression by gritting our teeth and trying to be nobler, braver citizens. We don't retrieve our passion for life, our wild, innate creative intelligence, by scolding ourselves and soldiering on with a stiff upper lip. That model of heroic behavior belongs to the worldview that gave us the Industrial Growth Society.

The most remarkable feature of this historical moment on Earth is not that we are on the way to destroying our world — we've actually been on the way quite a while. It is that we are beginning to wake up, as from a millennia-long sleep, to a whole new relationship to our world, to ourselves and each other. This awakening makes the Great Turning possible. We described it in Chapter 1 as a shift in consciousness, the third dimension of that revolution. It is so central to the arising of the Life-Sustaining Society that it is like the hub of a turning wheel.

The worldview emerging now lets us behold anew and experience afresh the web of life in which we exist. It opens us to the vast intelligence of life's self-organizing powers, which have brought us forth from interstellar gases and primordial seas. It brings us to a larger identity in which to cradle and transcend our ego-identified fears. It lets us honor our pain for the world as a gateway into deep participation in the world's self-healing. The group work of the last four decades that this book describes is based on this worldview.

More basic to the Great Turning than any ideas we hold is the act of courage and love we make together when we dare to see our world as it is.

> And I would travel with you
> to the places of our shame
> The hills stripped of trees, the marsh grasses
> oil-slicked, steeped in sewage;
> The blackened shoreline, the chemical-poisoned water;
> I would stand with you in the desolate places, the charred places,
> soil where nothing will ever grow, pitted desert;
>
> fields that burn slowly for months; roots of cholla & chaparral
> writhing with underground explosions
> I would put my hand
> there with yours, I would take your hand, I would walk
> with you
>
> through carefully planted fields, rows of leafy vegetables
> drifting with radioactive dust; through the dark
> of uranium mines hidden in the sacred gold-red mountains;
>
> I would listen with you in drafty hospital corridors
> as the miner cried out in the first language
>
> of pain; as he cried out
> the forgotten names of his mother   I would stand
> next to you in the forest's
> final hour, in the wind
> of helicopter blades, police
>
> sirens shrieking, the delicate
> tremor of light between
> leaves for the last
> time   Oh I would touch with this love each
> wounded place
>
> — Anita Barrows[7]

**3**

# The Basic Miracle: Our True Nature and Power

*Something inside me has reached to the place
Where the world is breathing.*

— Kabir

*We are caught in an inescapable network of mutuality,
tied in a single garment of destiny. Whatever affects one
directly, affects all indirectly.*

— Martin Luther King, Jr.

THE VIEW OF REALITY EMERGING NOW IS BREATHTAKINGLY new to those of us who have been shaped by the Industrial Growth Society. Supported by postmodern science and ancient spiritual traditions, it brings a fresh understanding of our relationship to the world and of powers within us for its healing. Liberating us from constricted notions of who we are and what we need, it brings us home to our true nature — in league with the stars and trees of our thrumming universe. This view is basic to the Great Turning and fundamental to the work this book presents.

We people shaped by western civilization have struggled to master the natural world around us. We have studied the Earth and the cosmos, determined to discover the essential building blocks of life. We have acted as if we could know and control the world. We came to think of ourselves as made of better stuff than the animals and plants and rocks and water around us. Our technologies have amplified disastrously the ecological and social effects of that kind of thinking. Anthropologist Gregory Bateson commented on this:

> If you put God outside and set him vis-à-vis his creation and if you have the idea that you are created in his image, you will logically and naturally see yourself as outside and against the things around you. As you arrogate all mind to yourself, you will see the world as mindless and therefore not entitled to moral or ethical consideration. The environment will seem to be yours to exploit. Your survival unit will be you and your folks or conspecifics against … other social units, other races and the brutes and vegetables.
>
> If this is your estimate of your relation to nature and you have an advanced technology, your likelihood of survival will be that of a snowball in hell.[1]

Perhaps we made our biggest error in thinking of the world as made of "stuff" to begin with. Fortunately — and paradoxically — our very search for mastery and knowledge through science has brought us to the dawning realization that the world, indeed the universe, seems not to be composed of stuff at all. Each time we have grasped what appeared to be a basic building block, it has dissolved into a dance of energy and relationship. And so we awaken today to a new kind of knowledge, a growing comprehension of our connectivity — and even identity — with everything in the universe.

## Living Systems Theory

Modern science and the Industrial Growth Society grew up together. With the help of René Descartes and Francis Bacon, classical science veered away from a holistic, organic view of the world to an analytical and mechanical one. The machines we made to extend our senses and capacities became our model for the universe. Separating mechanism from operator, object from observer, this view of reality assumed that everything could be described objectively and controlled externally. It has permitted extraordinary technological gains and fueled the engines of industrial progress. But, as 20th-century biologists realized with increasing frustration, it cannot explain the self-renewing processes of life.

Instead of looking for basic building blocks, these scientists took a new tack: they began to look at wholes instead of parts, at processes instead of substances. They discovered that these wholes — be they cells, bodies, ecosystems, even the planet itself — are not just an assemblage of parts. Rather they are dynamically organized and intricately balanced *systems*. These scientists saw each element as part of a vaster pattern that connects and evolves by discernible principles. The discernment of these principles gave rise to General Systems Theory.

Austrian biologist Ludwig von Bertalanffy, known as the father of general systems theory, called it "a way of seeing."[2] And while its insights have spread throughout the natural and social sciences, the systems perspective has remained just that: a way of seeing. Anthropologist Gregory Bateson called it "the biggest bite out of the fruit of the Tree of Knowledge that mankind has taken in the last 2000 years."[3]

## How Life Self-Organizes

By shifting their focus to relationships instead of separate entities, scientists made an amazing discovery — amazing at least to the mainstream western mind. They discovered that nature is self-organizing. And they set about discerning the principles by which this self-organization occurs. They found these principles or systems properties to be awesomely elegant in their coherence and constancy throughout the observable universe, from sub-organic to biological and ecological systems, and mental and social systems as well. The properties of open systems permit the variety and intelligence of life-forms to arise from interactive currents of matter/energy and information. These properties or *invariances* are four in number:

1. Each system, from atom to galaxy, is a whole. That means that it is not reducible to its components. Its distinctive nature and

capacities derive from the dynamic relationships of its parts. This interplay is synergistic, generating *emergent properties* and new possibilities, which are not predictable from the character of the separate parts. For example, wetness could not be predicted from the combination of oxygen and hydrogen before it occurred. Nor can anyone can predict the creative solutions that may emerge when a group of people put their wits together.

2. Thanks to the continual flow-through of matter/energy and information, open systems are able to self-stabilize and maintain their balance in what von Bertalanffy called *fliessgleichgewicht* (flux-equilibrium). This homeostatic function enables systems to self-regulate amidst changing conditions in their environment. They do this by monitoring the effects of their own behavior and realigning their behavior with preestablished norms, like a thermostat. Feedback — in this case, negative or deviation-*reducing* feedback — is at work here. It is how we maintain body temperature, heal from a cut and ride a bicycle.

3. Open systems not only maintain their balance amidst the flux, but also evolve in complexity. When challenges from their environment persist, they can fall apart or adapt by reorganizing themselves around new, more functional norms. This is accomplished by feedback — in this case, positive or deviation — *amplifying* feedback. It is how systems learn and evolve. This feedback is blocked and ignored at the risk of system collapse.

   When a system is unable to adapt its norms, perhaps because of the scale and speed of change, the positive feedback loop goes into *overshoot* and *runaway*. As ever-increasing oscillations upset the balance of its interrelated parts, the system loses coherence and complexity — and begins to unravel.

4. Every system is a *holon* — that is, it is both a whole in its own right, comprised of subsystems *and* simultaneously an integral part of a larger system. Thus holons form *nested hierarchies*, systems within systems, circuits within circuits.

   Each new holonic level — say from atom to molecule, cell to organ, person to family — generates new emergent properties that are not reducible to the properties of the separate. In contrast to hierarchies of control familiar to organizations in which rule is imposed from above, in nested hierarchies (sometimes called *holonarchies*) order tends to arise from below, as well as be summoned or inspired by its larger context.

The system self-generates from adaptive cooperation between its parts for mutual benefit. Order and differentiation go hand and hand, components diversifying as they coordinate roles and invent new responses.

### Water, Fire and Web

The mechanistic view of reality separated substance from process, self from other, mind from matter. In the systems perspective, these dichotomies no longer hold. What appeared to be separate and self-existent entities are now seen as interdependent and interwoven. What had appeared to be *other* can be equally construed as a concomitant of *self*, like a fellow-cell in the neural patterns of a larger body. What we had been taught to dismiss as mere feelings are responses to our world no less valid than rational constructs. Sensations, emotions, intuitions, concepts all condition each other, each a way of apprehending the relationships that weave our world.

As systems we participate by virtue of constant flow-through in the evolving web of life, giving and receiving the feedback necessary to the web's integrity and balance. To convey this dynamic process, theorists have used a variety of images. Fire and water are prominent among them. "We are not stuff that abides," said systems cybernetician Norbert Wiener, "We are patterns that perpetuate themselves; we are whirlpools in a river of ever-flowing water."[3a]

Or we are like a flame, said several early systems thinkers. As a flame keeps its shape by transforming the stuff it burns, so does the open system. As the open system consumes the matter that passes through it, so does it also process information — ever breaking down and building up, renewed. Like fire, a system both transforms and is transformed by that on which it feeds.

Another frequent image is that of a neural net. By their interactions, nerve cells differentiate and create new neural assemblies at their holonic level within the larger body, enhancing diversity and therefore complexity. They generate intelligence as they weave ever more responsive nets. Systems political scientist Karl Deutsch took this image as a model for social systems, showing that free circulation of information is essential to healthy self-governance.

Our emerging understanding of fungi provides another potent image for the connectivity of open systems. Microscopic cells called *mycelia* — the fruit of which are mushrooms — spread nearly invisibly underground to create a vast network that permeates the soil and fuses with the roots of plants and trees to share water, food and vital information.

> I believe that mycelium is the neurological network of nature. Interlacing mosaics of mycelium infuse habitats with information-sharing membranes. These membranes are aware, react to change, and collectively have the long-term health of the host environment in mind.
>
> — Paul Stamets

## Gaia Theory

Systems theory has transformed the way we see our planet home. In studying the chemical composition of our atmosphere, scientist James Lovelock discovered that the balance of its proportions, which stays within the narrow limits necessary for life, indicates self-regulating processes at work — the hallmark of a living system. In collaboration with microbiologist Lynn Margulis, Lovelock developed a hypothesis that presents the entire biosphere of Earth as a self-organizing system.

Thankfully, Lovelock did not call this hypothesis, soon to become a theory (the "hypothesis of self-regulative processes of the biosphere" or another name respectable to his fellow scientists). Instead he listened to his friend, novelist William Golding, who suggested he call it Gaia for the early Greek goddess of Earth, thereby catching people's poetic

> For the first time in our history we can actually see our whole planet and recognize it as a living being — and we can understand that we are not its privileged rulers,... but only one part, and not even an indispensible part, of its body.
>
> — Elizabet Sahtouris

imagination. Like the Apollo photo of Earth from space, this name for Earth has transformed the way many of us now think of our planet home. We no longer see Earth as just a rock we live upon, but as a living process in which we participate. Earth takes on a presence in our consciousness as source of all we are and can become.

## Deep Ecology

What does it mean or matter to be interdependent with all Earthly life? In exploring this question, deep ecology arose, both as a philosophy and a movement. Norwegian philosopher Arne Naess, a mountain climber and scholar of Gandhi, coined the term in the 1970s.

In contrast to reform environmentalism, which treats the symptoms of ecological degradation — clean up a river here or a dump there for human benefit — deep ecology questions fundamental premises of the Industrial Growth Society. It challenges the assumptions, embedded in much Judeo-Christian and Marxist thought, that humans are the ultimate measure of value. Often expressed as *biocentric*, this perspective holds that we must break free from the species arrogance that threatens not only humans but all complex life-forms within reach.

> Deep Ecology, or biocentrism, is a law of nature that exists independently of whether humans recognize it or not .... And the failure of modern society to acknowledge this — as we attempt to subordinate all of nature to human use — has lead us to the brink of collapse of the Earth's life support systems .... Biocentrism is ancient native wisdom ..., but in the context of today's industrial society, biocentrism is profoundly revolutionary, challenging the system to its core.
>
> — Judi Bari, forest activist

## Beyond Anthropocentrism

It is hard to experience our interrelatedness with all life if we are blind to the human-centeredness embedded in our culture and consciousness. Deep ecologist John Seed, an Australian rainforest activist, described both the ways it constricts us and the rewards we find in moving beyond it.

> Anthropocentrism means human chauvinism. Similar to sexism, but substitute "human race" for man and "all other species" for woman...
>
> When humans investigate and see through their layers of anthropocentric self-cherishing, a most profound change in consciousness begins to take place. Alienation subsides. The human is no longer a stranger, apart. Your humanness is then recognized as merely the most recent stage of your existence, and as you stop identifying exclusively with this chapter, you start to get in touch with yourself as mammal, as vertebrate, as a species only recently emerged from the rainforest. As the fog of amnesia disperses, there is a transformation in your relationship to other species, and in your commitment to them.[4]

John Seed pointed out that this liberation is far more than an intellectual process. For him, as for many others, it comes through taking part in actions on behalf of Earth.

> "I am protecting the rainforest" develops to "I am part of the rainforest protecting myself. I am that part of the rainforest recently emerged into thinking." What a relief then! The thousands of years of imagined separation are over and we begin to recall our true nature. The change is a spiritual one, sometimes referred to as deep ecology.[5]

### The Ecological Self

Arne Naess has a term for the wider sense of identity that John Seed describes. Naess calls it the *ecological self* and sees it as the fruit of a natural maturation process. We underestimate ourselves, he said, when we identify self with the narrow, competitive ego. "With sufficient all-sided maturity" we not only move on from ego to a social self and a metaphysical self, but an ecological self as well. Through widening circles of identification, we vastly extend the boundaries of our self-interest, and enhance our joy and meaning in life.

A welcome and significant feature of this concept is the way it transcends the need to sermonize about our moral responsibilities. When we assumed that we were essentially separate, we called people to be altruistic — that is to favor the other (*alter* in Latin) more than the self (*ego* in Latin). This is not only philosophically unsound from the perspective of deep ecology, but it is also ineffective.

> What humankind is capable of loving from mere duty or moral exhortation is, unfortunately, very limited .... The extensive moralizing within the ecological movement has given the public the false impression that they are primarily asked to sacrifice, to show more responsibility, more concern, and better morals .... [But] the requisite care flows naturally if the self is widened and deepened so that protection of free nature is felt and conceived of as protection of our very selves.[6]

### Asking Deeper Questions

Naess and his activist colleagues called for a deep, long-range ecology movement. Whether or not it is generally recognized as a movement, certainly deep ecology ideas have circulated widely, enlivening green activists and academics alike.

These ideas have evolved into a deep ecology platform — including such principles as the recognition that life-forms have an intrinsic right to exist, and that human population should not exceed the carrying capacity of Earth. However, deep ecology is neither an ideology nor a dogma. Of an essentially exploratory character, it seeks to motivate people to ask, as Naess put it, "deeper questions" about their real wants and needs, about

> We call on the spirit of Gaia .... Awaken in us a sense of who we truly are: tiny ephemeral blossoms on the Tree of Life. Make the purposes and destiny of that tree our own purpose and destiny.
>
> — John Seed

their relation to life on Earth and their vision for the future. Such questions act as a solvent, loosing up encrusted mental structures, freeing us to think and see in fresh ways.

## Ancient Spiritual Teachings

The view of reality offered by systems science and deep ecology is remarkably convergent with ancient teachings of our planet's people. At the same time that we are rediscovering the process nature of our world as a dynamically interrelated whole, our appreciation deepens for how spiritual traditions from East and West, North and South, have carried this understanding through the ages. We find it not only in Taoist, Hindu and Buddhist sages and scriptures, and among Indigenous peoples who still know and live this truth. We also find this vision expressed in the mystical teachings of Christianity, Judaism and Islam. Perhaps only we who are shaped by the Industrial Growth Society have forgotten our embeddedness in a larger, living whole.

> Mere purposive rationality unaided by such phenomena as art, religion, dream and the like, is necessarily pathogenic and destructive of life ... its virulence springs specifically from the circumstance that life depends upon interlocking circuits of contingency, while consciousness can see only short arcs of such circuits as human purpose may direct.
>
> — Gregory Bateson

The meeting of these spiritual traditions with the Westernized, modern mind may well be, as Arnold Toynbee asserted in relation to Buddhism, the most significant occurrence of the last century. These traditions serve to embody and enliven these understandings — so that they become real to our experience and efficacious in our lives. We do not live by conceptual abstractions. We are not brains on the end of a stick. We are flesh-and-blood beings, and ideas become real for us through our senses and imagination — through stories, images and rituals that enlist our capacity for devotion, our tears and laughter.

Approached solely by the intellect, ideas lack power to lift us into new perspectives and new meanings for our lives. Our ancestors knew this, hence their ritual celebrations to honor Earth and their yogas to open body and mind. Moreover, practices derived from spiritual traditions can help us stay steady and alert in the face of the Great Unraveling.

## Abrahamic Religions

Understandings comparable to those of systems theory and deep ecology run through all three major religions of the Western world. They point beyond the narrow confines of orthodoxy to the basic miracle of life itself. From the Jewish Renewal movement, prophetic voices, such as those of Rabbis Zalman Schachter, Lynn Gottlieb, Arthur Waskow and Michael Lerner, invigorate Biblical summons to social and ecological justice.

From the vast and varied landscape of contemporary Christianity come similar calls to honor the sacredness of all life. We hear them in Creation Spirituality articulated by Matthew Fox; the new cosmology put forward by Thomas Berry, Brian Swimme, Sr. Miriam MacGillis; and radical Catholic witnesses for peace from Kathy Kelly of Voices of Creative Non-Violence to Jim Wallis of Sojourners. Their witness goes back to the practices of the early church as well as the figure and teachings of Jesus and beloved figures like Francis of Assisi, the patron saint of ecology.

And from Islam comes a resurgence of Sufism, that ancient mystical river of devotion that unites us with the beauty of this world and with the courage to protect it. Rumi, who sings the enrapturing sacredness of all life, is perhaps the most popular poet of our day, while contemporary Sufi teacher Llewellyn Vaughan-Lee, author of *Darkening of the Light*,[7] helps us see that our forgetting this sacredness now threatens the whole planet with suffering and death.

Although these movements are nourished by their own distinctive religious roots and practices, they are ecumenical in their reach and readiness to act together. We see this, for example, in the program and vitality of Interfaith Power and Light, a national network linking religious congregations in practical responses to climate change, and in Rabbi Arthur Waskow's Shalom Center, which defines itself as " a prophetic voice in Jewish, multi-religious and American life."

---

### Shalom Center

Spiritually Rooted, Strategically Focused Plan of Action on the Climate Crisis

We begin convinced of these truths:

That human action, driven by global corporations we are calling Big Carbon or Carbon Pharaohs, are bringing a climate crisis on all life-forms on Planet Earth — a crisis of a breadth and depth unprecedented in the history of the human species.

That in the religious, spiritual, and ethical traditions of practically all cultures on the planet are teachings, stories, practices, and symbols that could . . . heal our wounded Earth and move toward a planetary Beloved Community.

That such teachings, stories, practices, and symbols are present in the traditions rooted in the Bible, beginning with the very first insight into human history — the story of the Garden of Eden — appearing again and again in ways that invite their urgent use to face "the fierce urgency of Now."[8]

---

### *Asian Traditions*

The rich religious heritage of Asian culture through the ages offers distinctive portals into the intrinsic connectivity of all life. Taoism reveals the reciprocal and complementary interplay of apparent opposites that gives rise to the phenomenal world. Within the vast panoply of Hindu traditions are stories, practices and devotional songs that train the imagination to see the irrepressible vitality at the core of existence.

Buddhism especially helps us to understand the new ecological paradigm and to put it to work for the sake of life. The core doctrine of the Buddha Dharma, basic to its psychology and ethics, is the *dependent co-arising* of all phenomena — arguably the clearest conceptualization of mutual causality prior to general systems theory. The genesis of the Work That Reconnects was strongly influenced by Joanna's immersion in systems theory and Buddhism.

Buddhist teachings and practices, deriving from our connectivity with all life, help us experience the world in terms of process rather than in terms of things to grasp or reject. They confront us with the fear, greed and ill will at the root of human suffering. Meditations, such as loving-kindness, compassion and joy in the joy of others, further decondition old patterns of fear and competition, serving as ground and compass in a fluidly interdependent world.[i]

The Buddha Dharma provides images of interconnectedness and models for a life of action. From Mahayana Buddhism comes the Jewel Net of Indra, a polycentric vision of reality in which each being at each node in the vast net of everything is a gem reflecting all the other gems. As in the holographic model presented by contemporary science, each part contains the whole.

The *bodhisattva*, the Buddhist hero figure, is one who deeply comprehends the dependent co-arising of all things. This one knows that there is no private salvation and therefore turns back from the gates of *nirvana* to reenter *samsara* (the world of suffering) again and again, until every being, every blade of grass, is enlightened. The choice to act for the sake of all beings — that intention known as *bodhichitta* — arises naturally when we open to our mutual belonging. As we realize our *interbeing* (a word coined by a Vietnamese Zen master Thich Nhat Hanh) we also realize that we are all, in a sense, *bodhisattvas*.

### *Indigenous Spirituality*

Voices from yet more ancient wellsprings of wisdom yield teachings to us now. Shamanic traditions of the Indigenous peoples of America, Africa, Australasia, Old Europe, Siberia and Arctic regions resurface in our day with a similar message. Their voices find a hearing because they tell us what we yearn to know once again: that as kin to the animals and plants, rocks and winds of this sacred world, we can tap its powers, take part in its healing.

---

[i.] See Chapter 13 for further details.

> Hear me, four quarters of the world — a relative I am!
> Give me the strength to walk the soft earth, a relative to all that is!
> Give me the eyes to see and the strength to understand, that I may be like you.
> With your power only can I face the winds.
>
> — Black Elk

At the same time, archeological evidence brings us knowledge of the Goddess of pre-patriarchal cultures. Embodying not only the abundance of Earth, but also the reverence and fairness this abundance requires, she guided hunter-gatherer societies, gave rise to agriculture and ancient arts over warless millennia. Despite persecutions and inquisitions, remnants of this Earth-based wisdom still survive on the margins of the major religions, in practices of Wicca or witchcraft, and today's neo-paganism. Goddess wisdom breaks down the mind-matter dichotomy erected by patriarchal structures of thought, and points to Earth's self-organizing powers. Many see the women's spirituality movement as a return to the goddess, calling for justice and resacralizing life.

## The Miracle of Mind

The image of the neural net and Gaia theory both convey a major systems insight: mind is not separate from nature; it is *of* nature. Mind pervades the natural world as the subjective dimension within every open system, however simple, said systems philosopher Ervin Laszlo. With our human brain composed of 100 billion neurons, it is hard for us to imagine the subjectivity of a single-celled creature, but, as Laszlo has pointed out, there's no reason or logic to deny that it exists.

> If we remember that some $10^{11}$ neurons form the complex cerebral nets (physical events) which correlate with human

mind-events, we must beware of attributing anything re-
sembling human mind-events to lesser systems, such as
atoms or molecules. Their mind-events must be entirely
different in "feel" from ours, yet they can be mind-events
nevertheless, i.e. types of sensations, correlated with, but
different from physical processes.[9]

In affirming the presence of mind in nature, Gregory Bateson
took another tack. Instead of relating it to the interiority of systems,
he saw mind in the circuits of information that interconnect and
guide living systems:

> The total self-corrective unit that processes information is
> a system whose boundaries do not at all coincide with the
> boundaries either of the body or what is popularly called
> 'self' or 'consciousness.'[10]

### Self as Choice Maker

The mind, like any open system, is self-organizing. While its mental operations can be influenced from without, they cannot be
controlled. This is because external pressures can only operate in
interaction with a system's internal codes, which are conditioned by
past experience. As the system complexifies, it becomes less determined by its environment, more autonomous.

In humans, and some other big-brained mammals, mind is endowed with a remarkable feature: self-reflexive consciousness. It
emerged by necessity, when the system's internal complexity grew so
great — and its range of options so large — that it could no longer
survive by trial and error alone. It needed to evolve another level of
consciousness in order to weigh different courses of action; it needed, in other words, to make choices. A new level of self-monitoring
emerged in ever-complexifying assemblies of feedback loops. The
self-observant *I* arose. It arose by virtue of decision-making.

So as many a sage has pointed out: however dire the circumstances we find ourselves in, we can always choose our response. The
power of choice is our nobility, our refuge. In both systems theory

and Buddhism, choice-making is seen as definitive of the self. We discover who we are in our choices.

## Positive Disintegration

Sometimes the best choice is to let go, to fall apart.

Dangers to their survival prompt living systems to evolve. When feedback tells them — and continues to tell them — that their old norms and behaviors are no longer effective in current conditions, they respond by changing. They adapt to such challenges by seeking and incorporating more appropriate norms. They search for values and goals that allow them to navigate in more varied conditions, with greater resilience and connectivity. This is serious business, because a system's norms are its internal codes by which it defines itself. Ervin Laszlo calls this process exploratory self-reorganization.

In humans, our internal codes and organizing principles are basic to our sense of self. The realization that they are no longer valid can be very disorienting, making us frighteningly unsure of who we are. This sense of being off track can be experienced in religious traditions as a call to repentance. This loss of previously valid norms is painful and confusing, but psychiatrist Kazimierz Dabrowski calls it *positive disintegration*[11] because it allows more adaptive understandings of self and world to arise.

In periods of major cultural transition, the experience of positive disintegration is widespread. Such is the case now in this time of the Great Unraveling. Everywhere anomalies appear that don't fit our expectations, because — in systems terms — they don't match previous codes and beliefs. Bereft of comfort, confidence and old coping strategies, we may feel that our world is falling apart. Sometimes we panic or shut down; sometimes we get mean and turn on each other.

Today in the early 21st century, we face challenges humankind has never faced in our 150,000-year journey. Never before have we seen mass extinction of species brought on by human depredation of habitats and ecosystems. Never before have we grappled with human-caused climate disruption across the planet. Never before have we exposed ourselves and all other life-forms to the levels of radiation and radioactive particles currently being released by the production of nuclear energy and weapons, massively intensified by catastrophes on the scale of Fukushima. Never before has the biosphere endured such onslaughts of chemical pollution and genetic tampering, including many whose consequences we cannot ever undo.

It's difficult to comprehend the enormity of these assaults on life. We want to turn away. We have no formulas or examples to follow as we struggle to cope. History cannot instruct us, except by analogy. Our old codes do not apply, no matter how hard we try.

It helps to recall that the life living through us has repeatedly died to old forms and old ways. Positive disintegration is integral to the evolution of living systems. We know this dying in the explosion of supernovas, the relinquishment of gills and fins in moving onto dry land, the splitting of seeds in the soil. We know this in the cyclical growth, flowering and decomposition of plants through the seasons. As they live out their life cycle in one form, plants break down into compost to nourish other life-forms, including new plants of the same species. Our own life story attests to this, as we learned to move beyond the safeties and dependencies of childhood.

It is never easy. Some of the uglier aspects of human behavior today arise from fear of the wholesale changes we must now undergo. Opening our awareness to global calamity and letting ourselves feel the anguish and disorientation are integral to our spiritual ripening. Mystics speak of the "dark night of the soul." Brave enough to let go of accustomed assurances and allow old mental comforts and conformities to

> Like all other living things, we must make our descent into the darkness then wait for some new kind of wisdom to take root.
>
> — Valerie Andrews

> Let go of the place that holds, let go of the place that flinches, let go of the place that controls, let go of the place that fears. Just let the ground support me.... Walking in the dark night is a way to practice faith, a way to build confidence in the unknown.... I learn to practice courage in the vastness of what I can't see ....
>
> — Stephanie Kaza

fall away, they stand naked to the unknown. They let processes that their minds cannot encompass work through them. Out of darkness, the new is born.

## We Are the World

It becomes clear, then, that our planetary crises could serve to engender a new birth of consciousness: self-reflexivity on the next holonic level. It would emerge from the necessity for swift collective choice-making at the level of social systems.

It has been assumed in the modern west that choice only occurs at the level of the individual. Even elections are determined by individuals casting votes that then are counted. This form of choice-making is too slow and too easily corrupted to respond adequately to the survival challenge we face.

However, today we are seeing people act together in a new way on behalf of life on Earth. Bodhichitta is manifesting collectively. Groups of people from all walks of life are acting in spite of the threat of social censure, personal injury, imprisonment, even death. Their motivation cannot be reduced to private gain, but it can be understood as manifesting a collective consciousness in defense of life on Earth.

This holonic shift does not sacrifice, but indeed requires, the uniqueness of each individual and his or her perspective. It begins, almost imperceptibly, with a sense of common fate and a shared intention to meet it together. It emerges in unexpected behaviors, as individuals in countless settings meet to speak and respond to what is happening to their world. It manifests in an unpredictable array of spontaneous actions, as people step out from their private comforts, giving time and taking risks on behalf of Earth and their fellow-beings. It includes all the hopes and changes that constitute the Great Turning. Acting together, we discover greater confidence and precision than we may have expected. Given the dynamics of self-organizing systems, this is hardly surprising.

Paul Hawken, in his book *Blessed Unrest*, gave staggering numbers to this phenomenon and offered a dramatic biological metaphor, that of the immune system and how it functions. He explained how the immune system in any organism learns to recognize self

> If … the metaphor of an organism can be applied to humankind, we can imagine a collective movement that would protect, repair, and restore that organism's capacity to endure when threatened. Specifically, the shared activity of hundreds or thousands of nonprofit organizations can be seen as humanity's immune response to toxins like political corruption, economic disease, and ecological degradation.
>
> — Paul Hawken

and non-self, what sustains the life of the body and what does not. Similarly, the immune system of humanity "identifies what is humane and not humane,"[12] or what sustains the human life-support system and what harms it. The immune system

> can best be understood as intelligence, a living, learning, self-regulating system — almost another mind. Its function does not depend on its firepower but on the *quality of its connectedness* …. The immune system depends on its *diversity to maintain resiliency*, with which it can maintain homeostasis, respond to surprises, learn from pathogens, and adapt to sudden changes ….
>
> Similarly, the widely diverse network of organizations proliferating in the world today may be a better defense against injustice than F-16 fighter jets. *Connectivity* allows these organizations to be task-specific and focus their resources precisely and frugally [emphases ours].[13]

As we move into the Great Turning, it seems that humans can indeed function together as a kind of immune system of Earth, identifying and championing what is life-sustaining, and containing, neutralizing or transforming what is destructive to life.

## The Nature of Our Power

Just as our pain for the world arises from our connectivity, so does our power. Yet the generative creativity operating in and through open systems is very different from our customary notions of power.

## Power Over

The old concept of power, in which most of us have been socialized, originated in the worldview that assumed reality to be composed of discrete and separate entities — rocks, plants, atoms, people. Power came to be seen as a property of those separate entities, and this property enables them to push each other around. Power became identified with domination, equated with the exertion of one's will over others, limiting their choices.

This is a linear, unidirectional view of causality. Here power is seen as a possession — something you have and can get for yourself — and plays out in a zero-sum game: the more of it you have, the less I have; if you win, I lose.

In this view, power correlates with invulnerability. To keep from being pushed around, defenses are needed; armor and rigidity appear to make one more powerful, less likely to be influenced or changed by others.

From the systems perspective this notion of power is both inaccurate and dysfunctional. The exertion of greater force can certainly serve to defend oneself and others, but that function is one of protection, not to be confused with the kind of power that generates new forms, behaviors and potentials. That capacity emerges with and functions through relationship. We can call it *power with* or synergy.

## Power With

Living systems evolve in variety, resilience and intelligence; they do this not by erecting walls of defense and closing off from their environment, but by opening more widely to currents of matter/energy and information. Through constant interaction, they spin more intricate connections and more flexible strategies. They can't do this if they are invulnerable, but only if they are open and responsive. Such is the direction of evolution. As life-forms evolve in complexity and intelligence, they shed their armor in order to grow sensitive, vulnerable protuberances — like lips, tongues, ears, eyeballs, noses, fingertips — the better to sense and respond, the better to connect in the web of life and weave it further.

We may wonder why power as domination — which we see enacted around us and over us — seems so effective. Many who wield it seem to get what they want — money, fame, control over others. Yes, they do, but always at a cost to the larger system and to their own well-being. To the social system, power over is dysfunctional because it inhibits diversity and feedback; by obstructing self-organizing processes, it fosters entropy or systemic disintegration. To the powerholders themselves, it is like a suit of armor: it restricts vision and movement. Narrowing awareness and maneuverability, it cuts them off from fuller and freer participation in life. They have fewer options for action and fewer sources of joy, except to grasp for more of what represents power to them.

Power with or synergy is not a property one can own, but a process one engages in. Efficacy is transactional. Take a neuron in the neural net. If, hypothetically, it isolated itself behind defensive walls — believing that its powers were personal property to be protected from other nerve cells — it would atrophy and die. Its health and its power lie in opening itself to the charge, letting the signals through. Only then can the larger system — the neural net — learn to respond and think.

### Power Over Blocks Feedback

The body politic is much like a neural net, as Karl Deutsch has asserted. Like the brain, society is a cybernetic system which only functions well with unhampered flows of information. That is how our mind-bodies work. When you put your hand on a hot stove, you rapidly withdraw it because feedback tells you your fingers are burning. You wouldn't know that if you began censoring your body's reports.

Democracy requires the free circulation of information for public decision-making. In the present hypertrophied stage of the Industrial Growth Society, however, even governments that call themselves democracies suppress information unwelcome to corporate interests. We learn daily of high-level cover-ups, scientific findings suppressed, research projects defunded, reports censored, journalists penalized and whistle-blowers fired or jailed.

We have become accustomed to misinformation and deception about an enormous array of dangers, such as the relationship of cancer and other diseases to radioactivity, food additives and household products. Corporate-controlled media seldom mention climate change, even when we're awash in record-breaking floods, hurricanes, droughts and firestorms. This institutionalized secrecy may protect vested interests, but it comes at a high price. Any system that consistently suppresses feedback — closing its perceptions to the results of its behavior — is committing suicide.

### The Power of Disclosure

While the concept of power with summons us to develop empathy, it also calls for vigilance and assertiveness in responding to the needs of the larger system. It is our responsibility to give feedback to our body politic and to unblock feedback that has been suppressed. This is essential to the Great Turning from the Industrial Growth Society to a Life-Sustaining Society. Among its heroes are women and men, such as Chelsea Manning and Edward Snowden, who — at enormous personal risk — disclosed crucial information that had been withheld from the public.

> The public needs to know the kinds of things a government does in its name, or the "consent of the governed" is meaningless. The consent of the governed is not consent if it is not informed.
>
> — Edward Snowden

Our connectivity with others in the web of life does not mean that we should tolerate destructive behavior. On the contrary, it means we should step in when our collective health and survival are at stake. That can involve lobbying for laws, or intervening in a more direct fashion, nonviolently, to remove authority from those who misuse it. This is not a struggle to *seize* power so much as to release it for efficient self-governance. Thus we act, not only for ourselves and our own group or party, but also on behalf of all the other neurons in the net. Then we are sustained by the myriad resources of that net, which include all our differences and diversities.

Acting on behalf of the larger system, for the common good, is alien to the mores of the Industrial Growth Society. According to the doctrine of *shareholder value*, corporations are driven to maximize their own short-term profits, regardless of the harm inflicted. Within this increasingly competitive system, individuals perceive their own self-interest to be in conflict with the interests of others. People entrenched in this oppositional point of view assume that activists are similarly motivated, labeling them special interest groups.

In fact, action for the common good brings needed feedback to the system about challenges it faces. It helps to change the norms from individual, competitive self-interest to collective self-interest.

### Synergy and Grace

When we make common cause on behalf of the Earth community, we open not only to the needs of others, but also to their abilities and gifts. It is a good thing that power with is not a personal property, because, frankly, none of us alone possesses all the courage and intelligence, strength and endurance, required for the Great Turning. And none of us *needs* to possess them, or dredge them up out of some private storehouse. The resources we need are present within the web of life that interconnects us.

This is the nature of *synergy*, the first property of living systems. As parts self-organize into a larger whole, capacities emerge that could never have been predicted and that the individual parts did not possess. The weaving of new connections brings new responses and new possibilities into play. In the process, we can feel sustained — and *are* sustained — by currents of power arising from our solidarity.

This phenomenon is similar to the religious concept of *grace*, but does not require belief in a God. Whether restoring a garden or cooking in a soup kitchen, there is a sense sometimes of being supported by something beyond one's individual strength, a sense of being *acted through*. This empowerment often seems to come through the very beings on whose behalf one acts and is familiar to many today who work for their own threatened communities, for distant peasants ripped from land and livelihood or for children imprisoned in sweatshops and brothels. Those who risk their lives to protect marine mammals, and those who risk jail to stop paying taxes for weapons and those who risk their jobs and even lives to blow the whistle on corruption and deception — they also draw on vaster powers of life. These people, whose numbers are countless, show us what can happen through us when we break free of the old hierarchical notions of power. Grace happens when we act with others on behalf of our world.

How can we as individuals help our species make the holonic shift to collective self-interest? The following guidelines were composed in 1990 in collaboration with German colleagues in the Work That Reconnects. We offer them here to invite further reflection.

1. **Attune to a common intention.** Intention is not a goal or plan you can formulate with precision. It is an open-ended aim: may we meet common needs and collaborate in new ways.

2. **Welcome diversity.** Self-organization of the whole requires differentiation of the parts. Each one's role in this unfolding journey is unique.

3. **Know that only the whole can repair itself.** You cannot fix the world, but you can take part in its self-healing. Healing wounded relationships within you and between you and others is integral to the healing of our world.

4. **You are only a small part of a much larger process, like a nerve cell in a neural net.** So learn trust. Trust means taking part and taking risks, when you cannot control, or even see, the outcome.

5. **Open to flows of information from the larger system.** Do not resist painful information about the condition of your world, but understand that the pain you feel for the world springs from interconnectivity, and your willingness to experience it unblocks feedback that is important to the well-being of the whole.

6. **Speak the truth of your experience of this world.** If you have persistent responses to present conditions, assume that they are shared by others. Willing to drop old answers and old roles, give voice to the questions that arise in you.

7. **Believe no one who claims to have the final answer.** Such claims are a sign of ignorance and limited self-interest.

8. **Work increasingly in teams or joint projects serving common aims.** Build community through shared tasks and rituals. ☛

9. **Be generous with your strengths and skills — they are not your private property.** They grow from being shared. They include both your knowing and your not-knowing, and the gifts you accept from the ancestors and all beings.

10. **Draw forth the strengths of others by your own acknowledgment of them.** Never prejudge what a person can contribute, but be ready for surprise and fresh forms of synergy.

11. **You do not need to see the results of your work.** Your actions have unanticipated and far-reaching effects that are not likely to be visible to you in your lifetime.

12. Putting forth great effort, **let there also be serenity** in all your doing; for you are held within the web of life, within flows of energy and intelligence far exceeding your own.[14]

**4**

# What Is The Work That Reconnects?

*If we could surrender to Earth's intelligence,*
*we would rise up rooted, like trees.*

— Rainer Maria Rilke

A S WE STAND NOW AT THE BRINK OF DESTROYING OUR PLANET
as a home for conscious life, contemporary science and ancient
spiritual traditions bring us insights into the basic miracle of our
existence. These insights are powerful enough to liberate us from the
corporate industrial complex and to help us create a Life-Sustaining
Society — if we let them shape our lives.

That is a big *if.* For while the new paradigm is the stuff of countless lectures and books, it is purveyed mainly on the intellectual level.
As a plaything of the mind, it is fascinating — even hopeful — but
we urgently need ways to let it transform our lives. That is because,
as poet Rilke reminds us:

Only in our doing can we grasp you.
Only with our hands can we illumine you.
The mind is but a visitor:
it thinks us out of our world.[1]

## History of the Work

Beginning in the late 1970s, a form of personal and group work has grown up to help our lives be shaped by what our minds are learning. Arising first in North America, it spread to Western and Eastern Europe, Australasia and Japan through articles circulating from hand to hand before the time of the Internet, and through workshops that have engaged some hundreds of thousands of people, within and beyond movements for peace, justice and a healthy environment. First it was called Despair and Empowerment work, and when Joanna wrote the first book on this work, she titled it *Despair and Personal Power in the Nuclear Age.*[2] After a few years, the Deep Ecology movement inspired her and her colleagues to identify this approach as Deep Ecology work. It is still known by that name in German-speaking Europe.

In the late 1990s, Joanna asked Molly to help her update the original book. Our collaboration soon produced an entirely new book, incorporating the same basic concepts and exercises. We titled our book *Coming Back to Life — Practices to Reconnect Our Lives, Our World.*[3]

Over the years, workshops carried a variety of names: Awakening as Earth, Our Life as Gaia, The Power of Our Deep Ecology, Being Bodhisattvas, Opening the Global Heart, and many others. However, as we wrote the book, we looked for a generic name other than Deep Ecology work. In an unforgettable conversation we had with Fran Macy, the name emerged: *The Work That Reconnects.*

In all the publications, the work has been offered as a giveaway or open source, so that people can easily share the ideas and practices in their communities. The books have been translated into German, French, Spanish, Portuguese, Russian, Japanese and other languages.

Many key ideas of the work also appeared in Joanna's books *World As Lover, World as Self*[4] and *Widening Circles: A Memoir.*[5] In 2012, Joanna and British colleague Chris Johnstone published *Active Hope,*[6] aiming to bring basic assumptions and ingredients of this work to a wider readership, including people who wouldn't be caught dead in a workshop.

The Work that Reconnects also reaches people through the Internet, especially the websites www.joannamacy.net, workthatreconnects.org, www.activehope.info, mollyyoungbrown.com as well as training DVDs and webinars. Most of all it has spread by word-of-mouth as people talk about what they've read and share their experience in workshops.

## Aims of the Work

The central purpose of the Work That Reconnects is to bring people into new relationship with their world, to empower them to take part in the Great Turning, and to reclaim their lives from corporate rule.

In order to do this, the Work That Reconnects:

* provides perspectives and practices drawn from systems science, Deep Ecology and spiritual traditions that reveal our interbeing through space and time
* reframes our pain for the world as evidence of our mutual belonging and hence our power to take action on behalf of life
* awakens stamina and buoyancy to live with full awareness of both the Great Turning and the Great Unraveling, and to embrace the uncertainty
* affirms that our intention to act for the sake of all beings can become the organizing principle of our life
* helps us identify the strengths and resources we can mobilize in our commitment to the self-healing of the world
* presents the Great Turning as a challenge that every one of us, in collaboration with others, is fully capable of meeting in our own distinctive ways

## Basic Assumptions of the Work

The theory underlying this work is implicit in the preceding chapters: it derives from the present challenge to choose life, from recognizing what stops us and from understanding the self-organizing powers of the universe. The following statements make more explicit the principles on which we base the Work that Reconnects.

1. **This world, in which we are born and take our being, is alive.**
   It is not our supply house and sewer; it is our larger body. The

intelligence that evolved us from stardust, and interconnects us with all beings, is sufficient for the healing of our Earth community.

2. **Our true nature is far more ancient and encompassing than the separate self defined by habit and society.** We are as intrinsic to our living world as the rivers and trees, woven of the same intricate flows of matter/energy and mind. Having evolved us into self-reflexive consciousness, the world can now know itself through us, behold its own majesty, tell its own stories — and respond to its own suffering.

3. **Our experience of pain for the world springs from our connectivity with all beings, from which also arise our powers to act on their behalf.** When we deny or repress our pain for the world, or treat it as a private pathology, our power to take part in the self-healing of our world is diminished. This *apatheia* need not become a terminal condition. Our capacity to respond to our own and others' suffering — that is, the feedback loops that weave us into life — can be unblocked.

4. **Unblocking occurs when our pain for the world is not only acknowledged, but experienced.** Information about the crises we face, or even about our psychological responses to them, is insufficient; only when we allow ourselves to experience our feelings of pain for our world can we can free ourselves from our fears of the pain — including the fear of getting permanently mired in despair or shattered by grief. Only then can we discover the fluid, dynamic character of feelings. Only then can they reveal on a visceral level our mutual belonging in the web of life.

> Strength of heart comes from knowing that the pain that we each must bear is part of the greater pain shared by all that lives. It is not just "our" pain but *the* pain, and realizing this awakens our universal compassion.
>
> — Jack Kornfield

5. **When we reconnect with life by choosing to bear our pain for it, the mind retrieves its natural clarity.** Not only do we experience our interbeing in the community of Earth, but also mental eagerness arises to match this experience with new paradigm

thinking. Concepts, which bring relatedness into focus, become vivid. Significant learnings occur, for the individual system is reorganizing and reorienting, grounding itself in wider reaches of identity and self-interest.

6. **The experience of reconnection with the Earth community arouses the urge to act on its behalf.** As we experience *bodhichitta*, the desire for the welfare of all beings, Earth's self-healing powers take hold within us. For these powers to function, they must be trusted and acted on. The steps we take may be modest undertakings, but when they involve some risk to our mental comfort, they free us from old safe limits. Courage is a great teacher and bringer of joy.

## The Spiral of the Work

Over the years, we have come to see the Work That Reconnects as occurring in a spiral, mapping a journey through four successive stages: Coming from Gratitude, Honoring our Pain for the World, Seeing with New Eyes and Going Forth. These four stages support one another, and work best in sequence.

The Spiral begins with **gratitude,** because that quiets the mind and brings us back to source, stimulating our empathy and confidence. Expressing our love for life on Earth, in brief and concrete terms, helps us to be more fully present and grounded for acknowledging the pain we carry for our world.

In **honoring our pain,** and daring to experience it, we learn the true meaning of compassion: to *suffer with.* We begin to know the immensity of our heart/mind. What had isolated us in private anguish now opens

DORI MIDNIGHT

outward and delivers us into the wider reaches of our collective existence.

Sensing the larger life within us lets us **see with new eyes.** At this turning point of the work, we know more genuinely our relatedness to all that is. We taste our own power to change and feel the texture of our living connections with past and future generations, as well as with our brother/sister species.

Then, ever again, we **go forth** into the actions that call each of us, in keeping with our situation and gifts. We explore the synergistic power available to us as open systems and apply these understandings to our work for social change. We don't wait for a blueprint or fail-proof scheme, for each step will bring new perspectives and opportunities. Even when we don't succeed in a given venture, we can be grateful for the chance we took and the lessons we learned.

And the Spiral begins again. In the face of devastation and tragedy, gratitude will hold us steady, especially when we're scared or tired.

The nature of the Spiral is fractal. The sequence can repeat itself even within a particular stage of the Spiral. For example, the Seeing With New Eyes stage may reveal to us with greater clarity the horrors being inflicted on the Earth community, bringing up fresh grief and outrage. We may need to honor that pain with a practice or ritual before moving on.

The lens of the Spiral can reveal patterns of growth in our own understanding and capacity. The Spiral can be discerned over the span of a lifetime or a project, and it can also happen in a day or an hour.

**A Note on Stand-Alone Practices:** Some of the processes that have grown out of the Work That Reconnects embrace the whole Spiral, or a good portion of it. They can be used both within a particular stage of the Spiral, such as Seeing With New Eyes, or as the sole experiential component of a given event. Widening Circles and the Seventh Generation Practice, for example, are often used as the main

feature of an evening presentation, a conference breakout session or a guest appearance in a class or community group. These stand-alone practices are signaled with the logo left in the Table of Contents and in the chapters.

## The Shambhala Prophecy

From ancient Tibet across twelve centuries comes a prophecy relevant to our time, evoking the challenges we face in the Great Turning and the strengths we can bring to it. Joanna received this teaching in January 1980 from her close friend and teacher Dugu Choegyal Rinpoche at Tashi Jong, a Tibetan community in exile in northwest India.

There are varying interpretations of this prophecy. One portrays the coming of the kingdom of Shambhala as an internal event, a metaphor for one's personal spiritual journey, independent of the world around us. Another interpretation conveys it as an entirely external event that will unfold unrelated to any actions we may choose to take. In the version of the prophecy given to Joanna, the inner and outer worlds are not separable. That is the perception of the *bodhisattva*, who appears in this prophecy in the figure of the Shambhala Warrior.

Here is how Joanna has passed on the prophecy:

> *There comes a time when all life on Earth is in danger. Great barbarian powers have arisen. Although these powers spend their wealth in preparations to annihilate each another, they have much in common: weapons of unfathomable devastation and technologies that lay waste our world. It is in this moment, when the future of all beings hangs by the frailest of threads, that the kingdom of Shambhala emerges.*
>
> *You cannot go there, for it is not a place. It exists in the hearts and minds of the Shambhala warriors. And you can't recognize a Shambhala warrior by looking at her or him, for they wear no uniforms or insignia, and they carry no banners to show which side they are on. They have no barricades on which to climb to threaten the enemy, or behind which they can rest or regroup. They don't even have a home turf. Always they must move across the terrain of the barbarians themselves.*
>
> *Now the time has come when great courage — moral and physical courage — is required of the Shambhala warriors, for they must go into the heart of the barbarian powers, to*

*dismantle the weapons—weapons in every sense of the word. They must go where the armaments are made and deployed, and also into the corridors of power where decisions are made.*

*Now the Shambhala warriors know that these weapons can be dismantled. That is because they are* manomaya *(which means mind-made). Made by the human mind, they can be unmade by the human mind. The dangers threatening life on Earth are not visited upon us by any extraterrestrial power, or satanic deities, or preordained fate. They arise from our own choices, our relationships, our habits of thought and behavior.*

*So this is the time when the Shambhala warriors go into training. How do they train? They train in the use of two weapons. What are they? (To convey them, Joanna's teacher held* up his hands in the way the lamas hold the ritual objects, the *dorje* and bell, in the great lama dances of their people.)

*One weapon is compassion; the other weapon is wisdom, or insight into the radical interdependence of all phenomena. Both are necessary. Compassion gives you the fuel, the motive force, to go where you need to go, to do what you need to do. It means, essentially, to not be afraid of the pain of the world. When you are not afraid of the pain of the world, nothing can stop you.*

*But by itself, that weapon is not enough: it can burn you out. So you need the other, the knowledge of our interbeing.*

*With that wisdom you know that this is not a battle between good guys and bad guys; you know that the line between good and evil runs through the landscape of every human heart. You know that we are so interwoven in the fabric of life that even the smallest act with clear intention has repercussions beyond our capacity to measure or even see.*

*By itself, that insight seems abstract and cool, so to keep moving, we need the heat of compassion as well.*

These two weapons of the Shambhala warrior represent two essential aspects of the Work That Reconnects. One is fearless experience of pain for the world. The other is insight into the radical connectivity of all life. Tibetan monks, when they chant, often make continuous hand gestures or *mudras*. Often these mudras are dancing the interplay between compassion and wisdom — a dance that each of us can embody in our own way.

## The Work That Reconnects in Corporate Settings

People working in publicly traded corporations have a role to play in the Great Turning. We need their access, knowledge, savvy, experience, technical proficiencies and soul force if we are to dismantle the dominate structures of the Industrial Growth Society.

Furthermore, we will need the communication and transportation capacities now possessed by transnational corporations when we can claim and adapt them for the common good.

In bringing the Work That Reconnects into publicly traded corporations, let us be clear that it threatens their operating codes in these ways:

1. It helps people to tell the truth about what they see, know and feel is happening to their world. It opens feedback channels and legitimizes questions of conscience.
2. It expands one's sense of connectedness with the web of life. It breaks through denial and apathy, and it opens hearts and minds to worldviews beyond Business As Usual.
3. It helps build trust, solidarity and common vision among participants, contrary to the isolation and obedience fostered by corporations and corporate-controlled government.

Therefore, in bringing the work into corporate settings, we are confronted with perplexing questions:

1. How can we foster connections and gain entry without losing sight of understandings that are needed for the Great Turning?
2. How do we keep the Work That Reconnects from becoming just a feel-good experience that improves morale without generating structural change?
3. How can we as facilitators protect ourselves from co-optation by the glamour of corporate attention and fees?

4. How can we address *the elephant in the living room*: the destruction being inflicted on people and planet by the very structure in which we meet?

# 5

# Guiding The Work That Reconnects

*Since one person's knowledge can only represent a fragment of the totality of what is known, wisdom can be achieved when people combine what they have learned ... the defense of the world can truly be accomplished only by cooperation and compassion .... We became human by working together and helping one another.*

— Paul Hawken

NEVER BEFORE IN HISTORY have our destinies been so intertwined. The crises facing us are too vast and complex for any one of us alone to comprehend, much less adequately respond. The fact that our fate is a common fate has tremendous implications. It means that in facing it together openly and humbly, we find again our mutual belonging and our power to act.

This is the experience of people who come together in the Work that Reconnects. Although the effectiveness of this work can be explained in terms of systems theory, psychology and spiritual teachings, its full transformative power is discovered when we experience it together.

## The Value of Working in Groups

**Workshops provide focus and duration.** In the daily run of life the global crises facing us can appear too pervasive, too appalling, too remote to discuss with others without soon shifting the topic. A workshop is an island in time where, removed from other distractions and demands, we can focus together long enough to explore our deeper responses to these realities. The group helps us to sustain the gaze.

**Group work provides support.** The natural emotions evoked by the Great Unraveling are hard to deal with alone. The workshop serves as a haven and laboratory where we discover that our emotional responses are widely shared, bringing a rare sense of community.

**Workshops offer safety.** In the group exercises, we practice behaviors uncommon in our daily life. We learn to hear each other's deepest feelings about this planet-time, without wanting to contradict or fix them. We can express our dreads without trying to shield others, and our dreams without having to explain them.

**Workshops support truth-telling.** Practices we use permit us to tell the truth of what we feel, know and see is happening to our world, without having to explain or defend ourselves. There are things we really need to hear ourselves say.

**Group work is synergistic.** What occurs in the life of a group, even over a short period of time, is creative in unpredictable ways. From the interactions, connections are woven that are unique to

The roots of my personal agony and despair lie in having spent months at a time in close proximity to weapons of unfathomable destructive force. That experience led to a pattern of repressing my deepest feelings about the existence and possible use of nuclear weapons. The workshop provided a safe haven and highly relevant content, which for the first time allowed me to squarely face my feelings — without running. I am deeply grateful for that opportunity to begin to resensitize a part of myself, which had become numbed, and to take that pain as the basis for real spiritual growth and new direction in my life.

— Commander of a Nuclear Submarine

each particular mix of people. The synergy of a group reveals the profoundly collaborative nature of life.

**Group work generates community.** The workshop provides a setting for initiating ongoing relationships and joint endeavors. Participants frequently stay in touch afterwards for mutual support and collaboration. Even if we don't meet one another again, we experience a new openness and honesty in ourselves when we encounter other people; the feeling of community carries over into our daily lives.

**Groups working together demonstrate the characteristics of systems.** They become more integrated and, at the same time, reveal themselves as more differentiated. This allows them to exhibit increasing cohesiveness and, in the same measure, more flexibility.

## Tasks of the Facilitator

So how do we facilitate? What are our responsibilities as guides? Essentially, our task is to provide processes that help people know their pain for the world, their interconnectedness with all life and their power to take part in the Great Turning.

For this to happen, our tasks are to:

1. Create a safe setting in which people can come to trust themselves and each other.
2. Convey the aims of the workshop in the context of the Spiral.
3. Help the group stay focused on the work at hand.
4. Explain and guide exercises, working within time constraints, in a manner that does not rush or drag things out.
5. Convey the basic assumptions and conceptual foundations of the work, with illustrations from fields of interest that are familiar to you.
6. Engage in the practices you offer when possible; don't hold yourself aloof.
7. Help the group enjoy itself.

## Foundations of Good Facilitation

Feeling the impact of their experience in a workshop, people often share some of the practices immediately. If they haven't time to explore the work's theory and practices in any depth, they risk being superficial and even misleading. The following guidelines will help you develop your skills and knowledge base:

**Experience and Understanding of the Work That Reconnects.** It is best for you to have participated in several workshops and studied this book, especially the early chapters. Theory and practice form an integrated body of work. A single exercise by itself is not the Work; all four stages of the Spiral (see Chapter 4) are essential.

An effective and enjoyable way to prepare oneself for guiding the work is this: form a study/practice group of two or more — six to eight is ideal — to go through this book together. For each session, rotate leadership, discuss a section of theory (read ahead of time) and try out an exercise.

**Basic facilitation skills.** To guide any group in an interactive learning process, you need certain basic skills:

1. Confident presentation of ideas, stories, and exercises
2. Noticing and interpreting the feedback provided by non-verbal cues as well as comments and questions
3. Genuine *active listening* to participants' ideas and responses
4. Pacing and timing of discussions and activities

> How dare I be discouraged in the work
> By anything so trivial
> As the fear of personal failure?
>
> — Paul Williams

**Engaged activism.** To grasp the raw reality of today's challenges, you need to be actively involved in all three dimensions of the Great Turning. This is essential for a practical understanding of what corporate capitalism is doing to our world and the stresses that activists suffer. Facilitating a workshop does not fulfill this requirement.

## Capacities of an Excellent Guide

Certain capacities on your part help people experience the Work That Reconnects as authentic and real. In turn, these capacities deepen as you facilitate the work.

View the people in your workshop with **warmth and respect.** Trust their willingness to be honest and present in this time of crisis. Joanna's practice, as she comes into the room, is to see each person as a *bodhisattva*, the hero in Buddhism who seeks the welfare of all beings.

From this trust flows your **naturalness and spontaneity.** Pain for our world is normal and inevitable, like getting drenched in a rainstorm — no big deal. Humor arises, easy as tears, and so does a casual kind of self-disclosure. Without this naturalness, a tone of sentimentality or drama may creep in and undermine the work.

Your own **emotional authenticity** as guide is, of course, essential. This is why it is important for the guide to take part, wherever possible, in the experiential work rather than directing it from the sidelines or staying aloof from it as an observer. Otherwise your facilitation will risk appearing controlling and even manipulative. Be sure you've done your own despair work before attempting to facilitate it for others. If you have not allowed yourself to "touch bottom," you run two risks. One is fear of these emotions. The other is voyeurism. A guide who has not plumbed his own feelings of grief, overwhelmedness and futility risks using others' expressions of such feelings as a vicarious outlet.

With trust and ease in the work comes **flexibility.** The preliminary design of a workshop may be impeccable, but its unfolding will fall flat if you can't respond to unforeseen needs and opportunities as they arise. Your ability as guide to think on your feet and "change horses in midstream" grows from your understanding of the Basic Assumptions of the Work That Reconnects. You may want to stick a Post-it® in Chapter 4 and reread the section with that title before every workshop.

There's no neat formula for when to keep a firm hand and when to give space to unexpected developments. Here the Spiral, which you present in words and draw graphically at the start of the workshop, can help you **stay on course** while incorporating new material.

For you to serve as guide while also engaging in the work seems to require **two levels of consciousness.** On one level you are 100% participating in the process, and on the other you are 100% scanning the group as a whole. Fortunately, that's not as hard as you might think.

## Engaging Full Participation

A good workshop is a highly participative venture; therein lies its power to connect, inform, invigorate. One of the greatest gifts that a guide can offer to participants is the opportunity to listen to themselves and each other.

**Talking object.** In the whole group, some individuals tend to dominate and some stay quiet, while others wait impatiently to get a word in edgewise. A talking object, passed around the circle or taken from the center by whoever wishes to speak, helps people take turns and slows the pace for better listening.

**Sharing time.** Every group facilitator knows the quandary of time. We want to respect each speaker, but all too often as we go around the circle, each statement grows a little longer, and the time for other activities slips away. To counteract this tendency, explicitly ask for brevity at the outset. Molly sometimes warns the group that she will break in about a third of the way around with a reminder about brevity, specifying the point in the circle, so when the reminder comes, the previous speaker doesn't feel criticized.

Another time-minding method utilizes a watch that is silently passed to the one who is speaking when his time is up, e.g. a minute or two. He finishes his sentence and then holds it while the next person speaks, passing it to her after the allotted time, and she in turn does the same for the following speaker. This reliable method shares the responsibility with everyone in the group.

In small groups and pairs, people can speak more fully, of course. Encourage groups to share the time among their members. Sometimes free conversation with lots of give and take is appropriate, but it can go off on tangents and use up available time. To help people take turns, you may indicate how much time is available and signal when each person's time is up. You can allow a few minutes at the end for general conversation. Groups can also keep their own time, passing a watch as in the large group.

**Allowing silence.** Encourage participants to allow silence as well. In stillness, they can listen to their body, what is underneath the words they spoke or what is awaiting articulation. For others to jump in with words right after people have shared their deepest feelings can dissipate the intensity and meaningfulness of the moment.

**Vary modalities and pace.** Maintain a balance between verbal and non-verbal activities, between sitting and moving, between working in the large group and in smaller constellations. Such alternations enliven people and allow for a variety of learning styles.

**Spend time outside.** Send participants out on a mission, such as finding an object for use in an exercise, for a silent walk or do a group practice outside. The Mirror Walk, Council of All Beings, Cairn of Mourning and Systems Game all originated in outdoor settings.

> The turning point for me was when I stopped talking and just looked, when I held that hand [in The Cradling] and realized — for the first time in my life — the sheer miraculousness of a human being.
>
> — Engineer and workshop participant

**Take the pulse.** As guide, you need to know what is happening with the people in your workshop — are they feeling restless, anxious, tired? If it's not clear to you, find out by asking. The very act of checking in helps people feel more engaged and responsible.

**Brainstorm.** Brainstorming can let us feel that we are nerve cells interacting in a neural net — dramatizing power with. Brainstorming is a familiar practice, but even so, review the ground rules each time you use it:

1. Don't censor, explain, or defend your ideas.
2. Don't evaluate or criticize the ideas of others.
3. Save discussion until afterwards.

## Working With Strong Emotions

This work brings up powerful emotions, which we are unaccustomed to expressing among relative strangers. The following guidelines are essential to the Work That Reconnects:

1. **Respect people's feelings.** Remember that anger, sorrow, fear and overwhelmedness are natural responses to the suffering of other beings and the deterioration of our world. When these responses well up, do not rush in to comfort and discourage others

from doing the same. Your very presence, acceptance and matter-of-fact bearing are reassurance enough. Emotional discharge takes many forms. Tears and shouting release tension and integrate the full range of feeling. As we learn from Re-Evaluation Counseling, laughing and yawning are also forms of discharge and should not be taken as signs of indifference or boredom.

2. **Trust people's capacity to handle heavy discharge of emotion,** knowing that they can always choose to stop. Remember that the emotions arising from connection and concern for our world take us into shared territory and mutual belonging. This is in contrast to people getting carried away and, with eyes closed, screaming and spinning out into some private terror or hellhole. This latter behavior very rarely happens in the Work That Reconnects, but if it seems to be occurring, go to the person immediately, touch them and tell them firmly to open their eyes. Follow up with grounding questions about who and where they are in the present moment.

3. **Respect people's defenses and resistance.** Let no one in the workshop feel pressure to display emotion. Catharsis is healthy, but in this work the outward expression of emotion is no measure of a person's caring.

Men often have particularly strong defenses, as Doug Hitt observed,

> The social codes against the voicing of our feelings about what is happening in our world must be particularly punitive and effective in corralling men .... The corporate/ industrial/war machine could never abide a population of men with intact emotional feedback loops. I saw that words like "feelings" or "pain" set-off the social codes alarm system .... Use "speaking the truth" instead. This is a kind of call to arms to masculine energy and bypasses the codes about "sharing feelings."[1]

4. **Remember to engage in the process.** To act as guide and simultaneously express the full range of your own feelings is tricky, but not difficult once you choose to do it.

5. **Trust the mutual empathy of the group.** As people hear one another's deep pain for the world, empathy and caring arise. Stay open to the play of this mutual support, and let it remind you that participants will receive as much from each other as from you.

## Guidelines for Conducting Rituals [i]

+ A defining characteristic of a ritual is that it invites those taking part to speak archetypally — that is, to speak as part of a larger sacred whole. Our individual experience, needs and perspectives are held within that awareness. That more encompassing awareness tends to release us from the grip of a hyper-individualized sense of self.

+ Since the beginning of time, rituals have been a regular part of life. So, as guide, assume a natural authority without altering your manner. Don't get precious about it. Don't assume a special tone of voice or pious measured speech; that just puts people off.

+ Have a co-facilitator or assistant to help you scan the group and assist in the rare case that someone needs individual attention or leaves the room in distress.

+ Ritual space and time needs demarcation. Make all preparations and give all directions for the ritual before its actual start. If there's a chance people might be showing up late, ask someone to sit near the door to quietly brief the latecomers.

+ Start every ritual with a formal dedication to clarify the collective intention that the ritual serves. For example, "May our sincere participation in this ceremony serve all beings and strengthen us for the Great Turning."

+ After the dedication, and as a portal of sound to the ritual, you might invite the group to sound the seed syllable *AH* (for a good half minute), explaining that *AH* stands for all that has not yet been spoken, and for those without a voice.

---

[i.] Practices we consider to be rituals, and conduct as such, are: Reporting to Chief Seattle, the Bestiary, Cairn of Mourning, Truth Mandala, Despair Ritual, Bowl of Tears, Dance to Dismember the Ego, Bodhisattva Check-In, Council of All Beings, Harvesting the Gifts of the Ancestors, Seventh Generation Practice.

+ Once the ritual has begun, you as guide are fully engaged in it. Recall the two levels of consciousness described above.
+ The end of the ritual should be similarly clear and definitive. You can ring a bell or gong. You can invite ceremonial gestures, such as bows — bows to the Earth with head and hands to the ground (returning the energy), bows to ancestors and future beings, bows to each other. You can honor the depth and intention of the ritual and explicitly connect it to the wider world. You can borrow the Buddhist practice of "dedicating the merit," which means to share the benefits of the practice with all beings.
+ Be sure people have ample, unhurried time to make the transition back to ordinary conversation.

## Workshop Setting and Arrangements

Workshops have been held in churches, schools, town halls, living rooms, retreat or conference centers and at the gates of nuclear testing sites and of uranium mines. They have varied in length from an hour and a half to a week or ten days. They can be a single event or form a series over a period of time. Size of workshops has ranged from a few people to a hundred or more.

You will want a space that can be closed to outside disturbance, and spacious enough to permit people to move around easily. However, memorable workshops have taken place in cramped quarters, such as a small hotel room, and in noisy public settings, such as the corner of a high school cafeteria.

Access to nature, for some of the exercises and for breaks, helps participants reconnect with the more-than-human world. As more of us succumb to environmental sensitivities, try to arrange for a minimally toxic setting, without fumes from fresh paint, new carpeting or cleaning chemicals. In announcements and registration mailings, ask participants to refrain from using scented products. Insist that smoking be limited to outside areas well away from entrances. If possible, find space that is wheelchair accessible. And for residential workshops, make sure that healthy vegetarian food is at least an option.

Pay attention to the aesthetics of the space. Some guides like to create an altar in the room, inviting people to bring special objects and photos for it. Flowers and plants always beautify a room and remind us of the natural world outside the walls. If possible, set up chairs and floor cushions in a circle, or concentric arcs for larger groups.

Other items for your checklist might be: flip charts and markers; sound system if needed; roster of participants; relevant books and materials; any art supplies required.

### *Money*

And then there's the question of money. In the best of all worlds, we wouldn't need to be paid to do this work. However, many facilitators need money to support themselves and cover expenses, so they charge a fee and offer scholarships to people who can't afford it. If a workshop is offered through an institution, there are often additional charges for facilities and/or meals and lodging, and the fee must be set accordingly. Sometimes workshops are offered as fund-raisers for a cause, with facilitators donating their services. Our colleague John Seed often asks people to donate to a particular campaign at the end of a workshop. People who want to help create a *gift economy* may offer a workshop free to their community, and accept *dana* (a Hindu and Buddhist term for generosity or giving) in the form of money, in-kind services or Time Bank hours. Consider your own needs and resources as well as those of your community when deciding whether to charge a fee, and how much.

## Opening The Workshop

Openings set the tone for what follows. This is the time when participants listen most closely, to learn the ground rules and get the feel of the work. The following steps help create an atmosphere of openness, safety and mutual respect:

1. **Greet participants individually, if only for a moment.** Joanna has a practice of making brief physical contact with each person as she introduces herself and hears their names. This lets them know that their presence is appreciated, and helps Joanna relax into a sense of connection.

2. **Help participants to relax.** People may come with mixed feelings and an initial measure of awkwardness and tension. Some bodily movement — standing, stretching, and deep breathing — eases these tensions and helps people feel more alert and involved. Singing is excellent, too.

3. **Clarify logistics.** Tell people when breaks will occur and the location of the bathrooms. Limit food and drink to breaks, note-taking and recording to lecture sections of the workshop.

4. **Secure agreements.** Ask participants to agree to some specific ground rules, such as: full-time participation, suspended cell phone use (during breaks as well), punctuality and confidentiality.

5. **Dedicate the work.** Formally verbalize a group intention that this work serve the healing of our world and the Great Turning to a life-sustaining society.

6. **Help participants to come into full presence.** The workshop requires full attention, so we often help people with an invitation like this: "Many of us hurried to get here, perhaps leaving some chores undone and some calls we needed to make. Let's look at these bits of unfinished business in our mind's eye … and now let's put them up on a shelf and leave them there until five o'clock."

7. **Clarify the purpose of the workshop.** Make sure people understand that our purpose here is to explore our inner responses to the condition of our world and prepare to take part in its healing. It is not to discuss or debate the causes of the global crises, and it is not to decide on the best collective actions. Let people know that this will be an interactive workshop, with a range of experiential exercises.

8. **Affirm presence and power of feelings.** Acknowledge from the outset that our responses to world conditions are inevitably charged with emotion, and affirm that it's OK to feel. Grief, fear and anger are appropriate, and this is a safe place to express them.

9. **Have people introduce themselves.** After your initial comments, which should be as brief as clarity allows — ten minutes should do it — let people hear from each other. Already as they

introduce themselves, people often move to a deeper level of personal sharing.

10. **Present the Spiral** as a road map for the workshop. It's helpful to draw it "live," best on newsprint, labeling each station as you briefly describe it. You can refer back to it throughout the workshop. Some facilitators like to present the Spiral after the initial Gratitude work.

## Closing The Workshop

A focused completion process respects the depth of the experience and connections that have occurred.

Take care to end on time so that people with engagements do not leave before the others are finished; make it a part of your commitment to the group. Make the formal ending, and then people can talk informally afterwards (perhaps while they help with cleanup).

Coming together in a full circle at the end of the workshop honors the mutuality the participants have experienced. Points you might want to make in your closing remarks include:

+ The deep feelings experienced here are likely to well up in the days ahead, so take time for quiet reflection and remember to breathe.
+ Even though this particular circle may not meet again physically, it will remain part of our lives. Let people silently look around the circle, appreciating what they have learned from each other and what they wish for each other in the time ahead.

Then you can invite brief words of closing from the group, and end with a song, a poem or silence. Other ways to close a circle are described at the end of Chapter 10.

## Evaluation

In our years as facilitators, participants' evaluations have always provided important feedback. They affirm strengths we may have doubted, indicate skill areas we need to work on and generate new ideas for future workshops. They also offer participants an immediate opportunity to contribute to the work.

Evaluation can be done in individual written form or as a group activity, generally prior to the closing circle. If it is to be written, give the participants open-ended questions such as "What did you find most useful? Least useful? What changes would you suggest?"

Evaluations done collectively and orally are quicker (ten minutes can be sufficient). As enjoyable, high-energy brainstorms, they generate more items of response. An effective form is three wide columns on newsprint or blackboard, the first headed by a plus sign (for what the participants liked), the second by a minus sign (for what didn't work for them) and the third by an arrow (for suggested changes). In true brainstorm fashion, these are not to be argued, discussed or defended — just noted — and thus a rich blend of contrasting reactions often appears. The same activity might show up in both the plus and minus columns, according to different people's evaluations. In this approach, participants can note the variety of responses and are less likely to generalize from their individual experience.

## Follow-Up

People will want to be able to maintain contact with each other after the close of the workshop. You can encourage this in a number of ways, such as:

1. **Roster of participants.** Have people sign in (with addresses, phone numbers and email) when they arrive or at the end of the workshop. Send copies to everyone by email, omitting anyone who wants to opt out. Ask people to use "bcc:" when sending email to the group.
2. **Information on local resources and actions.** The end of a workshop is a good time to share information about organizations and projects in which people can become involved. Provide materials — but don't recruit. Put up sheets of newsprint where participants can write up further resources and actions; this is preferable to a lot of announcements.
3. **Follow-up session.** An evening gathering within a week or so after the workshop allows for ongoing community to build. Such follow-up sessions may generate a study/practice group to go

through this book together, discussing a section of theory (read ahead of time) and trying out an exercise at each meeting.

❧

## Ongoing Support for the Guide

When meeting with workshop participants who have declared an interest in becoming guides, Joanna likes to pair them up and give them two Open Sentences:

+ The idea of *my* facilitating the Work That Reconnects is totally absurd, because ....
+ The idea of me as a facilitator of the Work That Reconnects is the most natural thing in the world, because ....

These two Open Sentences are refreshing even for us old-timers. Given how overwhelming are the realities we contemplate in the workshops, and given how ludicrous are fantasies of a surefire fix, it's hard for a guide to avoid occasional feelings of inadequacy. At the same time, if we are honest about why that is so, and can accept that, we are naturals as facilitators of the Work That Reconnects.

So, if you're doing it right, it's easy to be unsure about your wonderfulness as a facilitator. Therefore, open your eyes — again and again — to the wealth of support that is available to you.

+ **The sacred living body of Earth.** Everything we are and know and will ever have comes from Mother Earth. That fact is our true nature and ultimate security. Rest in that. It bonds us with the ancestors and the future beings, and with each person walking into a workshop. Awareness of that is deepened through practices in this book, such as the Four Abodes, the Web, the Great Ball of Merit and the Death Meditation.
+ **The sufficiency of service.** As other wise ones have observed, we who are now in service to our planet cannot know whether we are deathbed attendants to life on Earth or midwives to a new age. Both callings have similar characteristics: a sense of awe, complete attention to each moment, a thinning of the veil between life and

death. Whichever side of the coin we are enacting, we are blessed to be of service.

+ **Facilitators of the Work That Reconnects.** As you embark on this path, those who are already guides in the work are a resource for you. You may know some already, and it's easy to locate more through workthatreconnects.org. Others you may find through Great Turning Times, and ActiveHope.info.

+ **Songs** that are especially suited to the Work That Reconnects have been collected by Gretchen Sleicher on her SongsfortheGreat Turning.org.

+ **Webinars** are appearing from the Work That Reconnects, such as those offered by Barbara Ford and Chris Johnstone: gaiaworkshops.net, ActiveHope.info and wtrtrainingsinUK.org.

+ **Videos.** Films of Joanna explaining and demonstrating the Work That Reconnects in 2004 are available online. View and download at univ-great-turning.org/study-areas-by-person/joanna-macy/. Also view at vimeo.com/channels/workthatreconnects.

+ The rewards of a **book study group** are mentioned in Chapter 10. To pull a few friends and neighbors together to walk through the chapters of *Coming Back to Life* and *Active Hope* — each session including both discussion and facilitation of a process — has proven to be a fine training ground for guides.

+ As you become more comfortable in the role of guide, you may be inspired by guides who have adapted the **Work That Reconnects to specific purposes:**

   ❀ As Kathleen Sullivan has done with the *cyber school bus* under the aegis of the United Nations, adapting basic practices to teaching nuclear disarmament in the classroom: cyberschoolbus.un.org.

   ❀ As Sarah Vekasi has done in pioneering the vocation of *eco-chaplain*, to more fully support Appalachian people fighting mountaintop removal coal mining: ecochaplaincy.net.

   ❀ As Barbara Hundshammer has done bringing bodywork into the work (see Appendix D).

❋ As Louise Dunlap has done in her writing courses and groups, with writing practices that move through the Spiral (see Appendix D).

❋ As Eleanor Hancock, Kristin Barker and other colleagues in the Work That Reconnects have done in creating White Awake to raise consciousness around issues of race and white privilege: whiteawake.org.

❋ As Gunter and Barbara Hamburger and their colleagues across Germany have done in their multi-session trainings, up to a year in length, in the Work That Reconnects (also called Deep Ecology Work). Consisting of six to eight residential weekends, these trainings include an individual project and a ten-day intensive with a vision quest: holoninstitut.de.

Above all, remember that the Work That Reconnects evolves through our shared practice, mistakes and all.

# 6

## Coming From Gratitude

*Just to live is holy,*
*to be is a blessing*

— Rabbi Abraham Heschel

*The whole thing is grace. Everything of the Universe — ev-*
*erything that has brought forth the carbon in my body, my*
*body itself, the trees that are shining outside my window, the*
*bees that are flying around collecting pollen — it's all grace if*
*we recognize it. It's there for us.*

— Sister Miriam MacGillis

WE HAVE RECEIVED AN INESTIMABLE GIFT. To be alive in this beautiful, self-organizing universe — to participate in the dance of life with senses to perceive it, lungs that breathe it, organs that draw nourishment from it — is a wonder beyond words. And it is, moreover, an extraordinary privilege to be accorded a human life, with this self-reflexive consciousness that brings awareness of our own actions and the ability to take choice. It lets us choose to take part in the healing of our world.

## Gratitude: Teaching Points

1. The originating impulse of all religious and spiritual traditions is **gratitude for the gift of life.** Yet we so easily take this gift of life for granted, which perhaps is why many spiritual paths begin with thanksgiving, to remind us that for all our woes and worries, our existence itself is an unearned benefaction.

   In Tibetan Buddhism, for example, we are to pause at the start of meditative practice and reflect on the preciousness of a human life. This is not because we humans are morally superior to other beings, but because we can "change the karma." In other words, with self-reflexive consciousness, we are graced with the capacity for choice — to take stock of what we are doing and change directions. We may have depended primarily on instinct for eons of lifetimes as other life-forms, but now at last we are granted the ability to consider and judge and choose. Weaving our ever-complexifying neural circuits into the miracle of self-awareness, life yearned through us for the ability to know and act and speak on behalf of the larger whole. Now that time has come, when by our own decision we can consciously enter the dance.

2. In times of turmoil and danger, **gratitude helps to steady and ground us.** It brings us into presence, and our full presence is perhaps the best offering we can make to our world.

   In Buddhist practice, that first reflection on the preciousness of human life is immediately followed by a second one, on its brevity. "Death is certain; the time of death is uncertain." And that reflection awakens us to the gift of the present moment — to seize this unrepeatable chance to be alive — right now.

3. That our world is in crisis — to the point where survival of conscious life on Earth is in question — in no way diminishes the wonder of this present moment. For the great open secret is this: **gratitude is not dependent on our external circumstances.** It does not depend on whether we like where we are or approve of what we are facing. On the contrary, to us is granted the great privilege of being on hand to take part, if we choose, in the Great Turning. We can let the hardships of this time enlist all our strength, wisdom and courage, so that life can continue.

4. **Gratitude is politically subversive** in the Industrial Growth Society. It helps inoculate us against the consumerism upon which corporate capitalism depends. It serves as a counterweight to the dissatisfaction with what we have and are, the craving and neediness inflamed by our political economy.

5. Gratitude is at the core of indigenous culture on Turtle Island (North America). Among the Haudenosaunee in particular, **this is seen as a sacred duty.** At the beginning of virtually every meeting or ceremony, thanks and greetings — "the words that come before all else" — are offered to all that gives life: from our eldest brother, the sun, to water, winds, plants, animals and Grandmother Moon.

Perhaps the practice of gratitude can help us understand the remarkable self-respect and dignity of those native people who have not been defeated by centuries of broken promises and cultural genocide. It would seem that gratitude — and the dignity and self-respect it engenders — has helped them survive. And that is an inspiration for all of us as we face the Great Unraveling and the suffering it brings.

There is so much to be done, and the time is so short. We can proceed, of course, out of grim and angry desperation. But the tasks proceed more easily and productively from an attitude of thankfulness; it lets us rest in our deeper powers.

> Let the beauty we love be what we do.
> There are hundreds of ways to kneel and kiss the ground.
> — Rumi

## Practices

Coming from gratitude begins with the guide's warm welcoming of each person. To evoke at the outset the love we share for life in Earth relaxes and enlivens us all. It also opens us all to our pain for the world, because knowing what we treasure triggers the knowing of how endangered it is.

In comments and instructions, take care not to tell people what to feel. This is true in every stage of the Spiral; in this stage, to over-name gratitude can sound both pious and flat. Allow feelings to arise and be named by participants.

## Becoming Present through Breath, Movement, Sound and Silence

Most of us are braced, psychically and physically, against the signals of distress that continually barrage us in the news, on the streets, from the natural world. This chronic state of tension inhibits our vitality and gratitude as well. At the outset of a workshop, therefore, we turn to the breath, the body, the senses — for they can help us to relax and tune in to the wider currents of knowing and feeling.

### OPENING THROUGH THE BREATH

The breath is a helpful friend in this work, for it connects the inside with the outside, revealing our intimate and total dependence on the world around us. It connects mind with body, lending attention to that ever-flowing stream of air, stilling the chatter and evasions and making us more present to life. The breath also reminds us that we as open systems are in constant flow, not stuck within any given feeling or response, but dynamic and changing as we let it pass through us.

Begin by having everyone pay attention to their breathing for a few moments. You may lead the group in a brief breathing practice of your choice.

> Breath, you invisible poem!
> Pure, continuous exchange
> with all that is, flow and counterflow
> where rhythmically I come to be.
>
> — Rainer Maria Rilke

In the course of the work, as we let ourselves experience our pain for the world, the breath continues to serve us, much as it serves a woman in childbirth. It helps us relax and open to the flow of information, and to the changes it may bring. (See Breathing Through in Chapter 13.)

## Opening through the Body

All the threats facing us in this planet-time — be they toxic wastes, world hunger or global warming — come down in the last analysis to assaults on the body. Our bodies pick up signals that our minds may refuse to register. Our unexpressed and unacknowledged dreads are locked into our very tissues along with known and unknown toxins — in our muscles, in our throats and guts, in our ovaries and gonads. Essential joys come through the body as well: the tastes, sights, sounds, textures and movement that connect us tangibly to our world. Our faithful "Brother Ass," as St. Francis called the human body, is our most basic connection to our planet and our future.

To bring attention to the body, continue the guidance you began with the breath, using your own words to suggest something like the following:

> *Stretch. Stretch all muscles, then release. Slowly rotate the head, easing the neck with all its nerve centers. Rotate the shoulders, releasing the burdens and tensions they carry. Behold your hand, feel the skin. Feel the textures of the world around you, clothing, arm of chair, tabletop, floor. Your senses are real; they connect you with your world; you can trust them.*

## Opening through Sound

To open up and tune in, we also turn to sound — sounds we make, sounds we hear. The physical universe, say the ancient Hindus and modern physicists, is woven of vibrations, and so are we. Releasing our attention into sound moves us beyond the self's cramped quarters into wider apprehensions of reality. Non-melodic music can weave our awareness into those larger patterns. So can *sounding* —

letting the air flow through us in open vowels, letting our voices in-terweave in ah's and oh's, in Oms and Shaloms.

Sounding together we feel our capacity for community vibrate within and among us. Sounding also clears the throat, helping us feel more present to each other and ready to speak.

### OPENING THROUGH SILENCE

Many traditions, like the Quakers, know the power of *gathered si-lence*, where together in stillness we attune to inner and deeper knowing. In this planet-time, when we face dangers too great for the mind to embrace or words to convey, silence serves. It can be as rich as sounding, while serving a complementary purpose: sounding helps us to release the planetary anguish; silence helps us to listen to it. And, later in the workshop, once we have had opportunities to specify our concerns and fears, we can take more moments to be with each other in silence.

Some guides like to begin every session with a period of silence, eyes closed, just to settle in. Sometimes they pose a question before the silence, to stir reflection for a dialogue to follow, suggesting that when people feel ready to speak out of the silence, they may do so. This can move the group to a deeper level, while closing the eyes builds trust and helps people relax and reflect.

### *Introductions with Gratitude*

(1–2 minutes per person)

Group introductions are a good place to bring in gratitude. Perhaps writing the list up where everyone can see it, invite people to briefly share the following:

1. Their name and where they are from
2. One thing they want us to know about them
3. One thing they love about being alive in Earth (of the many things they love, choose just one)

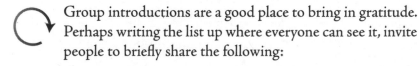

## Open Sentences

(30 minutes)

Open Sentences is a structure for spontaneous expression. It helps people listen with rare receptivity as well as speak their thoughts and feelings frankly. People sit in pairs, face to face and close enough to attend to each other fully. They refrain from speaking until the practice begins. One is Partner A, the other Partner B — this can be determined quickly by asking them to tap each other on the knee; the one who tapped first is A. When guide speaks each unfinished sentence, A repeats it, completes it in his own words, addressing Partner B, and keeps on talking spontaneously for the time allotted. The partners can switch roles after each open sentence or at the end of the series. The listening partner — and this is to be emphasized — keeps silent, saying absolutely nothing and hearkening as attentively and supportively as possible.

For the completion of each open sentence allow a couple of minutes or so. Give a brief warning each time before it is time to move on, saying "take a minute to finish up," or "thank you." A small bell can then bring people to silence, where they rest a few seconds before the next open sentence.

## Open Sentences on Gratitude

This is a highly pleasurable activity, and you may want to invent your own open sentences. Or pick from these favorites of ours (#5 always comes last):

1.  Some things I love about being alive in Earth are ...

> This morning I stood on the riverbank to pray. I knew then that the ancient ones were wise to pray for peace and beauty and not for specific gifts ... And I saw that if one has even a small degree of the ability to take into and unto himself the peace and beauty the gods surround him with, it is not necessary to ask for more.
>
> — Edith Warner

2.   A place that was magical (or wonderful) to me as a child was ...
3.   A person who helped me believe in myself is or was ...
4.   Some things I enjoy doing and making are ...
5.   Some things I appreciate about myself are ...

## Gratitude Rounds

### (30–40 minutes)

It's so easy to take the things and beings in our lives for granted. Then it helps to move back a little, and gain a bit of distance, in order to glimpse how precious and how uniquely real they are. As with a quick turn of the lens, we see with fresh appreciation.

### METHOD

Sitting in circles of five or six, people imagine they are at a point outside of space and time. After a short spell of silence, they start remembering together what they loved about living on Earth. That's the first Round, which can circle more than once, and last for ten to fifteen minutes. The second Round focuses on what they liked about the humans of planet Earth. And in the Third Round, they reflect on what they were grateful for in being themselves.

## Mirror Walk

### (40 minutes)

The Mirror Walk, adapted from the familiar Trust Walk, awakens sensory awareness and a fresh sense of gratitude for life, as well as providing a change of pace and focus. An excellent training for the ecological self, it helps people experience the world as their larger body — imagining when they open their eyes, at specified moments, they are looking in a mirror. Hence the name. Suitable at any point in the workshop, it develops trust among participants and moves beyond words to immediacy of contact with the natural world.

## Method

An outdoor setting, with growing things, is most rewarding, but even a city street with an occasional tree has served. Forming pairs, people take turns being guided with eyes closed, in silence. Without vision, they use their other senses with more curiosity than usual and practice entrusting another person with their safety. Their partners, guiding them by the hand or arm, offer them various sensory experiences — a flower or leaf to smell, the texture of grass or tree trunk, the sound of birds or children playing — all the while without words. The tempo is relaxed, allowing time to fully register each sensory encounter. Every so often, the guide adjusts her partner's head, as if aiming a camera, and says, "Open your eyes and look in the mirror." The ones being guided open their eyes for a moment or two, and take in the sight.

Demonstrate with a volunteer as you give instructions. Remind participants to remain silent, except for the periodic invitation to look in the mirror.

After a predetermined length of time, roles are changed. Provide an audible signal when it is time to switch, using a loud bell. The Australian aboriginal call, *coo-ee*, works well because it reaches a great distance as people repeat the call as soon as they hear it.

When they return at the end of the second shift, each pair forms a foursome with another pair to speak of the experience. After ten minutes or so, you may wish to invite a general sharing in the whole group. "What did you notice?" "What surprised you?" "What feelings came up, in guiding or being guided?"

## *Open Sentences on the Great Turning*

### (20 minutes)

The Gratitude stage of a workshop is an excellent place to introduce the Great Turning. We strongly recommend describing the Great Turning within the context of the three stories outlined in Chapter 1. This can help us be thankful for the chance to choose the version of reality we want to live by.

After presenting the Great Turning, we sometimes offer these three open sentences. (For the mechanics of this exercise, see Open Sentences above).

1. To be alive now in this time of global crisis, what is hard for me is...
2. What I appreciate about living in this time of global crisis is ...
3. As I look at my life, it seems that I am taking part in the Great Turning — and some of the ways ...

## *The Wheel of the Great Turning*

### (30 minutes)

This lively process is a great way to learn about the Great Turning and generate appreciation for what people are already doing.

### METHOD

Clear a circular space, six to ten feet in diameter, around which people sit closely together. If participants number more than 12 or so, consider making two circles in different parts of the room.

Each circular space becomes a wheel of the Great Turning. In each wheel, place three objects to symbolize the three dimensions of the Great Turning. For Holding Actions, some first-aid material (like rolls of bandaging) works well. For Transforming the Foundations of Our Common Life, use something organic and alive, like the leafy stalk of a growing plant. For the Shift in Perception and Values, perhaps a pair of eyeglasses.

The wheel turns when people reach into the circle, one at a time, to pick up an object and report to the others something they are involved in or immediately acquainted with. For example, taking the eyeglasses, they may speak of a vision quest or a study group that has opened new horizons. Holding the roll of gauze bandaging, they might tell of volunteering at a soup kitchen or joining the resistance to a corporate water grab in their community. With the stalk of leaves, they might describe a farmers' market or a cooperative child-care starting in their neighborhood.

This practice generates high spirits and is best kept at a lively pace. To help people be brief, treat it as a ritual. For example, after each person has spoken, the group responds in chorus: "That's how it goes in the Great Turning!"

༄༅

## The Elm Dance

### (30 minutes with instructions and story)

A simple, beautiful practice has been spreading along with the Work That Reconnects. To celebrate their commitment to life and their solidarity with activists the world over, people join hands in a circle dance.

Set to the haunting strains of a Latvian song by Ieva Akuratere and choreographed by Anastasia Geng, the Elm Dance took form in Germany in the 1980s. In 1992, having learned it from her friend Hannelore Witkowski, Joanna took the Elm Dance to workshops she was leading with a Russian-speaking team in areas poisoned by the Chernobyl disaster. There, and especially in Novozybkov, the most contaminated of still inhabited cities, the dance became an expression of the people's will to live.[1] It was here the dance evolved a distinctive form with the raising and swaying of arms, evoking their connection with the trees they so loved.

We share the Elm Dance in nearly every workshop and course we teach. The dance helps us feel more fully our gratitude and grief. It helps us feel the presence of our brother and sister activists around the world, to know that we are many and that we are linked in ways we cannot see. When sharing this dance, you are invited to dedicate it to the people of Novozybkov, or to any other group you choose.

People love this dance, so in an extended workshop we may do it at the start of every day. Some people make a practice of doing it after the Truth Mandala. It can be used at any stage in the Spiral.

### INSTRUCTIONS FOR THE ELM DANCE

(as evolved among environmental activists)
Music: itunes.apple.com/us/artist/ieva-akuratere/id260647004
Song name: "Kā Man Kājās?"

Circle up with plenty of room to move, holding hands. If the numbers are too great to form a single circle, make concentric circles with about one large step of distance between them.

It does not matter when in the music you begin the dance, except to start on a beat. The dance consists of four beats of movement, alternating with four beats of swaying in place. When swaying in place, imagine that you can feel the energy from the heart of the Earth spiraling up through the floor into your body. When the energy reaches the heart chakra, send it out for the healing of the trees and all beings. This is an act of intention. Anastasia Geng, who created the dance from the Latvian song, said the purpose of the dance is for building strong intention, which in Bach Flower Remedies is the power of the elm.

The circle moves counterclockwise (to the right). Always begin with the right foot. Start by taking four steps backward (to the right). After four beats of swaying in place, the next four steps are facing forward, still moving counterclockwise. Then, after the next four beats of swaying in place, move four steps toward the center of the circle, raising your arms high and unlinking hands so they can wave like boughs of a tree. Remember to sway for four beats, and then move four steps back from the center, rejoin hands, sway four beats, and begin again. Continue in this fashion until the music breaks midway. In the silence before the music resumes, the guide reminds the dancers that throughout the second half of the dance they can call out by name those beings and places to which they send healing.

❧

## The Presence of Gratitude Throughout the Work

The affirmative note we strike at the outset of the workshop will continue to reverberate. In the stages of the work and the practices that follow, notice how consistently gratitude is summoned. Even in Honoring Our Pain, we are reminded to be thankful — for the chance to speak the suffering, and for each other. Gratitude for the miracle of life, for each other and for the motivation that brings us to this work are explicitly evoked in the Milling, the Remembering, the Cradling, the Bodhisattva Check-In. The Deep Time work fosters thankfulness for the gifts of ancestors and for the inspiration of the future generations, just as the practices surrounding the Council of All Beings bring gladness for our bonds to other life-forms. The visioning and planning we do as we prepare to Go Forth help us to be aware of the vast resources we can draw upon — and to take grateful note of our own strengths, too. The sense of how blessed we are by the life we share is nourished by the meditations offered in Chapter 13.

**7**

# Honoring Our Pain For The World

*Your pain is the breaking of the shell*
*that encloses your understanding.*
*Even as the stone of the fruit must break, that its heart*
*may stand in the sun, so you must know pain.*
*And could you keep your heart in wonder at the*
*daily miracles of your life, your pain would not seem*
*less wondrous than your joy.*

— Khalil Gibran

*Our choice is to be in love or to be in fear. But to choose to*
*be in love means to have a mountain inside of you, means to*
*have the heart of the world inside you, means you will feel*
*another's suffering inside your own body and you will weep.*
*You will have no protection from the world's pain*
*because it will be your own.*

— China Galland

ZEN MASTER THICH NHAT HANH was asked, "What do we most need to do to save our world?" His questioners probably expected him to identify the best strategies to pursue, but Thich

Nhat Hanh's answer was this: "What we most need to do is to hear within ourselves the sounds of the Earth crying."

## Our Inner Responses to Suffering and Destruction

In this stage of the Spiral of the Work That Reconnects, this is what we do. We bring to awareness our inner responses to the suffering of our fellow-beings and the destruction of the natural world — responses that include dread, rage, sorrow and guilt. These feelings are healthy and inevitable — and usually blocked for all the reasons explored in Chapter 2, including the fear of getting permanently mired in despair. Now they are allowed to surface without shame or apology.

Note the term *allowed to surface*. We do *not* try to inspire or instill these feelings in people; compassion — the capacity to suffer with — already flows in us like an underground river. All we do here is help that river come to the light of day, where its currents mingle and gain momentum. We need not scold or manipulate people into what we think they should be feeling if they were moral or noble; we simply help each other uncover what is already there. Only honesty is needed. Then we discover, as Thich Nhat Hanh has said in reference to our interbeing, "the pain and the joy are one."

Fear of so-called negative thinking causes some people to resist this aspect of the Work That Reconnects, for fear of making things worse. This concern usually comes from a misunderstanding of the New Age adage, "We create our own reality," and it results in

> When I really let myself experience the state of the world, my first reaction is bottomless, unutterable sorrow. That moves quickly into outrage. The sorrow I can deal with; the outrage I used to suppress — after all, it might offend someone. Now I use it to give me courage. When I get mad, I have to move. With half-suppressed anger, I tend to swing out and do something impetuous and ignorant, but a fully-felt, grounded, familiar anger can move me through a life-time commitment to make things better.
>
> — Donella Meadows

a reluctance to see what is actually going on. It is a kind of magical thinking that cuts off the feedback necessary to the system's healing.

This stage of the Work That Reconnects involves the following steps:

+ acknowledging our pain for the world
+ validating it as a wholesome response
+ letting ourselves experience this pain
+ feeling OK about expressing it to others
+ recognizing how widely it is shared by others
+ understanding that it springs from our caring and connectedness

After the first practice in which people are expressing their pain for the world, Joanna likes to make the following observation:

> I want to call your attention to something. Please observe how far the concerns you've just shared extend beyond your personal ego, beyond your individual needs and wants. This says something very important about who and what you are. It says you are capable of suffering with your world. That capacity to suffer-with is the literal meaning of compassion, a central virtue in every spiritual tradition. It says you are a compassionate being. Another word for that, in Buddhism, is bodhisattva.
>
> So don't you apologize for the tears you shed or the rage you feel about what's happening to our living world. They are just the other face of your belonging.

Of course these are Joanna's words. You will find your own way of linking our pain for the world to our mutual belonging — a great liberating secret of the Work That Reconnects.

> Let this darkness be a bell tower and you the bell. As you ring, what batters you becomes your strength.
>
> — Rainer Maria Rilke

## Practices

**Before leading these practices,** be sure you are quite familiar with the teachings in Chapters 2 and 3, and understand how important it is that these practices be used within the context and sequence of the Spiral as outlined in Chapter 4.

Some of us are inclined, as we move into this stage of the Spiral, to tell the Shambhala Prophecy. We like the way it describes compassion, the first tool of the Shambhala warrior, in terms of the strength and courage needed to face the suffering of our world. Please tell the Prophecy only if you have received it directly as an oral teaching.

**Quoted passages** in these exercises are included for illustrative purposes only. Reading them like a script sounds artificial, even boring. It can distance you from the participants, making it hard for you to respond to the needs of the moment.

In preparing to lead a practice, read the instructions and quoted versions over several times to get a good feel for its structure and tenor. Translate them into your own words and images. Mentally, or on a slip of paper, record the main points and key phrases you want to use. Practice until you feel comfortable and authentic.

❧

## Small Groups on the Great Unraveling

### (30 minutes)

This simple sharing practice comes after an exposition of the Great Turning and the Great Unraveling. Clustered in small groups, people tell each other how they experience in their own lives the collective crises of our time — environmental, economic, social. People rarely get a chance to report and reflect on these realities without appearing to complain or blame.

### METHOD

Invite people to sit close in threes or fours and take turns reporting to each other in response to a single question: *In what ways, in your own life, do you experience and observe the Great Unraveling?* Allow enough time for the sharing to go around their little circle more than once.

At the conclusion, invite people to see how the concerns they mentioned extend beyond their personal needs and wants, demonstrating their capacity to *suffer with* their world — the literal meaning of compassion and the fuel we need for the Great Turning.

> What is true is already so. Owning up to it doesn't make it worse. Not being open about it doesn't make it go away. And because it's true, it is what is there to be interacted with. Anything untrue isn't there to be lived. People can stand what is true, for they are already enduring it.
>
> — Eugene T. Gendlin

## Open Sentences on Honoring Our Pain
### (30 to 45 minutes)

This exercise provides a swift and easy way for people to voice their felt responses to the condition of our world. Its structure helps people both to listen with total receptivity and to express thoughts and feelings that are usually censored for fear of comment or adverse reaction.

### METHOD

See Chapter 6 description of the Open Sentence Process.

Here is a sample series of open sentences. Feel free to make up your own, remembering to keep them as unbiased and non-leading as possible.

+ What concerns me most about the world today is …
+ When I see what's happening to the natural world, what breaks my heart is …
+ When I see what's happening to our society, what breaks my heart is …
+ When I think of the world we will leave our children, it looks like …
+ Feelings about all this, that I carry around with me, are …
+ Ways I avoid these feelings are …
+ Ways I use feelings are …

## VARIATIONS

The Open Sentence format adapts easily to different situations.

With groups of organizational or professional colleagues, the sentences can help articulate difficulties without beating around the bush, as well as renew inspiration. For example:

+ What first inspired me to work for the Environmental Protection Agency (or become a physician or canvasser) was ...
+ What I find hard in this work is ...
+ What keeps me going in this work is ...
+ What I hope can happen for us in this work (or organization) is ...

In a workshop for couples, these sentences can be included:

+ I am sometimes reluctant to share my pain for the world with my partner because ...
+ The effect of these feelings on my relationship with my partner is ...

Working with teachers or parents, this practice can include:

+ If I withhold from my children my concerns for the future, I do so because ...
+ If I tell the children my concerns for the future, I do so because ...
+ In talking with the children about the news, what I want is ...

## *Breathing Through*

Early in this stage of the Spiral, it is beneficial to introduce the practice of Breathing Through that appears in Chapter 13, Meditations for the Great Turning. It makes it easier for people to take in distressing information.

## *The Milling*

### (About 20 minutes)

This practice provides a change of pace after people have been sitting and talking. The silent encounters help people to see each other more fully in their shared humanity. The present global realities strike us with greater impact when we relate to our face-to-face experience of another person. To confront their possible suffering and death can jolt our minds and hearts more than imagining our own.

Be sure, as the guide, that your comments are non-manipulative. Never tell people what to think or feel. Keep your suggestions in accordance with present reality. For example, do not say: "See this person as a victim of nuclear attack." Rather: "Let the possibility arise in your mind that this person might ...." Use an ordinary tone of voice without drama or sentimentality. We offer one patter here just to give the flavor and tenor of this practice.

## METHOD

Moving back chairs and cushions to make a large open space in the room, invite people to *mill* — to circulate around the room at a fairly energetic pace without talking. Stress that they are to remain silent throughout the whole practice.

*Let your eyes go out of focus; you won't bump. Use the whole space so we don't get into a snarl in the middle. Soft vision and you won't collide. If you find us all going in the same direction, turn around and go upstream.*

1.  In the first part, people are moving as on busy city streets. *Hurry; this is the Industrial Growth Society, and time is money. Keep moving. No talking.* Embellish this a bit, reminding people how time is accelerating. *You are an important person with important things to do. Feel in your body the tension of having to make your way through all these moving obstacles.*
2.  Next, the pace slows and participants become aware of each other's presence. *Now we slow down a bit. We see the faces around us. "Oh, I'm not alone here." Our eyes engage as we pass.*

    Then begins a series of one-to-one encounters. Take care to point out that when they meet, they don't need to lock eyes. They can simply relax their gaze and open their awareness to the whole person. Be sure to give ample milling time between encounters, to relieve the intensity and allow the experience to sink in.

3. The first encounter draws attention to the sheer presence of the other and their choice to be here. (We use the ungrammatical "their" and instead of "his or her.") *And you find yourself in front of someone — and stop. Take their right hand in yours. This person is alive on planet Earth at the same time as you, born into the same period of crisis, danger and speed. And they've chosen to be here today. There are plenty of other things they could do on this day — catching up on work, hanging out with family or friends. But they've chosen to be here, to look together at what's happening to our world. Notice how you feel that they made that choice and now take your leave of this person in any way you want.*

4. In the next encounter, we focus on the other's unknown strengths and powers. *Again, you find yourself in front of another person, and take their hand in yours. Behold this brother-sister being, who spoke today of things they love. Open your awareness to the strengths and gifts this person can bring to the Great Turning — their patience, their love of adventure, their knack at problem solving, their kindness.*

5. In the following encounter, the focus moves to the other person's knowledge of our present situation and their willingness to face it. *You are looking into the face of someone who has a good clue what's going on in our world.* (Give two or more examples of what's going on, such as the following: forests being clearcut, small farms forced out of business, crops genetically engineered, fracking, mountaintop removal, the corporate military complex and its wars, radiation spreading from Fukushima and other power plants, the huge threat of climate change.) *This person knows this is going on, yet they haven't closed their eyes, haven't turned away. Honor their courage.*

6. In this next encounter, the sense of touch is used to heighten awareness and imagination. *And again we find ourselves in front of another person, and again we take their right hand in ours, but this time we close our eyes as soon as we've connected. Close your eyes so that all your attention can go into the sensation of touch. What is this object you are holding? There is life in it ….* (See The Cradling in Chapter 8 for ideas of what to include here. If you plan to use the Cradling in the same workshop, omit this encounter.)

7. In this final encounter, we acknowledge the danger each person faces in this planet-time and the gifts they can bring to it. *Moving on, we come to our last encounter. Facing each other, put your hands together palm to palm at shoulder height.... Before you stands someone living in a beautiful, fragile and poisoned planet. In their body, as in yours, are toxins that can bring cancer and immune disease. This person, like you, can die from a nuclear accident or attack, or a plague triggered by climate change. We can face this together. We must not let our common danger separate us. Let it bond us. Keep breathing ....*

   *Now there's another thing to see in this face. Allow your awareness to open to the real possibility that this person will play a pivotal role in the Great Turning to a life-sustaining civilization. They have the gifts, the strengths, the motivation. Allow that possibility to enter your mind and let them know how you feel about it.*

Some guides have people sit down with their last partner for a few minutes of sharing.

⟨❧⟩

## Reporting to Chief Seattle

### (30 minutes)

In this process, through people's own words, the contrast between attitudes of the Industrial Growth Society and our indigenous ancestors' reverence for the natural world becomes poignantly clear. Reminding us that respect for the web of life is our birthright, it evokes both sorrow for its loss and a yearning for its return.

The practice is based on the speech that Chief Sealth, or Seattle as he is now known, delivered to his tribal assembly in 1854. Its words and images are familiar to many. The version best known to us was adapted in 1970 by film scriptwriter Ted Perry, from the notes of a settler who heard the original speech. Here we use it not as an historical document, but for its powerful evocation of Native American reverence for Earth and its foreboding of what the white man's lack of reverence would bring.

## METHOD

Sitting in a circle, people take turns reading aloud significant portions of Seattle's speech (see Appendix A). In the center of the circle, a lit candle, or better yet an arrangement of natural objects and a woven basket, helps to ground the process. Quietly, reflectively, people listen to the message that the great chief uttered over a century and a half ago in response to the US government's decision to buy — or take — his people's land. Among the now familiar words are these:

> How can you buy or sell the sky, the warmth of the land? This idea is strange to us. If we do not own the freshness of the air and the sparkle of the water, how can you buy them? Every part of this earth is sacred to my people. Every shining pine needle, every sandy shore, every mist in the dark woods, every clearing, and humming insect is holy in the memory and experience of my people .... All things share the same breath.
>
> We will consider your offer to buy the land. I will make one condition: the white man must treat the beasts of this land as his brothers .... What is man without the beasts? If all the beasts are gone, men would die from a great loneliness of spirit. For whatever happens to the beasts soon happens to man. All things are connected.
>
> This we know. The earth does not belong to man; man belongs to the earth. This we know. All things are connected like the blood which unites one family. All things are connected. Whatever befalls the earth befalls the sons of the earth. Man does not weave the web of life; he is merely a strand of it. Whatever he does to the web, he does to himself.

After a pause, upon completion of the reading, the guide invites the group to imagine that Chief Seattle's spirit is present at the center of the circle. Speaking spontaneously at random, they can tell him now what has happened to his land: how we are treating it and each other and what life is like for us now. To give weight to each person's words, the others can say simply, "Yes, it is so."

No further guidance is necessary. Whether people choose to tell Seattle about deforestation or factory farms, toxic dumping, poisoned air or homelessness, they will be glad for the chance to speak of these current facts of life within a larger, encompassing context. The web of life, so revered by Seattle, lets this truth-telling become redemptive, because it both owns the grief and opens us to possibilities of change and healing. The guide, after allowing ample time for people's words and for reflective pauses between them, concludes the process, saying something like, "May our words to Chief Seattle, like his to us, remain with us for the healing of our world."

## The Bestiary

### (30 minutes)

This process provides a ritual structure for recalling what the Industrial Growth Society is doing to our fellow species. It serves to honor the unique and irreplaceable forms that are passing from us. It arose in 1981, at a midnight gathering of several hundred people in Minnesota, in the form of a simple reading from the list of threatened and endangered species. At its close, people were invited to call out the names of other endangered aspects of our common life on Earth; then they expressed their sorrow by the ancient act of keening. Joanna's poem, "The Bestiary," grew out of that experience, although it only names other animals and does not include trees or plants.

As the names are read, it is easy to feel guilty as a human. So, before the reading, the guide makes clear that this is not the point of the exercise. Guilt tends to close us down. Instead, as each name is read, let people take the opportunity silently to honor the beauty and wisdom of that unique, irreplaceable species. This approach helps people to open to the grief that is in them.

### METHOD

The group sits in a circle and listens as "The Bestiary" (see Appendix B) is read aloud. Use several voices (four is a good number) spaced around the circle; the pace should be unhurried as befits a funeral, and the voices should be strong. After the naming of each species, a clacker or a drum is struck in one strong beat. The drum has a funereal connotation; the clacker (two pieces of wood struck sharply together as in a zendo) has the finality of a guillotine. In "The Bestiary," the reader who names the species immediately before a paragraph reads that reflective paragraph as well.

At the conclusion of the poem, the guide invites people to name things they notice are disappearing from the world. The intent remains the same as with the endangered species: to publicly name the loss and to keep its memory. After each naming — "clean beaches," "bird song," "safe food," "stars over cities," "hope" — the clacker or drum sounds. Again the pace is slow and measured. The guide concludes with words that honor the losses that have been spoken, and the honesty and solidarity that their naming brings us now for our work in the Great Turning.

❦

## We Have Forgotten Who We Are

This liturgical responsive reading in Chapter 13 can be used effectively as part of Honoring Our Pain, especially before or after an intense practice.

❦

## "I Don't Care"

### (10–15 minutes)

This short exercise strikes an unexpected note and brings up a lot of energy. By exaggerating feelings of disconnection, even indifference — almost inevitable in our mass culture — we can achieve greater honesty and sense of wholeness.

As we relate to what is happening to our world, concern and compassion are not all we feel. There is fed-upness too, even some callous indifference. To be whole, to be present and real, we need to acknowledge those responses as well. Doing this helps us identify with what we imagine the many other people feel, counteracting our judgment and self-righteousness.

"My despair," said Tom in a workshop at Columbia University, "is that I don't feel despair. My heart feels like a rock. I'm afraid I don't care the way the rest of you do." The rest of us were soon grateful for his confession, because it triggered the invention of this process. It ignited much laughter, and became known for a while as "I am a Rock."

It is good to do before — not after — an intensive process from this stage of the work.

## METHOD

The exercise is similar in form to Open Sentences: people sit in pairs and take turns speaking and listening to each other. The partners switch after each cue.

Before giving the first cue or open sentence, Joanna usually invites the participants to free themselves from excessive sincerity. That's because it is a little shocking, and one wonders, "Is it acceptable to actually express this here?" So, as she models, the personal expressions can start almost humorously with exaggeration and gallows humor; they get more honest soon enough.

The first open sentence allows us to express how fed up we can feel under the continual onslaught of bad news and the overwhelming array of urgent issues, from terrorism to topsoil. A phrase to start off with is: *I'm sick and tired of hearing about ...* Or *Don't talk to me about ...* Then let it go from there. The scene soon gets loud and often hilarious.

The second and last open sentence is: *I don't want to hear (or think) about all this, because it makes me feel ...* Here the mood shifts, as people find themselves expressing the very things they had doubted they felt or had feared to feel. Allow several minutes for each response.

## *Cairn Of Mourning*

### (30 minutes)

This ritual practice is similar in function to The Bestiary, but allows people to express more personally their grief for what is happening to the world. In knowing this sorrow, they can know their belonging, from which comes the power to endure hardship and to act for the sake of life.

## Method

The Cairn of Mourning is often done out of doors, though the process can be held inside as well. Invite people to wander outside, alone, calling to mind a particular part of their world, a place or being precious to them that is lost now or disappearing from their life. They find an object — say, a rock, a cluster of leaves, a stick — to symbolize what they mourn and bring it with them when they rejoin the group.

When all are seated in a circle, the simple ritual begins. One by one, at random, people arise, walk to the center and place their object. As they do, they speak. They describe the loss that the object represents — family farm, paved over creek, neighborhood store — and their feelings about it; then they formally say good-bye to it. As each offering is made and the objects pile up to form a heap or cairn, all in the circle serve as witnesses and acknowledge the speaker by saying, "We hear you."

The ritual can end with people sitting in twos or threes to express more fully the grief they felt as objects were added to the cairn. Or it can close with people holding hands as they sound together.

## Variation

When natural objects cannot be collected to represent the losses, such as when working indoors, squares of paper can be used instead. People can take three or four squares on which they can write words or draw images to represent the losses they would honor. Place an open basket in the center of the circle. People bring one square at a time to the basket, describing the loss it represents — blue sky, a beloved tree, bird song. This method allows for a variety of creative expression, some people writing short poems, some drawing pictures.[1]

⬥

## *Truth Mandala*

(90 minutes)

This ritual provides a respectful whole group structure for owning and honoring our pain for the world. The practice emerged in 1990 amid a large, tension-filled workshop near Frankfurt, on the day of the reunification of East and West Germany. Since then it has become a trusted and featured part of countless workshops the world over.

Here's how one participant described his experience with the Truth Mandala in a weekend college workshop:

> One by one we shared our fear, our grief, our anger and our emptiness. I could feel reservoirs of untapped compassion and courage emerge that enabled me to open and truly suffer with each person and the concerns that each revealed. To be able to embrace our suffering and not pull back in denial or defense is a gift and one that is transforming. It pushes us, stretching our hearts to be able to hold all of life's experience, not just the good or the joyful, but the difficult and the painful. And, in so doing, we get to experience the great paradox of opening to the suffering, which is the opening to more life and joy and love and compassion.

### METHOD

People sit in a circle. They sit as closely-packed as possible, for they are creating a containment vessel for holding the truth. The circle they enclose has four quadrants (demarcation lines are not needed), and in each quadrant is placed a symbolic object: a stone, dead leaves, a thick stick and an empty bowl. In the center is placed a small cloth. After placing the objects, the guide picks up each one in turn and explains its meaning. Here are some words we use:

> *This stone is for fear. It's how our heart feels when we're afraid: tight, contracted, hard. With this stone, we can let our fear speak.*

*These dry leaves represent our sorrow. There is great sadness within us for what we see happening to our world. Here the sadness can speak.*

*This stick is for our anger, for our outrage. Anger needs to be spoken for clarity of mind and purpose. As you let it speak, grasp this stick hard with both hands; it's not for pounding or waving around.*

*And here in the fourth quadrant, this empty bowl stands for our sense of deprivation and need, our hunger for what's missing — our emptiness.*

*Maybe there's something you'll want to say that doesn't fit one of these quadrants, so this square of cloth in the center of the mandala is a place you can stand or sit to give voice to it — be it a song or prayer or lines of verse.*

*You may wonder where is hope? The very ground of this mandala is hope. If we didn't have hope, we wouldn't be here.*

After introducing the objects, present these guidelines for the Truth Mandala and make clear that the inner circle is sacred space — made sacred by our truth-telling:

1. People at the inner edge of the circle should keep their feet from extending into the central space, which should also be free of other objects like water bottles and tissues.
2. Once the ritual starts, one person at a time, randomly and spontaneously, steps into the circle and takes an object in their hands and speaks. A person can speak from just one quadrant and leave, or move from one quadrant to another. It's OK to just hold an object and not speak. People may come in more than once or not at all; there is no pressure on anyone to enter.
3. Encourage brevity in what is spoken, pointing out the relationship between the brevity and the power of a statement. The Truth Mandala is not for lectures or reports, but for direct and simple expression of our pain for world. Let the ritual object itself help focus the mind.
4. To support the truth-telling, suggest a refrain — "I hear you" or

"I'm with you" — that people in the group will say (not in unison), during or after each speaking in the Mandala.

5. Confidentiality is essential; what's said here stays here. A person's words in the Mandala are not to be referred to afterwards.

6. No personal references to those present will be made and no cross talk or responses to what others have said.

7. Concerns about our personal lives, such as our health and families, are as welcome as concerns about the world; they are intrinsically related to the conditions of our world.

8. Feel free to speak in your mother tongue.

9. Feel free to speak as another being or another person, and let us know if you are doing that.

10. Refrain from excessive comforting. When people are expressing heavy emotion, gestures of comfort may be taken as a signal to shut down.

11. Tell people how long you expect the ritual to last (we usually keep it to about an hour and a half). Let people know they can go to the bathroom as needed.

After explaining the guidelines, describe the deeper import of each quadrant in the mandala, its source or *tantric* side. Indicating one object after another, say in effect:

> Our sorrow is in equal measure love. We only mourn what we deeply care for. "Blessed are they that mourn."
>
> In speaking fear, you also show the trust and courage it takes to speak it, in a fear-phobic society.
>
> The anger we express has its source in our passion for justice.
>
> And as to this bowl, its emptiness is to be honored, too. To be empty allows space for the new to arise.

The ritual itself begins with a formal dedication of the Truth Mandala to the welfare of all beings and the healing of our world. This is followed by a simple chant or sounding. The seed syllable *AH* in Sanskrit stands for what has not yet been spoken and all the voices not yet heard.

Trust yourself to sense the moment to draw the ritual to a close. As you prepare to close, give people a warning, so that those who have been holding back can seize the chance to speak. We often say:

> *The truth-telling will continue in our lives, but this chapter of it will draw soon to a close. Let any who have not yet entered the Mandala, and wish to, do so now.*

The formal closing of the Truth Mandala is a key moment. First you honor the truth that each has spoken and the respectful support that each has given. Truth-telling is like oxygen: it enlivens us. Without it we grow confused and numb. With it, we experience our own authority.

Next, the naming of the *tantric* side is repeated briefly. Indicating one object after another, say in effect:

> *The sorrow spoken over the dead leaves was in equal measure love.*
> *In hearing fear, we also heard the trust and courage it takes to speak it.*
> *And when we heard anger, we heard passion for justice.*
> *And we saw how the empty bowl makes space for the new.*

Then lead the group in sounding *AH* again to close. As the sounding ends, invite all to make three bows: first to the Earth to return the energy, putting head and hands on the floor. Then, to oneself by putting hands on heart, in thanks for being fully present throughout. The third bow is to the others, with hands palm to palm, for their brave presence and support.

Now let mingling, conversation and silent communion — and sometimes singing — arise naturally.

## NUMBERS, TIMING AND OTHER CONSIDERATIONS

+ We seldom conduct the Truth Mandala with fewer than twelve people or more than a hundred. We feel most comfortable leading groups of 20 to 40, and we have heard of wonderful Truth Mandalas with as few as four.

+ Allow 20 to 30 minutes for the setup before the dedication and formal beginning. We draw the ritual itself to a close after an hour and a half, even with large numbers. The process is intense, and though people are riveted, they grow more tired than they realize.

+ Be sure people have already had a chance to acknowledge their pain for the world, as in Open Sentences, before the Truth Mandala. Place the ritual near the middle of the day, with a break following. Some time for rest or journaling helps people absorb the experience. Let there be another activity before people separate for the day.

+ Review the section in Chapter 5 on dealing with strong emotions.

+ Participate. Don't hold aloof, but enter the ritual as honestly and openly as you can, while monitoring the process of the whole group.

+ Feel free to adapt the arrangements to people's needs. In workshops with the elderly, the mandala is set up on a table rather than the floor. People can then approach it with a cane or walker or from a wheelchair. In a psychiatric ward, the stone and stick are replaced with other objects, like a vine and a picture.

## *Despair Ritual*

### (60 to 90 minutes)

The Despair Ritual, one of the oldest forms of our work, serves much the same purpose as the Truth Mandala, but with greater intensity. It has the advantage of movement, encouraging people to circulate freely, with more people actively engaged at one time than in the Truth Mandala. On the other hand, the Despair Ritual can get pretty loud and chaotic and lacks the redemptive feature that the Truth Mandala includes with the *tantric* side of each heavy emotion.

Originated by Chellis Glendinning after the Three Mile Island nuclear accident, the ritual's structure was prefigured in a dream, and its function was inspired by the practice of *speaking bitterness*, which was used in China to alleviate apathy and paralysis from the suffering incurred in the revolution.

> People confessed, not their sins, but their sorrows. This had the effect of creating emotional solidarity. For when people poured out their sorrows to each other, they realized they were all together on the same sad voyage through life, and from recognition of this they drew closer to one another, achieved common sentiments, took sustenance and hope.[2]

The despair ritual has a similar result; moreover, its form offers people the opportunity to *touch bottom* in experiencing and expressing their pain for the world. As they do, people lose their fear of it. And the bottom becomes common ground.

## METHOD

The process unfolds in three concentric circles. At the outset everyone is standing and moving in the outer ring, which is the Circle of Reporting. The next is the Circle of Anger and Fear (with two cushions to pound on), and the innermost, a pile of pillows at the center, is the Circle of Sorrow. Elsewhere in the room, a corner space is marked off with plants or branches to create the Sanctuary.

After initial explanations by the guide (see Advice below), the ritual begins like the Truth Mandala with a vow of intention — *May the work we are about to do serve the healing of our world* — and a long sonorous sounding of *AH*, which symbolizes all that has been silenced or unsaid. People now move around the outer circle, counterclockwise, and at their own pace. Spontaneously they begin to make short comments about what is in their hearts and minds about the condition of the world. They report both facts and feelings — simply, briefly, without explanation:

> In my city the homeless are being arrested now, and the shelters are closing.

The air pollution is giving my daughter asthma.
I am terrified of getting cancer.

After each statement the group responds, "Indeed it is so" or "We hear you."

When emotion wells up and people feel moved not only to report it, but express it, they enter one of the two inner circles. In the middle one they may stride, stomp, pound pillows, shout out their anger or fear. Or they may move directly to the Circle of Sorrow, kneel or sink down on the cushions to release their grief, crying and sometimes holding each other. People stay in any circle as long as they want and return as frequently as they want. At different moments, almost half the participants may find themselves in the inner rings; all the while the reporting continues. As emotions and noise escalate, individuals may want to take refuge from the turbulence — then they go sit a while in the Sanctuary. There they can be quiet and a bit removed, while still following and supporting the process.

The great advantage of having the three circles and the Sanctuary is that people can participate simultaneously at different levels of emotional engagement. As they move back and forth, they discover the fluidity as well as the depth of their feelings. And those who don't give free rein to their feelings still provide a supportive presence.

After painful facts and feelings have been expressed at length, and may have reached a crescendo, or repeated crescendos, the tone of the group usually shifts. The movement down into darkness and distress begins to turn of its own dynamic into a movement up toward affirmation, as people experience the profound commonality of their caring. Statements like "my brother is dying of AIDS" are increasingly interspersed with "I'm planting a garden," or "Folks in my neighborhood are organizing a cooperative." This shift cannot be programmed, but it almost always occurs. The prevailing mood begins to change, even though some still weep in the Circle of Sorrow. Often people start clustering there, touching arms and shoulders, meeting one another's eyes in compassion and gratitude. A humming or song may arise with the rest soon joining in.

Each ending is different. Sometimes a good number of the group needs to stay longer with their feelings of anguish; but even then you can sense an abatement of energy, a shift in mood, a temporary kind of completion. Then, in an appropriate pause, you as the guide move to close the ritual by acknowledging the significance of what has transpired and inviting people to honor each other for their participation. Help them refocus on the group as a whole and soon invite them to once again sound the *AH* that began the ritual.

Sometimes the closing is less dignified. Hilarity can happen when deep emotions have been released — all the more so when they pertain to our shared world. Then the solidarity that has been rediscovered can explode in dancing and drumming.

## ADVICE TO THE GUIDE

The Despair Ritual is quite a challenge to facilitate, requiring trust, authenticity and constant alertness. Anyone serving as guide — or *road person* as Chellis put it — should reread the section on Working with Strong Emotions in Chapter 5 and also attend to the following counsel:

1. It is best not to offer and lead this process before you have experienced it.
2. Do not attempt it with fewer than 12 people or more than 50. Twenty or 30 is optimal.
3. With over 20 people, allow a couple of hours, including time for preliminary instructions and time at the end to unwind.
4. In your preliminary instructions, emphasize the fact that everyone has different emotional styles and timing. No one should feel any pressure to behave in a particular way. Emphasize, furthermore, that each person always has a choice about the extent to which they let themselves experience and express their emotions.
5. Remind the group of the distinctive nature of the ritual, which is to allow people to speak archetypally and on behalf of the collective. Here the dread, rage and grief we express are not ours alone; given our interconnections in the web of life, the tears we shed could also be those of an Afghan mother, a street child, a hunted

whale. If someone sees another in the ritual process expressing strong feelings that they also share, they may show their solidarity by quietly standing or kneeling beside them.

6. Participate. Never hold yourself aloof from the ritual, as if you were an observer or some magus. Take part fully *and* with two levels of attention — one level as an ordinary participant and the other maintaining a continuous, overall sense of how people are doing and watching for moments when you may need to intervene.

7. Intervene if people reporting from the outer circle fall into dialogue or debate. This is unlikely to happen if you have clarified the distinctive nature of ritual.

8. Intervene if a person begins to distract or disturb the others by acting out some private emotional agenda. This rarely occurs, but if it does, you can handle it. Simply go to the person, make physical contact with their arms or shoulders, ask them to look at you and then look around the group — to come back to it — and invite them to rest a while in the Sanctuary with your co-facilitator.

9. You may choose to provide support to persons undergoing extremely heavy emotional discharge. You can do this by touch or your simple physical presence beside them.

10. If nothing seems to be happening, just breathe and wait. Let people take their time.

11. If everything seems to be happening at once, the storming and sobbing looks as if it could go on for days and you wonder how you'll ever bring the group "back to normal," our advice is the same: just breathe and wait. Your job is not to rescue people but to allow them to take advantage of this rare opportunity to share so fully their pain for the world. Trust the process.

12. As with the Truth Mandala, hold the ritual near the middle of the day, and let it be followed by a break. People need time quietly to absorb the experience, preferably together — so don't let people leave right afterwards. The Cradling, Spontaneous Writing or Imaging with Colors and Clay are good follow-ons; and it's excellent to have some time in nature. This ritual should never be the last process of the day.

13. Later on, let people meet in small groups to share their experiences of the ritual; then conclude with a general discussion to give people a chance to say things to the whole group.
14. Do we need to say: don't both the Despair Ritual and the Truth Mandala in the same workshop?

## Bowl of Tears

### (30 to 60 minutes)

This simple ritual can be adapted to any size group, from a handful to a large assembly. The ritual arose from the group of 60 attending a 30-day intensive led by Joanna and Fran Macy at Western Australia in 2005. People shared their grief for the world by passing a bowl of water around the circle, each person scooping up some water and letting it trickle through their fingers as they said, "My tears are for …" The bowl was then placed on the altar.

On the Oregon coast, at the next 30-day intensive, the Bowl of Tears was used to close a ritual honoring sufferings inflicted on Indigenous people the world over. Afterward, the group ceremonially processed to the beach where a young Spaniard carried the bowl out into the surf and poured the water into the ocean.

A year and a half later at Findhorn in Scotland, a ceremony with 250 people began with poetry and spoken reflections on the power, liberation and solidarity that comes with owning our collective grief. Then people clustered in foursomes to tell of their experience of the Great Unraveling. After that they sang together, over and over like a chant, words of Adrienne Rich put to music by Carolyn McDade.[3]

> My heart is moved by all I cannot save.
> So much has been destroyed.
> I have to cast my lot with those
> who age after age, perversely,
> with no extraordinary power,
> reconstitute the world.[4]

Then, with lights lowered, images of breakdown in our world were projected on a large screen, while a wordless, choral lament (from the same *My Heart is Moved* CD by Carolyn McDade) played over and over. On the hall's large, central floor space were set three large glass bowls half-filled with water. People slowly, randomly, came down from their seats around the hall to kneel by a bowl and let its water trickle through their fingers as they spoke their sorrow for the world ("My tears are for …"). As their forms moved about in the semi-darkness, everyone seemed to be held by the music, the murmuring around the bowls, the splashing of water. Then, following three people carrying the bowls, the whole assembly slowly processed out of the hall and gathered around a garden pond. There the bowls, one after another, were formally emptied into the pond with words that reminded us that the pain we feel for the world is no private pathology; it connects us with Earth and each other. *Let us remember: our tears for the world are the tears of Gaia.*

## Method

Fill a clear glass bowl about ⅓ full of water and place it in the center of the circle on the floor or a table. The water represents our tears for the world. All are invited to come to the bowl as they are moved. Dipping a hand in the water and letting it trickle through their fingers, they can say, "My tears are for …" and speak of specific beings and places.

After everyone is finished, the group processes to any nearby body of water or to a garden or natural area where you can pour the water, saying something to the effect of: *Our tears for the world are the tears of Gaia.*

## Variation

Place a little ceramic bowl of salt next to the bowl of water. Then give instructions to this effect: *Salt is essential to life. It is in our oceans and in our tears so we place a pinch of salt in the water. Then dipping a hand in the water and letting it trickle through your fingers, you can say, "My tears are for…" and speak of beings and places you mourn.*

❧

### *Spontaneous Writing*

(20–30 minutes)

Good at any point, this practice works especially well following one of the rituals of mourning. It encourages people to explore what emerged for them in the group's free expression of feelings.

## METHOD

Choose a word, a theme or phrase — perhaps something that emerged in a previous process — and post it. Have everyone in the group relax as they read it, and have them then take pen or pencil and write whatever comes to mind. There is no requirement for spelling, grammar or even "making sense" and no requirement to read what they write to others. Suggest that people continue moving their pen or pencil even when nothing comes, just repeating the last word or drawing circles or whatever.

**With this dark and painful stuff, our task is to ...** This half-sentence from the poster artist Sister Carita has been especially powerful after sharing of our pain for the world. It lets the depths of the psyche speak its own knowing. It lets each person, still feeling the support of the group, move alone now to catch a fresh glimpse of his or her distinctive truth. After 10 or 15 minutes of writing, people are usually eager to share. Let them do this in twos or threes.

### *Imaging With Colors And Clay*

(30–40 minutes)

Verbal expression of our concerns for the world has its limits, for words can hide as well as reveal. We use language not only to communicate, but to protect ourselves, distracting others' and our own attention from what is painful. To connect with our deep responses to the condition of our world, it helps to go beyond words or dive beneath them to that subliminal level where we register inchoately both the peril and the promise of our time. On that level we can tap our energy and the wellsprings of our creativity; images and art give us access.

When we use colors on paper or model with clay, images surface; the tactile, visual engagement releases them. According to neuroscientists, artistic engagement shifts the locus of mental activity to the right hemisphere of the brain, with its capacity for thinking spatially rather than consecutively. We open our awareness to the web of life and its far-reaching reciprocities, beyond linear cause and effect. Workshop participants are often surprised by what their hands have portrayed: potencies of feelings and reaches of concern that they had supposed were peripheral to their lives. Unlike the words we speak, these images seem to have a reality of their own: we feel less need to explain or defend. The images, once birthed, are just there — like a fact of life, self-existent — and viewing them we feel at the same time both revealed and protected.

Acknowledge people's hesitations. Many people, especially adults, feel dismay when asked to engage in any kind of artwork. Make clear that the point here is not to portray or create anything or to measure up to any artistic standard. Encourage participants to trust whatever shapes and images arise and any changes that emerge, remaining open to new directions and to use more paper or clay as needed.

Encourage participants to work in silence. To let images arise, we need to let our thinking, talking mind take a rest. Soothing, non-vocal music helps. Tell people how much time they have and give them a warning two or three minutes before the time is up.

## COLORS

As you lay out the materials, suggest people use color and shape to express whatever they are feeling. Drawing with the dominant hand allows us to express with less frustration the images that have arisen. For this, allow plenty of time (say, 15 to 20 minutes) because people become very engrossed and want time to complete what they envision. On occasion, however, try drawing with the non-dominant hand; people find it frees them more completely from the control of the censoring mind, keeping the focus on color and movement and feelings.

Or let people bring in from outside some small object that attracts their attention: a leaf, a rock, a piece of bark. Placing it in the center of their paper, they allow a drawing to appear as an expression of that object — lines and shapes and colors extending out from it, as if that piece of nature were the artist.

Allow time at the end for quiet discussion. Imaging work is enhanced by the opportunity to share with others and hear their reflections. Have people gather in small groups or in the larger circle, their drawings face down. Then one by one, as they choose, people turn their sheets over and describe what they saw and felt as the lines and colors emerged on the paper. Avoiding psychological interpretations, other participants ask clarifying questions and offer observations to help deepen discovery of what the drawings reveal. Sometimes two or three drawings seem to resonate together. At the close, people often like to tape the sheets to the walls and move around absorbing them.

## MURAL

In another form of imaging together, people make a group mural, drawing on a long roll of newsprint placed on the floor or wall. In intergenerational gatherings, adults and children can each — in turn or simultaneously — draw something they love or something that makes them *feel sad about the world*. To do this first and in silence, and only later tell about what they have drawn, encourages children to express themselves in the company of grown-ups. They feel readier then to share what is on their minds, especially since they are freer with color and images than many adults.

## COLLAGE

In a similar way, people can create either individual collages or a group collage, using images cut from old magazines. Environmental magazines and *National Geographic*'s offer great images for this. In a group collage, themes often emerge, with people spontaneously placing similar images together.

## CLAY WORK

Imaging on paper is easier to arrange and less messy than working with clay. Yet clay work, being more tactile and involving larger muscles, can release emotion and tap our subconscious wisdom. Joanna experienced this personally during the Vietnam War when she felt sapped by a sense of futility. Here is how she later described the experience that took place at a Quaker conference on depth psychology:

> To give form to feeling, and tired of words, I worked with clay. As I descended into the sorrow within me, I shaped that descent in the block of clay — cliffs and escarpments plunging into abysses, dropping off into downward-twisting gullies, down, down. Though I wept as I pushed at the clay with fingers and fists, it felt good to have my sense of hopelessness become palpable. The twisted, plummeting clay landscape was like a silent scream, and also like a dare accepted in bitter defiance, the dare to descend into empty nothingness.
>
> Feeling spent and empty, the work done, my mind turned to go, but then noted what my fingers had, of themselves, begun to explore. Snaking and pushing up the clay cliffs were roots. As they came into focus, I saw how they joined, tough and tenacious, feeding each other in an upsurge of ascent. The very journey downward into my despair had shaped these roots, which now thrust upward, unbidden and resilient.

**8**

## Seeing With New Eyes

*It's the rose's unfolding, Ghalib,*
*that creates the desire to see*

— Mirza Ghalib

WE MOVE INTO THE NEXT STAGE OF THE SPIRAL as we realize from personal experience that it is from our connectivity that our pain for the world arises. The very distress that, when we hid it, seemed to separate us from other people, now uncovers our connective tissue. This realization, whether it comes in a flash of insight or a gradual dawning, is a turning point. We shift to a new way of seeing ourselves in relation to our world and a new way of understanding our power.

Many metaphors come to mind for describing this shift. It is like a turning of the tide or the pause between breathing in and breathing out. As we allow the world's pain to flow in, it rearranges our internal structures. Then the outflow releases our gifts of response into the world. Or it is like a fulcrum, letting us shift the weight of our despair, turn it and raise it into new understandings. The Chinese character for *crisis* is a combination of two forms: one means danger, the other opportunity. On this fulcrum danger turns to opportunity.

Or, yet another metaphor: this shift is a gateway. The approach to many an ancient temple is guarded by ferocious figures. In facing them down, in moving through our dreads and griefs, we gain entry to the truth that awaits us. We discover our mutual belonging, our own deep ecology and the promise that it holds for us. Now we can see in our anguish for the world the good news of a larger consciousness at work; it is the universe knowing itself through us. This wisdom is bought at the price of *positive disintegration*, the crumbling of the system's old codes and constructs. Carl Jung said, "There is no birth of consciousness without pain."

This shift in perception is an inner revolution which religious traditions call *metanoia* — turning around. In Mahayana Buddhism, it is termed *parinamana* — turning over — and described as filled with jubilation and dedication to the welfare of all.[1] We turn around or turn over into wider awareness of who and what we are — as jewels in the Net of Indra, as members of the body of Christ , as the beloved of Krishna or as synapses in the mind of God.

At the same time, this turning appears as a new paradigm anchored in holistic science. This conceptual framework, furthermore, helps us understand the ultimately suicidal nature of a growth-driven industrialized economy.

## Brain Food

After the emotional work of the second stage, our minds are ready for nourishment — time for some brain food. Here, to consider the implications of what we have been uncovering and to provide ground for our further work, we offer concepts basic to the paradigm shift taking place in our time.

Note that in some cultures, group work proceeds best when its theoretical foundations are set forth at the outset. The Work That Reconnects arose in a society that is conditioned by Anglo-Saxon predispositions to empiricism and inductive reasoning, where interpretations and conclusions are more welcome *after* direct experience. However, in continental Europe, for example, participants are often more ready to trust the work when they are provided a cognitive framework from the start. In such settings, we briefly articulate the theoretical premises set forth in Chapters 4 and allude to some of the concepts that will be unpacked more fully after the stage of honoring our pain.

### Key Teaching Points

Certain basic concepts are essential to understanding the transition from the Industrial Growth Society to a Life-Sustaining Society. Whatever illustrative material we may use, we always endeavor to make these key points, implicit in Chapters 3 and 4.

1. **The Industrial Growth Society cannot be sustained.** Given the features described below, it is destroying the biological and ecological systems on which all life depends.

   a. Unlimited economic growth. Nothing in the universe grows endlessly without limits.
   b. Maximizing profit. When one variable in a system, e.g. profit, consistently trumps all others, the system cannot stay in balance, goes into overshoot and heads toward eventual collapse.
   c. Externalizing costs and blocking feedback. In order to maximize profit, ecological and human costs of production are off-loaded to third parties, such as taxpayers and the natural world. This distorts both perceptions and accounting of a corporation's impact. It blocks the feedback that any system needs in order to know the effects of its behavior. Incapacity to receive and register feedback is ultimately suicidal.

   > I think
   > an economy should be based on thrift,
   > on taking care of things, not on theft,
   > usury, seduction, waste and ruin.
   >
   > — Wendell Berry

   d. Top-down power. The worldview underlying the Industrial Growth Society sees reality in terms of separate entities, which are in linear, hierarchical and competitive relation with each other. Hence power has been understood as power over and win/lose, an assumption that breeds insatiable wants (see Chapter 3).

2. Now, in the Great Turning, **we perceive once again the interdependence of all things** and build a Life-Sustaining Society upon that understanding. The shift in perception is a figure-ground reversal: from separate entities to flows of relationship, from substance to process, from noun to verb.

   a. Power is understood as mutual and synergistic, arising from interaction and generating new possibilities and capacities within the limits of biosphere.
   b. A life-sustaining economy does not alter the integrity and balance of natural systems through technological innovations, such as genetic or geo-engineering.
   c. The goal of economic activity is not the profit of a few, but sufficiency for all, now and into the future.
   d. Feedback is essential for accessing the true costs of our behaviors and our responsibility for any harm they incur.
   e. Humans are seen as both unique *and* inseparable from our matrix, the web of life; our genuine self-interest includes that of other beings and the living body of Earth.

3. **The global crisis is at root a crisis in perception.** There is no technological fix.

> People of conscience need to break their ties with corporations financing the injustice of climate change .... It makes no sense to invest in companies that undermine our future.
>
> — Desmund Tutu

## Advice for Conveying These Concepts

+ Make time for them. These ideas are implicit in the practices and can easily be made explicit. It is also good to plan a specific time to focus on these concepts, perhaps presenting a mini-lecture. Visual aids, if only a chalk-talk, are helpful.

+ Keep it simple. Use only a few analogies to convey this shift in perception.
+ At the same time, don't talk down to your audience. Assume that they are interested, serious and smart. Don't be fooled by first impressions.
+ Many of these concepts can be made clear in presenting the three stories, e.g. Business as Usual, the Great Unraveling and the Great Turning (see Chapter 1).
+ If your life experience has made you uncomfortable directing intellectual discourse, you may want to assemble a series of quotes or short passages that have enriched your own understanding. Perhaps you'll choose some earlier sections from this book. Then, instead of reading them out like a scripted lecture, distribute copies and have participants take turns reading them aloud with pauses for reflection and comments.
+ Remember that you are not trying to convince people. The only questions you should try to answer are those seeking clarification of what you said. Your role as guide is not to resolve people's doubts, but to offer food for thought and room for sharing insights.
+ When you contrast worldviews, keep the focus on their psychological and behavioral effects instead of trying to disprove one theory and prove another.
+ Set a time limit. Intellectual discussion gets heady. When time is up, ask participants to stand and stretch, and then move them into an exercise that reflects and grounds these ideas.
+ Each guide has a world of experiences to draw from, with distinctive concepts and images to offer, in conveying the interconnectedness of all life. Some take examples from nature, others from spiritual traditions. Guides who are musicians may speak of a shared world of rippling, intersecting vibrations. Those with a philosophical bent may refer to Deep Ecology, the Hundredth Monkey concept or morphogenetic fields. Lovers of systems theory may talk about co-evolution and emergent properties; community organizers about the synergies unleashed as they help people take charge of their lives; anthropologists and storytellers about ancient myths of co-creation in the web of life.

There is no limit to the illustrative material that is here for us to use.

## Practices

Experiential work brings ideas to life. Guided meditations such as The Great Ball of Merit and Learning to See Each Other (Chapter 13) are excellent right after conceptual discussion. Aikido exercises are also appropriate, dramatically demonstrating the relational character of power and the synergy that arises when the energy of an adversary is accepted and used non-defensively.

The following interactive practices help us see the larger context of our lives. They use our innate powers of imagination and empathy to shift perspectives from separation to connectivity. Seeing With New Eyes includes not only the practices described below, but also those set forth in the next chapter on Deep Time that make vivid our connections with past and future generations.

### The Systems Game

(30 minutes)

This lively, engrossing process provides a direct experience of the dynamic nature of open systems. It dramatizes two features of the new paradigm view of reality:

1. that life is composed not of separate entities so much as of the relations between them
2. these relations allow life to self-organize

#### METHOD

Have people stand in a circle within an open space large enough for them to move around freely. Then give two instructions: (1) *Mentally select two other people, without indicating whom you have chosen.* (2) *Move so as to keep at all times an equal distance between you and each of these two people.* Demonstrate that this does not mean just staying at the midpoint between the two others.

At your signal, people begin to circulate, each movement triggering many others in an active, interdependent fashion. People find they are, by necessity, maintaining wide-angle vision and constant alacrity of response. The process is purposeful, suspenseful, laced with laughter. It speeds up for a while, then may abate, accelerate and again slow down toward equilibrium, but it rarely comes to stasis. Let it continue for some minutes, then tell people to stop and reflect together.

The simple question *What did you experience?* evokes fruitful discussion:

+ People's reflections usually bring out some key features of self-regulating systems, such as the interdependence of all parts and their continual activity in seeking and maintaining balance.
+ People may have thought the point of the game was to achieve stasis; you can bring out and challenge that assumption. The self-regulation of open systems requires constant internal activity.
+ People may articulate perceptual and psychological shifts they experienced in the game. These can include a radically widened sense of context and a larger, more porous sense of self. A temporary eclipse of self-consciousness may be noted, as one's perceptions focus more on others' actions than one's own — that is, not on separate entities so much as on relations among them.
+ *Is this a closed system or an open system?* you may ask. If people think it is a closed system because no one entered from outside, you can point out that energy originating from the sun powers everyone present. We wouldn't last long without food or drink from outside the system we just created. Individually and collectively, we are open systems dependent on inputs of matter/energy and information. Closed systems do not exist in nature.
+ *What feedback enabled us to fulfill our function (that is, of staying equidistant from two others)?* If there is no answer, you may ask, *Could we have done it with our eyes closed?* You may note that not only visual perceptions, but feedback of all kinds guide us in our daily lives.
+ *Would anyone volunteer to organize this process?* It is obvious that no party or person on the outside could direct the movements necessary to keep this system in balance.

## VARIATIONS

### ENDANGERED ECOSYSTEM

Have everyone repeat the process, but this time tell them you will move through them and surreptitiously tap one person on the shoulder. After silently counting to five, this person will sink to the floor or squat down. Then anyone who has chosen to move in relation to this person will also silently count to five and sink down; and then those whose movements have been affected by these will follow suit until the whole group is down. After starting out slowly, the progression begins to accelerate and ends in a cascade effect that is sobering and instructive.

If after you tap someone and they go down, nothing else happens, you realize no one else chose this person — so you go tap another.

### SOCIAL INNOVATION

As a follow on to Endangered Ecosystem, have the whole group start out squatting down. Walk through and secretly tap someone; this person silently counts to five and then rises, and so on. The above process now plays out in reverse, illustrating the accelerating effect of new ideas or behaviors spreading throughout a social system.

### SOCIAL RESTRICTIONS

As a follow-on to the original game and maintaining the same relationships, immobilize two or more players and then proceed. In the discussion that follows, people may reflect on the diminished fluidity they sensed in the group as a whole or on their own experience if one of their partners didn't move. The decreased responsiveness is often experienced as a dysfunction within the system, and comments on this fact can bring fresh insights.

### LARGE-SCALE EXERCISE

A variation used by Mark Horowitz involves a group of 75 or more. Here some 20 volunteers play the game with the remainder as audience. This works best when the audience sits around a central area where the game is played.

The guide takes the volunteer players aside to give instructions. Meanwhile, the audience is instructed to observe the action and try to figure out what is going on. If the seating allows, audience members may move around to observe from different angles. Then the game begins, while the audience observes with bemusement.

After a few minutes, the guide asks four or five audience members to act as consultants to this "organization." Their task it is to line up the players in order of height. This will prove to be impossible, because the players don't stay still.

After some more minutes, the players are signaled to stop in place and the guide asks the audience what they observed and what they thought was happening. The explanations offered are often creative, even hilarious.

The consultants are then asked to report their (probably frustrating) experience, thereby illustrating the absurdity of trying to intervene in a system (human or other) without first learning what the system is doing and what its rules are.

Finally, unless someone in the audience has figured out what was going on, the players explain the rules of the game, as well as share their experience and what they learned in the process.

❧

## Riddle of the Commons[2] Game
## (also known as the Nuts Game)

### (20–30 minutes)

The Tragedy of the Commons, as named by Garrett Hardin, occurs when a community consumes a common resource too fast for regeneration to occur. In such situations, people must choose between restricting their own consumption for the good of the community or continuing to consume at a rate that satisfies their immediate self-interest, but leads eventually to losses for all.

This game embodies the Tragedy of the Commons problem. By the rules it lays out, it helps people explore the challenge of maintaining a dynamic balance between personal self-interest and collective self-interest. Each is necessary for the common good.

## METHOD

A group of three or more players sit around a shallow unbreakable bowl (diameter about 12 inches) that initially contains ten hardware nuts (half-inch diameter is a good size). An extra person, the Replenisher, sits with each group with a separate container of nuts nearby.

The guide explains the following:

+ Each player's goal is to get as many of the nuts as possible.
+ Players can take nuts from the bowl at any time and in any quantities after the start of the game.
+ After each ten-second interval (signaled by a bell or the like), the Replenisher doubles the number of nuts remaining in the bowl. The number of nuts allowed in the bowl throughout the game is limited to ten.
+ This game ends if the bowl is empty, or continues until a predetermined time limit, say five minutes.
+ Players are not to communicate during the game itself.

The bowl symbolizes a resource pool (such as an ocean of whales); the nuts, the resources themselves and the replenishment cycles, natural resource regeneration rates.

After the first round of the game, allow the groups five minutes to invent their own rules in order to increase their harvests on a second game. Groups typically come up with two main types of solution: (a) numerical solutions (such as an agreement to take only one or two nuts per person per ten-second interval; this type of solution is quite effective in preserving the pool) and (b) non-numerical solutions. In one non-numerical example, a group decided to use a rather complicated system of harvesting. Each player had to hook each nut out of the bowl with a pencil, place it on his nose, walk over to a nearby chalkboard and deposit the nut in the tray before returning for another nut. Harvesting was thus slowed down enough to prevent pool depletion, increasing individual scores and incidentally making the game more entertaining to players.

### *When I Made a Difference*

(30 minutes)

Recounting incidents from our own lives, we recognize our capacity to create positive change. This is all the more valuable since we are not accustomed to sharing this kind of experience or understanding it as power.

#### Method

*Think of a time in your life when something important and good happened because of what you said or did. Recapture the scene, play it back for yourself.*

Note that the guide *does not use the word* **power** until later in the general discussion that follows.

Now in groups of three or four, people take turns telling their stories. The guide suggests: *As you listen to each story, discern the qualities in that person that were at play.*

- I got the principal's permission to start a recycling program at our school.
- Instead of backing off, I just stood there and talked to the guard at the nuclear power plant.
- I was presiding at the board meeting and felt stuck; I decided to relinquish my role as leader, and then everyone was able to decide what to do.

When the small groups are finished, the guide asks people to call out the qualities they discerned in each other's stories and writes them up on newsprint as they are named: empathy, trust, letting go, flexibility. The guide then asks the group to point out those qualities and behaviors that fit the new paradigm understanding of power (see The Nature of Power section in Chapter 3).

At one workshop, a man still insisted that he experienced no power in his life. "What gives you pleasure?" the guide asked. "Well, I don't know. I feel good when I ride my bicycle." "What is that like?" "Well, I tell you now, it feels good when I'm riding home from work and the traffic is jammed. I just speed by all those cars and trucks;

they can hardly move and I'm going where I want to go." "That sounds like a powerful feeling," said the guide. "You bet!" said Jim beaming. "I guess that is a kind of power, isn't it?" And he recognized with pride the guerrilla-power of autonomy and flexibility.

❧

## Widening Circles or Four Voices

### (About 60 minutes)

Activists want to be able to express their views about an issue clearly, even passionately. At the same time, for their own understanding and skillfulness, they need to grasp differing and opposing perspectives on this issue. This favorite exercise of ours helps us do both. And in the process it loosens the grip of self-righteousness, opening the mind to progressively larger contexts and to widening circles of identity.

> I live my life in widening circles
> that reach out across the world
> I may not complete this last one
> But I give myself to it.
>
> I circle around God, the primordial tower.
> I have been circling for thousands of year.
> And still I don't know: am I a falcon,
> a storm, or a great song.
>
> — Rainer Maria Rilke

### METHOD

People sit in groups of three or four. Ask them each to choose a particular issue or situation that concerns them. After a minute of silence, invite them to take turns speaking about their issue. Each person will speak to their issue from four perspectives while the others in the group listen:

1. from their own point of view, including their feelings about the issue
2. from the perspective of a person who holds opposing views on this issue, introducing themselves and speaking *as* this person, using the pronoun *I*
3. from the viewpoint of a nonhuman being that is affected by that particular situation

4. lastly, in the voice of a future human whose life is affected by the choices made now on this issue

After describing these four perspectives at the outset, the guide provides cues for each perspective as each speaker's turn unfolds, reminding them to always speak in the first person. Allow some two to three minutes for each perspective, perhaps a little longer for the first. The one speaking may find it helpful to stand up and turn around before moving on to the next voice.

To speak on behalf of another and identify even briefly with that being's experience and perspective are acts of moral imagination. It is not difficult to do: as children we knew how to playact. Use an uncharged, almost casual tone in your instructions; you are not asking people to channel or be omniscient, but simply to imagine another point of view. Allow some silence as they choose for whom they will speak and imaginatively enter that other's experience, so they can respect it and not perform a caricature of it. It is a brave and generous act to make room in your mind for another's experience and to lend them your voice; let the participants appreciate that generosity in themselves and each other.

Allow time at the end for people to share in their small groups what they felt and learned.

## *The Cradling*

### (20–60 minutes)

A guided meditation on the body, the Cradling serves many purposes. It permits deep relaxation, all the more welcome after dealing straight on with fearsome issues. It builds trust among participants and a kind of respectful cherishing. It widens our awareness of what is at stake in the global crisis; for the dangers we face — pollution, ecological collapse, famine, warfare — are dangers because of what they do to the body. The Cradling also taps deeper levels of knowing, stirring reverence for life. Usually, in dealing with the deterioration of our world, we try to get our minds around it; we deal with it on the informational level, as if we were brains on the end of a stick. The Cradling quiets for a while the computing mind and opens it to the wordless wisdom of life.

## Method

People work in pairs, taking turns. First you model with a volunteer how Partners A lie down and Partners B, following your verbal suggestions, *cradle* them, which means lifting arms, lower legs and head.

Proceed with care and respect. Touching another person's body is a sensitive and often problematic issue. In some cultures it is virtually taboo. Even in California, people can interpret touch as an invasion of their personal integrity, especially if they have suffered physical or sexual abuse. So inform people that the practice involves their letting their arms, legs and head be lifted and held; ask them to choose a partner with whom they will feel comfortable.

Now Partners A, removing glasses and shoes, loosening ties and belts, lie down on the floor, close their eyes and relax. Have them place themselves so that there is adequate room for their partners to move around them to cradle arms, legs and head. Assist with a brief guided relaxation (for example stretching, feeling the breath, letting weight sink down, releasing tension from feet, legs, hands). Soft background music, like flute sound, is helpful, but not essential.

Respect the participants for their trust and stay matter-of-fact in your manner, avoiding a portentous or sugary tone. Speak relatively slowly, interspersing suggestions with silence, remaining casual and reflective, as if observing some constellation in the heavens or a conch shell on the beach.

Whatever words or images are used, it is good to touch on certain themes. These motifs renew and sharpen awareness of what it means to be a living person at this time in history. They include:

1. the uniqueness of the human species in the cosmos
2. our long evolutionary journey
3. the uniqueness of each individual and of each personal history
4. the intricacy and beauty of the human organism

5. its universality, linking us to other humans around the globe
6. and its vulnerability

The following transcript of Joanna guiding the Cradling is offered for illustrative purposes only. You will not be repeating this word for word when you are the guide; you have your own style, your own experience to use. Now, however, read it reflectively to get a feel for the process, its pace and unfolding.

*Lift gently your partner's arm and hand. Cradle it, feel the weight of it ... flex the elbow and wrist, note how the joints are hinged to permit variety of movement. Behold this arm as if you had never seen it before, as if you were a visitor from another world .... Observe the articulation of bone and muscle .... Turning the palm and fingers, note the intricacy of structure.*

*What you now hold is an object unique in our cosmos: a human hand of planet Earth. In the primordial seas where once we swam, that hand was a fin — as it was again in its mother's womb. Feel the energy and intelligence in that hand — that fruit of a long evolutionary journey, of efforts to swim, to push, to climb, to grasp. Note the opposable thumb, how clever and adept it is ... good for grasping a tool, a gun, a pen.*

*Open your awareness to the journey it has made in this present life-time ... how it opened like a flower when it emerged from the mother's womb.... how it reached to explore and to do. That hand learned to hold a spoon ... to throw a ball ... to write its name ... to wipe tears ... to give pleasure. There is nothing like it in all the universe.*

*Gently laying down that hand, move now to your partner's leg and slowly lift it. Feel its weight, its sturdiness. This species stands upright. Bend the knee, the ankle, note the play of bone and muscle. It allows this being to walk, run, climb. Holding the foot, feel the sole, no hoof or heavy padding.... It is this being's contact with the ground....*

*Feel that heel; when it kicked in the womb, that was what the parents first felt through the wall of the belly.... "See: there's the baby's heel." And such journeys that leg has been on since then ... learning to take a step and then another ... walking and falling and getting up again ... then running, climbing, kicking a ball, pedaling a bike ... a lot of adventures in that leg ... and a lot of places it has taken your partner ... into workplaces* and sanctuaries, mountainsides and city streets ... gotten tired ... sore ... still kept going. Gently putting it down now, move around to the other leg and cradle that one, too.

Observe this companion leg and foot ... which shared those journeys ... and many yet to come. For all its weight and sturdiness, it can be broken, crushed ... no armor ... just skin that can tear, bones that can fracture. As you hold that leg, open your thought to all the places it will take your partner in the future ... into places of suffering perhaps ... of conflict and challenge ... on missions that your partner doesn't know about yet .... As you lay it back down, extend your wishes for its strength and wholeness.

Lift now your partner's other hand and arm .... Observe the subtle differences from its twin .... This hand is unique, different from all other hands .... Turning it in yours, feel the life in it .... And note also its vulnerability ... no shell encases it, for those fingertips, that palm, are instruments for sensing and knowing our world, as well as for doing .... Flexible, fragile hand, so easy to break or burn .... Be aware of how much you want it to stay whole, intact, in the time that is coming .... It has tasks to do, that your partner can't even guess at ... reaching out to people in confusion and distress, helping, comforting, showing the way. This hand may be the one that holds you in the moments of your own dying, giving you water or a last touch of reassurance.... The world of sanity and decency that lies ahead will be built by hands like this one. With gratitude for its existence, put it gently down; move now around behind your partner's head.

Placing a hand under the neck and another beneath the skull, slowly, gently lift your partner's head .... Partner A keep your neck relaxed, your head heavy, loose. Lift that head carefully, cradle it with reverence, for what you now hold in your two hands is the most complex object in the known universe ... a human head of planet Earth ... a hundred billion neurons firing in there ... vast potential for intelligence ... only a portion has been tapped of its capacity to perceive, to know, to vision.

Your hands holding your partner's head — that is the first touch your partner knew in this life, coming out of the womb into hands, like yours, of a doctor or midwife.... Now within that skull is a whole world of ex-perience — of memories of scenes and songs, beloved faces ... some are gone now, but they live still in the mansions of that mind.... It is a world

*of experience that is totally unique and that can never be fully shared ....*
*In that head too are dreams of what could be, visions that could shape*
*our world.*

*Closing your eyes for a moment, feel the weight of that head in your*
*hands. It could be the head of a Chinese worker or a Nicaraguan mother,*
*of an American general or an African doctor. Same size, same weight*
*just about, same vulnerability, same capacity for dreams that could guide*
*us through this time.*

*Looking down at this head, think of what this person may have to be-*
*hold in the times that are coming ... the choices to be made ... the courage*
*and endurance needed. Let your hands, of their own intelligence, express*
*their desire that all be well with that head. Perhaps there is something*
*that you want your partner to keep in mind — something you want*
*them not to forget in times of stress or anguish. If there is, you can quietly*
*tell them now, as you lay their head back down.*

Allow time for the recumbent partner to stretch, look around,
slowly sit up. Then A and B reverse roles, and the verbal cues are
offered again in different words. At the conclusion of the whole
process, time to reorient is important. Let the pairs talk quietly or
remain in silence for a while.

If the number of workshop participants is uneven and you have
no co-facilitator, pair up with the extra person and lead the exercise
while acting as Partner B, but not reversing roles.

I trust what this body knows
    breathing in, breathing out
    the way home.
I trust the ground, which I can stand upon —
    the earth that rises to meet my feet
    and gives gently beneath my weight.
And I trust that ground which I cannot stand upon —
    the falling away that everything returns to.

— Oren Sofer

## TIMING AND VARIATION

Depending on the time and space available, the Cradling can take two forms: the fuller version (described above) lasts about 45 to 60 minutes. When time or floor space is inadequate to accommodate the full Cradling, a brief version (10 to 20 minutes) can be conducted with pairs sitting face to face. The meditation then focuses on the hands and arms, and if space permits one partner to move around behind the other, the shoulders and head as well. In that case, attention is directed to the burdens we carry, the stresses we tend to lock into our shoulders and necks; and the meditation on the head is appropriately adapted. If that is impossible or awkward, don't worry. So long as there is touch and attention, even the briefest form of this exercise is evocative and powerful.

## *Who Are You?*

(60 minutes)

This process in pairs serves to move us beyond constricted notions of who we are and what can happen through us. Of a metaphysical bent, it was originally inspired by followers of the Hindu sage Sri Ramana Maharshi. In their enlightenment intensives, persistent inquiry helps participants to free themselves from socially constructed self-definitions and attain a realization of the inherently unlimited nature of consciousness. In our workshop the process is condensed and less ambitious. We use it to remind ourselves that we are not our social roles or *skin-encapsulated egos* so much as participants in a larger encompassing awareness — or the awakening consciousness of Earth.

### METHOD

Each pair sits close enough together and far enough from the others to avoid distraction. The partners take turns querying each other for 30 minutes each way, without comment.

This is a strenuous mental exercise. It can produce extraordinary insights, sometimes with bursts of laughter, but it can feel relentless. It must be undertaken gently and with respect.

Here are the instructions to Partner A, which are repeated to B later:

> Partner A, you begin by asking B, "Who are you?" You listen. You ask again, "Who are you?" Again you listen, then repeat the question, "Who are you?" Rest assured that the answers will be different. You can vary the question, if you wish, with "What are you?" but you say nothing else. This continues for about ten minutes, until I ring the bell.
>
> Remember, you are not badgering your partner. You're not suggesting that his responses are wrong; you're helping him go deeper. You are in service to your partner. The tempo and tonality of your questions will vary; you'll know intuitively when to ask again quickly and when to pause in silence. Now before you begin, bow to your partner — and to the essential mystery at the core of this being.

After the first ten-minute bell, give the next instruction:

> Now shift to a second question, "What do you do?" For the next ten minutes, you listen to those answers and keep repeating the query, "What do you do?" You can also phrase it, "What happens through you?"

After ringing the bell, give the third instruction:

> Please revert now to the first question, "Who (or what) are you?"

Partner A bows to B once more when the cycle of questions is over. As the partners change roles, let them stand and stretch, without talking. Then repeat the process with B querying A.

At the end of the entire practice, which takes an hour, allow plenty of time for people to digest what has happened for them. They may want to journal or talk quietly with their partners. Then, if there is time, bring them back together in the large group so that they reflect on the process.

## *Dance to Dismember the Ego*

### (60 minutes or more)

This fanciful process derives from a Tibetan lama dance. For three days every spring, the monks of Tashi Jong, a refugee community in northwest India, honor their ancient Buddhist tradition with majestic, masked rituals. One of the high points for Joanna, a longtime friend of Tashi Jong, is the Dance to Dismember the Ego. In the center of the dancing ground lies a small clay doll enclosed in an open, three-sided box. The three sides symbolize the three fetters that hold the ego together: craving, hatred and delusion. The costumed monks, moving and leaping about it with their ritual implements, embody the innate powers of mind, which can free us from the grip of self-centeredness. At the climactic close, the doll is "eaten" by the dancers, who pull it apart, lift it to their mouths, scatter it to the winds.

Back in the States, a group of a dozen Buddhist and Quaker friends, to whom Joanna described the dance, wanted to try it themselves. Not only that, they each wanted to make their own ego doll. They wished to enact in material form what they knew in principle: that the self-centeredness that creates our suffering is not substantially and permanently real. We need to see it clearly, recognize it for what it is, along with the fears and ignorance that create it, before it can begin to dissolve.

From that first impromptu enactment at Temenos retreat center in Massachusetts arose the version of the dance Joanna has taken into the Work That Reconnects. This process aims to free us from some of the attachments to self-image that inhibit our joy in life and our effectiveness in action. Although totally serious in intent, it does not employ weighty moral judgments, but lightheartedness, and helps us learn that we can't free ourselves from anything without accepting and appreciating it first.

### METHOD

Acknowledging the original Tibetan dance that gave rise to this process, invite everyone to create their ego doll either with colors on paper or hunks of clay. *A degree of self-centeredness is present in us all. What form does yours want to take? How in this moment does your particular pride or self-image wish to display itself?* Everyone is encouraged to work in silence and watch what happens. They may see emerging before their eyes aspects of the persona they have constructed over the years. To behold this now, objectified and exaggerated, can bring a sense of relief.

After 10 to 20 minutes, participants gather in a circle with their work. Now comes the dance itself, or more precisely, a celebrative show-and-tell. One at a time, spontaneously, each person stands and parades around the circle displaying their ego doll for the admiration of all the others. As they do, they point out and extol its qualities while the group responds with extravagant praise. This adulation is important because egos *love* to be admired. Then each ego is placed solemnly in the center of the circle.

+ *Ta-daa! Presenting in its first-ever public appearance the incomparable, one and only … smart ass ego of mine; many hands and mouths to hide the hollow heart.*
+ *Feast your eyes on this sensitive soul, bent over by the woes of the world and afraid of getting her hands dirty.*
+ *This brilliant know-it-all likes to sit real cool on the sidelines and pass judgments.*

When all the little clay sculptures are amassed in the center, the group rises to walk ceremoniously around them, perhaps chanting a ritual farewell. Groups familiar with Buddhism have used the ancient mantra from the Heart Sutra, *Gaté gaté, paragaté parasam gaté; bodhi swaha!* (Gone, gone, gone beyond, completely gone beyond, far out!) We say good-bye, or at least begin to prepare to say good-bye, to these mental fabrications that have outlived their usefulness.

The ritual may end there, or the dolls can be broken apart or cast into a fire or into a body of water to dissolve, accompanied by shouts of support and jubilation. If this kind of dramatic ending is used, the guide should suggest that people relinquish their ego doll only if they feel ready. If they wish to, people can hold on their ego dolls a while longer.

## *Bodhisattva Check-In*
## *(or Owning My Life)*
### (60 minutes)

Using and growing our moral imagination, this process focuses on our own lives and helps us see how their basic features and conditions prepare us to take part in the healing of the world — almost as if we had chosen them for that purpose. It brings fresh appreciation for the chance to be alive in this planet-time. Like climbing a mountain and looking back on the landscape below, this practice provides a vantage point that lets us see new things. From that overarching perspective, we can see unsuspected connections and goodness; even our suffering and limitations reveal their value for the work we have come to do.

We call this practice the Bodhisattva Check-In because it is inspired by the hero figure of Buddhist tradition. Embodying our motivation to serve, the *bodhisattva* does not seek enlightenment in order to exit from this world, but turns back from the gates of *nirvana*, having vowed to return again and again to be of help to all beings. It is important to note that this process is effective even if we don't believe in rebirth. The bodhisattva archetype is present in all religions and even all social movements, be it in the guise of suffering servant, worker-priest, shaman, prophet, idealistic revolutionary or community organizer.

Spiritual traditions affirm that true liberation arises when we can fully own the particulars of our lives, seeing and accepting all that has shaped who we are now. In other words, we are taking a bodhisattva perspective on our lives. Bill Johnston's poem below eloquently expresses what happens with this kind of acceptance.

### METHOD

Three introductory stages precede the main body of the exercise:

First, tell about the bodhisattvas and their vow to keep returning to the world to relieve suffering.

Secondly, invite the group to contemplate the long panoramic journey we have made as life on Earth. (Draw from Evolutionary Remembering in Chapter 9.)

## I Take to Myself [3]

I take to myself
my broken self:
my guilt, my peace,
my folly and joy,
my sickness, my health;
in laughter and agony,
hating and loving,
my fear and my birthing —
and I am made whole.

I take to myself
you, my neighbor,
cupping your life
within my hands:
your broken self
pure gift to me;
not burden, gift,
as mine to you —
and I am made whole.

I take to myself
you, broken Earth;
stripped and abused,
paved over and poisoned,
you mother so freely,
abundant in grace:
clasp in your mercy,
surprise into tears —
and I am made whole.

I take to myself
your broken self,
my dear, near God;
broken for broken,
for lost and for spent.
As fragmented love
and nectar of life,
you come, gentle God —
and I am made whole. [3]

— Bill Johnston

Third, invite everyone to imagine that we are all together some-where in the larger body of Earth, in a timeless moment preceding our birth in this life. Information now reaches us about the dangers to all life on Earth that have been arising through the 20th century and reaching a crisis point at the start of the third millennium.

> The challenges take many forms — from nuclear weapons and climate chaos, to mass extinctions and billions of people sink-ing into poverty — but one thing is clear. A quantum leap in consciousness is required if life is to continue on Earth.
>
> Hearing this forces us to consider whether or not to return and take birth as humans, bringing everything we've ever

*learned about courage and community. This is a major deci-*
*sion. And it is a hard decision because there is no guarantee*
*that we will remember why we came back, or that we won't*
*regret it at moments, or that we will succeed in our mission.*
*Furthermore, we will feel alone because we'll be arriving at*
*different times, different places, in different colors and circum-*
*stances, and we probably won't even recognize each other.*

Now the key moment in the process: *If and when you choose to*
*take birth as a human in this era, stand up.*[i]

When you are confident that everyone who has made this decision is standing, acknowledge that: *You can't take birth as a generic*
*human, but only as a unique human shaped by particular circumstances.*
*Step into these circumstances now, with awareness of how they will help*
*prepare you for the mission you are coming to perform.*

People begin slowly walking around the room, progressively
owning the main circumstances of their present life. Take care to
convey that each step relates to their actual life and not to any fanta-
sized alternative to it. Here follows some words describing each step.
Remember to allow ample time for reflection after each one.

> *Step into the* **year of your birth**. *The timing of your birth gives*
> *your life its important historical context. Own it.*
>
> *Step into the* **place of your birth**. *In what country were*
> *you born? Were you born in a town or a city, or on the land?*
> *Which parts of the Earth's body first greeted your eyes? Own*
> *that now.*
>
> *What* **skin color and ethnicity** *is yours to own? And what*
> **socio-economic conditions**? *The privileges and the privations*
> *resulting from both these circumstances help prepare you for*
> *the work you are coming to do. Own them.*

---

[i.] If someone chooses not to take birth and does not stand up, the guide can move
to stand nearby to reassure the person that he or she is still part of the group.
When it is time for the others to check in in pairs, the guide can sit with the person
and invite him or her to talk about the experience and its challenges.

*Into what **faith tradition** — or lack of same — were you born this time? Religious stories and images from childhood — or the very lack of these — influence how you see your purpose. Own them.*

*Which **gender** is yours this time? And which **sexual orientation?** Own them.*

*And step into **your family.** What man is your father? What woman your mother? For some of you, this means your adoptive parents as well as your birth parents. What strengths and weaknesses of your parents — the loving care or neglect or abuse you may have received — helped to prepare you for the work you are coming to do? Own it all.*

*Are you an **only child** or do you have **siblings** in this life? The companionship, the competition or the loneliness that ensued from that circumstance will foster the unique blend of strengths you bring to your world .... Own them.*

*What **disabilities** came with this life of yours? Challenges of body or mind bring their own strengths and resilience. Own them.*

*What **inner gifts and talents** came with this life? Own them.*

*And lastly, imagining that you can for a moment see it clearly, what **particular mission** are you coming to perform?*

*Now look around you. You did not expect to recognize each other in new and different bodies, but here we are! Sit down now with one other person. Take turns telling each other about the life that is yours this time. This is the Bodhisattva Check-In.*

To guide this check-in, a list of the circumstances mentioned can be posted (such as time of birth, place of birth).

## VARIATIONS

As you become familiar with this practice, you may wish to add topics for the bodhisattvas' report, such as educational choices, spiritual journeys, central relationships and vocational explorations and commitments. An evocative question is: "How did you first let your heart be broken?"

⁂

## Council of All Beings[4]

### (2 to 3 hours)

This colorful, sometimes solemn, and often high-spirited communal ritual allows us to step aside from our human identity and speak on behalf of other life-forms. It is excellent for growing the ecological self, for it brings a sense of our solidarity with all life and fresh awareness of the damage wrought by one upstart species.

Following a ritual opening, participants allow themselves to be chosen by another being, for whom they will speak in Council. They prepare themselves to do this by reflecting on their particular life-form, often by making a mask to represent it, sometimes practicing moving and speaking as that life-form, and finally gathering in a formal Council to speak of the grave threats they are facing today.

Each Council, being the extemporaneous expression of those present, is different from all others. Each has its own character and flow. Some release torrents of intense feelings; others appear lighthearted or relatively staid. Remember that appearances can be misleading: participants who seem awkward in their roles or relatively silent and uninvolved, can be deeply affected by the Council.

> We are Nature,
> long have we been absent,
> but now we return.
>
> — Walt Whitman

### METHOD

**Invocation.** To begin the process, the guide can call upon the Beings of Three Times (see invocation in Chapter 9) and the Four Directions. The blessing of the Four Directions is found in many indigenous traditions; use a form familiar and comfortable to you. Other ritual openings include smudging everyone with sage or sweet grass smoke and chanting.

**Being chosen.** In this process, we imagine that other beings, other life-forms apart from humans, seek to be heard at our Council.

The participants take time alone to let themselves be chosen. If time and setting permit, they walk outside for 15 or 20 minutes. Indoors, allow three to five minutes. Ask people to relax deeply, opening their mind wide like a radar dish.

Encourage people to stay with the first impulse that arises. It is not a question of choosing a species one knows a lot about, but rather allowing oneself to be surprised by the life-form that comes, be it plant, animal or ecological feature, such as swamp or mountain — any nonhuman being. Suggest that they visualize this being fully and from every angle, its size and shape and ways of moving. Then they request this being's permission to enter it, so they can imaginatively sense its body from within. Finally, they ask the being how it wishes to be represented and, if masks are to be used in the Council, what symbolic form the mask can take.

**Mask-making.** Lay out materials (cardboard, color markers, paste, tape, scissors, string, fabric scraps) on tables or ground cloths. Let people also gather their own materials from nature. A half hour should suffice; give a five-minute warning before the end of the allotted time. Everyone works without speaking. People can attach their masks with string, elastic or by taping the mask to a stick to be held in front of the face. Be sure everyone cuts holes to see and speak through; a mask which blocks the mouth makes it hard to be heard.

**Practice moving and speaking as the life-form.** If time allows, this practice session helps people identify more fully with their life-form. Either or both of the following activities can help alleviate self-consciousness.

1.  The guide invites participants to start moving as their life-form, beginning with eyes closed.

    *Breathing easily, begin to let yourself feel how it is to take body in this new life-form ... what shape are you? How much space do you take up now?... What is your skin or outer surface like?... How do you take notice of what is around you? ... How do you move, or how are you moved by other forces? ... Do you make any sounds? Play with those sounds.*

2. In groups of three or four, participants don their masks and practice using their human voice to speak for their adopted life-form. Each being speaks in turn for three to five minutes to their small group, introducing themselves, describing how it feels to be who they are, and naming their special strengths and qualities. Here they stay focused on their physical nature and way of life as it has been from the beginning of time (saving comments about present conditions for the Council itself).

> I am a feather on a bright sky
> I am the blue horse that runs in the plain
> I am the fish the rolls, shining, in the water ...
> I am an eagle playing with the wind ...
>
> You see, I am alive, I am alive
>
> — Navarre Scott Momaday

**Gathering in Council.** The masked beings move to the Council ground "in character" when summoned by drum beat or animal call. When they are all in the circle, the guide, as her adopted life-form, welcomes them to this council on what is befalling their Earth and their lives. She invites them to identify themselves. One by one around the circle, each being introduces itself in a ceremonial fashion: *I am Wolf and I speak for the wolf people. I am wild goose and I speak for the migratory birds. I am the Colorado River and I speak for the rivers of the world.* It is important that this initial roll call precede any lengthier statements.

**Three Stages of the Council.**
1. Now, speaking at random, the beings express the particular concerns they bring to the council. For example:

> As wild goose, I want to tell the Council that my long migrations are hard now because the wetlands are disappearing. And the shells of my eggs are so thin and brittle now, they break before my young are ready to hatch. I fear there is poison in my bones. The Beings in the Council respond with "We hear you, wild goose."

*As Mountain I am ancient, strong, solid, enduring. But now my forest skin is being torn off me, and my topsoil washes away, my streams and rivers choke. Blasts of dynamite shatter me. I cannot care for the beings to whom I have always given refuge.* The Beings in the Council respond with *"We hear you, Mountain."*

One by one they speak and are heard: rainforest, river, soil, wheat, badger, mouse.

2. After a while, perhaps a dozen testimonies, the guide observes that all the suffering that the beings describe seem to derive from the activities of one adolescent species. *It would be good for humans to hear what we have to say. Let us summon them to our Council, to listen only. Would five or six of you put down your masks and move to the center to be humans?* The guide beats the drum and humans come to sit back to back in the middle, facing outwards. From now on, they are addressed directly: *Hear us, humans. This is our world, too. And we've been here a lot longer than you. Yet now our days are numbered because of what you are doing. Be still for once and listen.*

    The humans silently listen as the Council continues. *Oh, humans, as the Danube, I was a bearer of life. Look at what I bear now that you've poured your wastes and poisons into me. I am ashamed and want to stop flowing because I have become a carrier of sickness and death.* The other beings respond, *"We hear you, Danube."*

    After a few more beings have spoken, the drum beats again and other humans replace the ones in the center, who return to the periphery and pick up their masks. In this fashion, everyone takes a turn to listen as a human.

3. When all the beings have had a chance to address the humans and call them to account, a major shift occurs. The guide may reflect, *For all their machines and apparent power, the humans now are frightened. They feel overwhelmed by the momentum of the forces they have unleashed. It does not serve our survival for them to panic or give up, for truly our life is in their hands. If they can awaken to their place in the web of life, they will change their ways. What strengths and gifts can each of us give them to help them now?*

Now each being has the chance to offer to the humans, and receive as a human when they come to the center, the powers that are needed to stop the destruction of the world, the strengths and gifts inherent in each life-form. Sometimes the humans break their silent listening to say simply "*Thank you.*"

> *As Mountain, I offer you my deep peace. Come to me at any time to rest, to dream. Without dreams, you may lose your vision and your hope. Come, too, for my strength and stead-fastness whenever you need.*
>
> *I, Condor, give you my keen far-seeing eye. Use that power to look ahead, beyond your day's busyness, your short-term concerns.*
>
> *I, Wild Flower, offer my fragrance and sweet face to call you back to beauty. Take time to notice me, and I'll let you fall in love again with life. This is my gift.*

**Ending.** Each Council ends a little differently, given its dynamics. Some wind up reflectively in silence. Some end intimately when everyone has joined the humans in the center to receive the gifts and find themselves embracing and sounding together. Other Councils burst into vigorous drumming and dancing, with hoots and howls and other wild calls.

In whatever way the Council ends, a formal releasing and thanksgiving should take place. People are asked to speak to the life-forms they adopted, thanking them for the privilege of speaking for them and then letting that identity go. Then, placing their hands and foreheads on the ground, they return the energy that has moved through them to the earth, for the healing of all beings.

Now what to do with the masks? The group may burn them in a reverent way, or compost them, or take them home to keep for a while.

John Seed and Joanna sometimes end with another suggestion: Participants can retain as their true identity the life-form for whom they have spoken — and put on a human mask (their own face) to reenter the world.

## VARIATIONS

1. When time is short or the materials are not at hand, drop the mask-making. If desired, use stick-on labels instead, on which people can draw a figure or symbol. Drop the practice sessions of movement and/or speaking in small groups.

2. When time is very short, say you have just an hour, you can still offer a key feature of the Council: the chance to step aside from one's human identity and speak on behalf of another species.

   In this abbreviated form, people cluster in foursomes. Closing their eyes, they follow the guide's suggestions on how to let themselves be chosen by another life-form. Then one by one, in their small group, they begin to speak *as* that being. It helps to lean forward, heads together, eyes half-closed.

   Each person's turn takes about ten minutes and covers three parts, which the guide delineates beforehand, perhaps noting them on a sheet of newsprint:

   a. Describe what it's like to be this life-form, the powers and perspectives you enjoy, the relationships that nourish you and that you nourish in turn.

   b. Describe the disruptions and difficulties you may be experiencing now, due to loss of habitat, pollution, toxic dumping, drift nets, clearcutting, factory farming or other circumstances.

   c. Since humans are causing these difficulties and abuses, and only they can correct them, consider what strengths you can offer to the humans to help them make the changes necessary to your survival — and the survival of life on Earth.

The guide, who has given a time signal for each ten-minute turn, may conclude the exercise by reflecting that the gifts each life-form has given are already present within us by virtue of the web of life. Otherwise they would not have occurred to us. When the whole group has drawn together, people may share what life-forms spoke through them, what gifts they offered and what they discovered in the process.

Alan Steinberg included a very brief but effective version of a Council in a conference workshop using clay. After a number of clay-working activities, he used a guided meditation to help each group member encounter another life-form. Participants then had five minutes to make a clay figure representing it. Then going around the circle, each person spoke as their being, addressing the three topics listed above. Although brief, the process was moving and memorable.

### Who Has Need, I Stand with You

In this hour, let us grant to each other the grace that is ours
to give.
In each other, let us see ourselves, and ourselves again,

That all the times we have looked at our faces in a mirror
Should have added up — each face our own, but a reminder as well

We are more than ourselves, that our eyes can see
Into that silver world as far as, and beyond, what we
understand.

Looking into a mirror, into a window pane, into the water
of a lake,
A photograph — we are here and over there as well. In that
moment

All things are more possible. In this hour of ourselves, you
and I,
One stronger than the other, let us speak evenly, and make
plain

The hope that all this time has held us. Let us extend
ourselves

Beyond ourselves into the silver, ourselves bigger and farther,

Ten thousand bodies to choose from suddenly in that mirror, us
Needing only one, so that things seem again so simple.

— Alberto Ríos[5]

**9**

# Deep Time — Reconnecting with Past and Future Generations

*It was the custom of my tribe
to speak and sing;
not only to share the present breath and sight,
but to the unborn.
Still, even now, we reach out
toward survivors. It is a covenant
of desire.*

— Denise Levertov

PEOPLE OF TODAY RELATE TO TIME in a way that is surely unique in history. The technologies and economic forces unleashed by the Industrial Growth Society radically alter our experience of time, subjecting us to frenetic speeds and severing our felt connection with past and future generations.

The Industrial Growth Society and the technologies it requires depend on decisions made at lightning speed for short-term goals, cutting us off from nature's rhythms. Time, both as a commodity and an experience, has become a scarcity. It is a painful irony that we who have more timesaving devices than any culture in history are the most time-harried and driven. The paradox is only apparent,

> But is the nature of civilization "speed"? Or is it "consideration"? ... a human being can consciously oblige himself to go slowly in order to consider whether he is doing the right thing, doing it the right way, or ought in fact to be doing something else .... Speed and efficiency are not in themselves signs of intelligence or capability or correctness.
>
> — John Ralston Saul

however, for our time scarcity is linked to the very time-efficiency of our technology. Measure of time, once based on changing seasons and wheeling stars, then much later the ticking of the clock, is now parceled out in nanoseconds. We have lost time as a biologically measurable experience.

Marooned in the present, we are progressively blinded to the sheer ongoingness of time. Both the legacy of our ancestors and the claims of our descendants become less and less real. Our culture's readiness to demolish treasures of the past — and to permanently poison the aquifers the future ones will need — reveals a pathetically shrunken sense of time and a pathological denial of its continuity.

Psychiatrist Robert J. Lifton argues that the development and use of nuclear weapons has crippled our capacity to imagine a long-term future. The import of climate disruption has a similar effect. Lifton calls it *the broken connection*. He explains that "We are ... among the first to live with a recurrent sense of biological severance."[1]

This peculiar relation to time is inherently destructive of the quality and value of our lives, and of the living body of Earth. And it will intensify because the Industrial Growth Society is, in systems' terms, on exponential *runaway* — accelerating toward its own collapse.

## To Reinhabit Time

Even as we see its consequences, this relation to time is not innate in us. As humans we have the capacity and the birthright to experience time in a saner fashion. Throughout history, men and women have labored at great personal cost to bequeath to future generations

All will come again into its strength
the fields undivided, the waters undammed,
the trees towering and the walls built low.
And in the valleys, people as strong
and varied as the land.
You too, God, will find your strength.
We who must live in this time
Cannot imagine how strong you will become.

— Rainer Maria Rilke, *Book of Hours*

monuments of art and learning to endure far beyond their individual lives. And they have honored, through ritual and story, those who came before.

As we take part in the Great Turning to a life-sustaining society, we learn to act like ancestors of future generations. We attune to longer ecological rhythms and nourish a strong felt connection with past and future beings. For us as agents of change, this isn't easy, because to intervene in the Industrial Growth Society, we can't avoid falling into its tempo. We race to find and pull the levers before it is too late to save this forest or stop that weapons program. Nonetheless, we can learn again to drink at deeper wells.

**Deep Time work** has arisen for that express purpose: to refresh our spirits and inform our minds by experiencing our present lives within larger contexts of time. This work brings a sense of relief and lasting resilience, as expressed in Molly's poem:

Ancient Ones,
residing in this forest,
speak to me.
Fill me with your wildness,
your wisdom,
your abiding Now.
Let me see all the projects and tasks

that consume my days
in the vast perspective of your time.
Let me see them as at one with
the forming of a seed cone,
the pushing out of leaf and stem
the chatter of grey squirrel
the flight of chickadee
the flow of water in the creek:
All taking place within the embrace of Life;
All held in love.

— Molly Brown[2]

## Practices

### *Invoking the Beings of the Three Times*

(5–10 minutes)

This ritual invocation affirms our connectedness with those who have gone before and those who come after us, as well as those living now. It evokes our solidarity with all these beings across time and opens us to the inspiration they can offer. Heightening our sense of gratitude and responsibility, it strengthens the will.

Good for opening a workshop or that portion given to Deep Time, the invocation can also be used in a public talk and a sermon. It would precede any of the exercises that follow.

#### METHOD

Bring the group into a standing circle. Speaking with respect and conviction, invoke first the beings of the past, pausing at the end for people to murmur names of ancestors and teachers. These words of ours may inspire your own.

*Be with us now all you who have gone before, you our ancestors and teachers. You who walked and loved and faithfully tended this Earth, be present to us now that we may carry on the legacy you bequeath us. Aloud and silently in our hearts we say your names and see your faces ....* Pause to allow people to say the names.

Then call on the beings of the present: *All you with whom we live and work on this endangered planet, be with us now. Fellow humans as well as brothers and sisters of other species, call forth our collective will and wisdom. Aloud and silently we say your names and picture your faces.* Again, pause to allow people to murmur names.

Lastly, invoke the beings of the future: *You who will come after us on this Earth, be with us now. It is for your sakes, too, that we work to heal our world. We cannot picture your faces or say your names — you have none yet — but we feel the reality of your claim on life. It helps us to be faithful in the work that must be done, so that there will be for you, as there was for our ancestors, blue sky, fruitful land, clear waters.* Here again a pause, this final one in silence.

## VARIATIONS

Before starting the invocation, teach the group this simple chant, using two notes of your choosing: *Gather with us now in this hour. Join with us now in this place.* The group repeats the chant three times after each part of the invocation.

If there is sufficient time for preparation, invite three people to speak in turn one part of the invocation. The group can then respond with the chant.

## Open Sentences on Time

(30–50 minutes)

### METHOD

Following the method for Open Sentences described in Chapter 6, offer the following or make up similar sentences:

- When I am in a hurry, my body feels …
- When I am in a hurry, my mind is like …
- Nowadays, I don't have time to …
- Lack of time affects my relationships in these ways …
- If I had all the time in the world, I would …

## The Evolutionary Gifts of the Animals
## (or the Eco-Milling)

### (15–20 minutes)

Using our own bodies, we learn about our kinship with other life-forms and the debt of gratitude we owe to those who first invented key features of our anatomy.

### METHOD

This process is usually conducted as a Milling (see Chapter 7), which allows it to be lively as well as instructive. At each encounter, when people stop to connect without words, their attention is directed to a particular biological feature that they all share. They are asked to note it in the person before them, to sense the wonder of this gift and to honor the animal ancestor that invented it. Here are features we tend to take for granted as *our own*. They are really gifts from other and ancient beings.

**The Blood Stream.** *Can you feel the pulse in your partner's wrist? Blood is circulating. That capacity common to all life-forms arose with the first multicelled creatures who devised ways to transfer nutrients to their inside cells. As they developed, some of them invented a muscular pump, a heart. That pulsing you feel is the gift of ancient, great-grandmother worm.*

**The Spinal Column.** *Feel the bones in your partner's neck and back. Those vertebrae are separate, but ingeniously linked. They cover the central neural cord and, at the same time, allow flexibility of movement. Grandfather fish did the design work, because he couldn't swim if his backbone were one solid piece. We can thank him for this marvel that now permits us to stand and walk and dance.*

**The Ear.** *Hum in your partner's ear; ah, you can hear each other! That's because tiny bones vibrate in the inner ear, and that is a gift from ancestor fish as well. They were once his jawbones, and they migrated into the mammalian ear to carry sound.*

**The Reptilian Brain.** *Inside the base of the skull lives the reptilian region of the brain, gift from our grandmothers and grandfathers who first came onto land. It allows us to protect ourselves by fighting, fleeing or freezing stock still.*

**The Limbic Brain.** *Near the middle of our brain lives the limbic region, gift from our early mammalian grandmothers and grandfathers. It allows deep pleasure and our primal sense of connection with others in family and tribe.*

**Binocular Vision.** *See the eyes are no longer on the sides of the head, as with our fish and reptile cousins, many birds and some mammals. Our tree-climbing primate ancestors moved their eyes around to the front to function together for three-dimensional vision, so they could know the exact location and distance of a branch to leap for. We thank them for our binocular vision.*

**Hand.** *And see how the thumb and fingertips can touch each other; see the size of the space they enclose. That's just the right size for a branch able to hold your swinging body. Grandmother monkey designed that hand. And the branch was designed by sun and wind and gravity, as well as Grandfather tree himself as he grew high to reach the light, and limber to allow the wind. So we, with these hands, are grandchildren of tree and sun and wind as well.*

## Variation

For this kind of reflection, people can also use their own bodies — when, for example, they are sitting in a lecture hall.

### *Harvesting the Gifts of the Ancestors*

#### (60 minutes)

This extended practice connects us vividly with our human past on Earth and deepens awareness of the strengths it offers us. The expanses of time, which we enter, remind us that the Industrial Growth Society is a momentary episode — and that, to move beyond it, we can draw on a far larger and more deeply rooted legacy.

As we progress through countless generations, respect and gratitude arise for our forebears' capacity to weather adversity — and to respond collectively and creatively to enormous challenges. The process helps us to believe that these capacities have not forsaken us and can help us now at this crisis point for life on Earth.

## METHOD

The process consists of a slow walk through time, first backwards to the start of the human story, and then forwards to return to the present. Allow five minutes for setup, 40 minutes or so for the walk and then another 15 for reflection in small groups.

Deep-toned flowing music, as background to the guide's verbal promptings, stirs images and memories of our long human journey arising from our collective unconscious. We like to use portions of *Ignacio* by Vangelis, rerecording them on the same CD to make an hour of background music.[3]

In order to keep walking without hitting a wall, people circle around a central point. Build this with a high stool or chairs visible to everyone as they walk. Ask them to space themselves around the room, right shoulder to the center, and wait while you explain the process. They are to move very slowly backwards after the music has begun and your words give the cue. Their eyes will be half closed to invite feelings and images to surface, while permitting enough vision to maneuver. They will feel the others moving alongside them, occasionally bumping and even stepping into each other, for paces vary. That is to be expected and is appropriate enough, because this has not been a solo journey; we make it together. When people get into a clump and feel impeded, they are just to raise their eyes, glance around for an open area and relocate.

Part way through, they will have reached the start of the human journey. Your words will make this clear and cue them to stop still. Then they will move forward in a clockwise direction, harvesting the gifts of the ancestors. It helps to make bodily gestures of gleaning,

We are one generation through thousands of years,
mothers and fathers shaped by children to come,
who, in their turn, will overtake them.
We are endlessly offered into life: all time is ours.

— Rainer Maria Rilke

scooping, picking from below and above, as they take to themselves the gifts.

After the explanations, the guide dedicates the ritual to the benefit of all beings. The walk now begins, with music in the background and voice-over from the guide. The guide's job is to offer a running series of verbal cues. These cues synchronize people's passage through time, as well as evoke memories, both personal and from the collective unconscious. The tone is steady, assured and slightly impersonal. *What* is said varies with the history and culture of the group. *How much* is said varies with the guide. Better to say too little than too much. You're not giving a history lesson; you're opening vistas for the imagination. The knowledge most needed is already there.

As in other extended verbal reflections, like the Cradling, reading the script word for word sounds contrived, even mechanical, making it harder for people to get into the practice. However, since there is so much to remember, feel free to work from extensive notes, using your own words whenever possible.

Here is a rough rendering of cues we have offered, with dots to indicate pauses. You may not want to say so much.

*From this present moment on [date] in [place], begin to walk slowly backwards in time. Move back through the events of this day ... to your waking up .... Walk back through the last week, the last month ... the times at home, and at work, and in your wider community .... Move back through the months to the turn of the year. Now you are walking back through last year through its seasons and encounters ....*

*Keep moving back through the decades of your adult life — many decades for some of us, or less than one for others — back through the journeys you made, the places you lived, the work you undertook. See perhaps the loss of someone close, perhaps the birth of a child, or children .... Encounter again the passions and adventures, disappointments and accomplishments ....*

*Walk back into to your teenage years with their hopes and heartache... back through the surprises and anguish of your adolescence .... You're entering your childhood, seeing the places and faces you knew, the lessons in school, the games, the lonely times .... Your body is getting smaller and smaller, and pretty soon the grown-ups are so tall, you have to reach up to hold their hands. Soon you're so small you're carried in arms …. And soon so small that you're inside your mother under the beat of her heart, your body simplifying, fewer and fewer cells … until you are just one cell and you've reached the moment of your conception.*

*Yet the life that is in you did not begin with your conception. It was there in your mother and your father. And even if you do not know your birth mother, your birth father, you can step back into their lives now …. Walk back now through their young adulthood, the choices they faced, the dreams they held. Move back with them into their adolescence, their childhood, their infancy ….*

*Continue walking back, back into the lives of your grandparents and your great-grandparents … back through the 20th century and beyond, back before the automobile, the telephone, before electricity. In the shadows of gas lamps, move into the lives of ancestors whose names you no longer know, but a gesture of theirs, a smile or turn of the head, lives on in you.*

*Moving back along this river of life, back through the industrial revolution, through the dark factories and teeming city streets, into lives of your people …. The generations move by more swiftly as you walk back through the centuries … through wars and upheavals, and the steady rhythms of tilling the earth ….*

*You're walking back through ancestors' lives as peasants, as magistrates, scholars, artisans, thieves, beggars, slaves and slaveholders, generals and foot soldiers …. Even then they carried you within them like a seed ….*

*You're moving back through ancient empires, through the rise and fall of entire civilizations back through the mists of time …. You come now into the longest chapter of our human journey, when we moved in small groups across the face of Gaia, gathering and hunting what we could, and no more than we needed …. Keep walking back through the millennia when we were nomads, treading with each footstep the soil and rock, the desert and forests of our planet home, through a time unmarked by wars ….*

*Keep walking back to our beginnings, some thirty thousand generations ago. Can you remember, was it in the heartland of Africa? …*

**And now you stop.** *Now with the very first ones, you're standing at the edge of the forest, looking out over the savanna. The journey of your people lies ahead. You and your kin don't have the strength and speed of the other animals, or the fangs or claws, or the heavy pelts to protect from cold and heat. You're naked. All you have is each other — and throats that can call out to each other.*

*You cannot imagine what your journey together will bring or the challenges you will face ....*

*Walk forward on that journey now. Enter the long treks of your ancestors across the continents, their voyages on rafts, the long marches in the ages of ice. You come from an unbroken line of survivors and each has gifts to bestow. Open your arms and hands to receive these gifts; gather them in.*

*Take their physical endurance ... take gifts of the one with the courage to lead, sending out scouts, choosing the way to go, keeping an eye on the little ones, the aging ones, those heavy with child; keeping the group together.*

*Take the gifts of the storytellers around the fire at night ... those who watched how the stars moved, so clear, so mysterious.*

*Walking with these ancestors, harvest their keen senses — their observant eyes, their knowing fingers gathering leaves and roots for fever and for childbirth. Harvest the knowledge of the healers and midwives ....*

*Harvest the wild knowing of the shaman who dances between realities, between seen and unseen worlds, and brings back instructions for the people .... Harvest the beating of the drum and the chants as we buried the dead and welcomed the newborn ....*

*Walking up through the centuries, see trust in the eyes of the children, the passion in the eyes of the young .... See the wisdom in the eyes of the aged .... Hear the laughter of two young girls splashing in a stream ....*

*Harvest our kinship with the other animals, watching and learning their ways — our teachers, our totems ....*

*Receive the ingenuity of your ancestors: making tools, weaving cloth, fashioning homes .... Know their love of beauty, music of a flute coming from the hills, hands carving jewelry, feet dancing on the packed earth ....*

*We are entering the time when we start to settle down, sowing seeds and returning to harvest. Then staying to cultivate, perhaps at the* confluence of two rivers .... And we begin to grow a surplus — our numbers increase, our settlements expand. We build granaries and temples ....

Some of us become owners of land, building walls to demarcate our fields. And some of us are landless, selling our labor to feed our children ....

Walk with the ancestors who devote their lives to trade and travel great distances, overland by caravans and by sea on ships ....

You are moving into recorded history; cities are growing with institutions of government and ecclesiastical power ... and imperial power. Empires with vast territories and vast armies ... with some of your ancestors in command and others as foot soldiers, who know the fear and blood of battle ....

And people come to be owned as well as the land .... And some of your ancestors are slaveholders and some are slaves .... All have gifts for you to harvest, gifts of endurance, gifts of responsibility, gifts of sorrow ....

And among them, those who rise up to claim the human right for dignity, for food .... Harvest the gifts of ancestors who sing songs of freedom and fight for justice .... Walk with the ancestors who stay on the land, tilling the fields, generation after generation, knowing the soil and the seasons of growth, times of plenty, times of want. Harvest their gifts ....

Moving onwards through time, walk with ancestors caught up in crusades and pogroms, inquisitions and witch burnings .... And they all have gifts for you, gifts of knowing how greed and fear warp the mind, gifts of steadfast faith ....

You are moving up into times of great exploration, ancestors leaving familiar worlds to voyage into new worlds, some seeking wealth, some seeking religious freedom, some brought in chains .... These ancestors have gifts for you; take their daring and resolve, take the bitter gifts, too, of sorrow and fortitude ....

Harvest as well the wisdom of the ancestors indigenous to these new lands .... Take their deep knowing of forests, plains, rivers, self-governance ....

Walk with your ancestors into the age of the machine — cotton gin, steam engine, railroad — ancestors whose highland farms and grazing *lands are taken, migrating into the factories, mills and mines .... Some are children, working dawn to dark .... Harvest the courage of those who speak out for a fair wage and the right to organize ....*

*You are stepping now into the lives of ancestors whose names you may know. Move with them into the 20th century, with its world wars and breakthroughs of technology: flying machines, cars, electronics — a century with bitter fruit ... the splitting of the atom, death camps, nuclear bombs, refugee camps, nuclear power, proliferation of weapons .... And some of your kin sent to the death camps, and others in charge of them. But they all have gifts for you, if only broken hearts and the plea to be remembered ....*

*Move now into the lives of your parents, the girl child who would grow to be your mother, the boy child who would grow to be your father — those two who gave you your own life. Take the gift of your own life; step into it ....*

*Walk into the radiance of the child who is you, greeting this world afresh. Step into your teenage years, with their dreams and betrayals. Walk into the beckoning world ... and now through the adult years of your life, through the choices you made, the people you loved, the tasks you gave yourself to ....*

*Take the anguish ripening you as you open your eyes to the world's suffering ... the war making, the spreading hunger, the lost species. Harvest the gifts of your own deep desire for the healing of our world ....*

*You are stepping into this last year, moving through these last months ... and through this last week ... until you come to the dawning of this present day .... Come to this present moment and stop.*

*Here in this Now, going no further than your next breath .... It's hard to imagine what lies ahead, and what will be asked of you or of our people. But you know one thing: you do not go empty-handed. You go with the gifts of the ancestors.*

## VARIATIONS

This practice can be adapted to focus on the ancestral line of a particular vocation, such as that of healers, teachers, scientists, artists, social justice activists. Then, instead of retracing a genetic line of forebears, we follow a vocational lineage, remembering men and women through history whose devotion to their calling bestows on-going gifts upon us all.

This can be offered as a meditation for people sitting in an auditorium or church. They can still use their hands and arms to gather the gifts.

❀ ❀ ❀

## Audio Recording to the Future

### (15–30 minutes)

In facing a particular situation or issue, the act of describing it aloud to future generations heightens appreciation of what is at stake in the long term. The larger time frame can deep the sense of responsibility, stimulate creativity and strengthen our resolve.

We like to use this practice at a specific location to support a holding action against a specific threat, such as clearcutting, toxic dumping and hydraulic fracking. People pass a small recorder, speaking into it one at a time. They imagine they are recording a message to be found and heard in that place by people of a coming generation or century. Alluding to choices presently confronting them, they record personal messages to the future.

This process originated in New Mexico at an *ad hoc* People's Council about government plans to deal with radioactive waste by burying it. Activists were concerned about leakage and eventual human intrusion at the site. Up to that point public opposition to such plans expressed a position known as NIMBY (Not In My Back Yard). Other than protecting their own communities, the public by and large didn't consider the waste to be their responsibility.

"Let's imagine," Joanna said, pulling out a small recorder, "that if we don't manage to stop the waste from being buried here, we could at least place this cassette here for future generations to find and listen to. What do we want to say to them?"

Passing the recorder around the Council circle, the men and women spoke into it with increasing urgency. "My name is George. I'm back in 1988 and trying to stop people from burying radioactive waste here. If they do and if you hear this, listen. Don't dig here, don't use the water, stay away! This stuff is deadly and contaminates all it touches. Take care!" As the words poured out, the future generations became more real, and those present began to feel more responsibility for the wastes their own generation had produced. They felt a greater determination to protect the beings of the future by developing less dangerous alternatives than burial — such as monitored, retrievable storage. This is now, among citizen activists, the preferred strategy.

> O you who will walk this earth when we are gone, stir us awake. Behold through our eyes the beauty of this world. Let us feel your breath in our lungs, your cry in our throat. Let us see you in the poor, the homeless, the sick. Haunt us with your hunger, hound us with your claims, that we may honor the life that links us.
>
> — Joanna Macy

## *Letter From the Future*

(40 minutes)

In this writing exercise, we identify with a human living on Earth one or two centuries from now and, from that perspective, see our current efforts and receive counsel and encouragement. It can also be used as a stand-alone practice, or in Going Forth. Molly has used it to begin a retreat focused on the rights of future generations, where it evoked a sense of mission.

### METHOD

Closing their eyes, people are invited to journey forward through coming generations and identify with a human living one or two hundred years from now. They need not figure out this person's circumstances, but only imagine that he or she is looking back at them in their present lives.

> *Now imagine what this being would want to say to you. Open your mind and listen. Now begin putting it on paper, as if this future one were writing a letter just to you.*

Allow ample time for the writing. After ten or fifteen minutes, people may read their letters aloud in small groups or the whole group. These simple letters can have a remarkable and lasting effect, bringing people their marching orders. They are often very meaningful to the hearers as well.

✧❊✧

## The Seventh Generation
## (formerly Double Circle)

(60 minutes)

This Deep Time ritual allows us to see the Great Turning within a larger time frame, including that of a human being of the Seventh Generation in the future, roughly two centuries from the present. It takes seriously the words of eminent radiologist Sister Rosalie Bertell: "Every being who will ever live on Earth is here now. Where? In our gonads and ovaries and in our DNA."[4]

This practice serves well as the sole experiential component of a short workshop or evening gathering.

### METHOD

People sit facing each other in pairs oriented in the same directional axis, as in E-W or N-S. Those facing in one direction, say West, identify as their present-day self. Those in front of them who are facing the opposite direction, say East, will identify as a human of the seventh generation in the future. These roles are not interchangeable, and are to be determined swiftly and clearly. Be sure all know what role they're in.

Ask people to grant two assumptions for the purpose of this ritual. *The first assumption is that there will be humans living on Earth two hundred years from now. Even if you have come to believe otherwise, please grant that assumption for the purpose of this ritual.*

*The second assumption is that the future ones have a cultural memory of what is happening in our time of the early 21st century — whether carried by universities or storytellers. This is an important assumption. It* means humans are not all scattered in caves; to have a common culture, they must be living in life-sustaining communities — for the Industrial Growth Society clearly can't last another 200 years.

Now explain that in order for present and future beings to meet across two centuries, we must go to a point outside of time. *We travel there by the power of our intention and our moral imagination — and by sounding together — long and strong — the seed syllable AH, which stands for all that has not yet been spoken.*

When the sounding has brought everyone to the point outside of time, explain the two roles as follows:

*You present-day people choose to see the person before you as a human of the seventh generation. And you future ones know that the person before you lives back in the year [today]. You have something to say to them and to ask; this will be spoken in* **my** *voice and taken as coming directly through your own heart-mind. Your present-day one will then answer out loud, while the future one listens in silence.*

*And by the way, the word* ancestor *refers to all people of preceding generations and is not limited to one's own genetic line.*

**Inquiries from the Future.** You as guide will speak for the future humans, three different times. Allow three to five minutes for the present-day humans to respond to each inquiry. After the first response and again after the second, invite the future ones to silently acknowledge what they have heard, then to take their leave and walk to an empty place in front of another present-day being. Now everyone is facing a new person.

We encourage you to speak these three successive inquiries in your own words, rather than reading them.

1. *Ancestor, I greet you. It's so amazing to see your face, because all my life I have heard stories from teachers and grandparents about the time you are living. Some of the things I've heard I find hard to believe, so I'd like to check them out with you. They say that in your time there are a few people richer than the richest ancient kings, while billions of people are without enough food or shelter or clean water. They tell us that in your time bombs are being made that can blow up whole cities. We know about that, but they say* **you** *know about*

*it too, right when the bombs are being made. They tell us that whole species of animals and plants are going extinct. We know about that, too, because gone is gone. But they tell us **you** know about that while it's happening. Is all this true?… And if it is true, what's that like for you to live in such a world?*

Allow about five minutes for the present-day humans to respond. Then invite the future ones to silently acknowledge what they have heard, then to take their leave and walk to an empty place in front of another present-day being.

2. *Ancestor, I greet you. When we in our generation find water we can drink and soil that's safe to grow food, it is thanks to the work you and your friends are doing on our behalf. It must be hard for you, especially at the beginning, standing up for beings you haven't met and will never meet. So I want to ask you these questions: What inspired you to start on this path? And what were the first steps you took?*

Allow three minutes or so for the present-day humans to respond. And once again invite the future ones to acknowledge what they have heard, take their leave and move to a new place in front of yet another present-day being.

3. *Ancestor, I greet you. We know you did not stop with those first steps. There are stories and songs about what you and your friends are doing to leave us a livable world. What they don't tell us, and what I would really like to know, is where you find the strength to do this. Where do you find the power to keep on going for the sake of life, despite all the obstacles and discouragements? Can you tell me?*

**Future humans respond.** After the present-day persons have answered the third question, the future ones do not leave, but stay right there and respond to your next invitation:

*Now, you of the Seventh Generation, it is your turn to talk. You have been listening to three ancestors speak of their experience of Great Turning. As you listened, thoughts and feelings arose in you. Now is your chance to speak them. What is in your heart to say to the one before you? Very soon this person will be returning right into the midst of that darkness and danger. What words do you have for him or her?*

Ask the present-day ones to just listen now, without speaking.

**Closing the Ritual.** Bring the ritual to a close by inviting the people in dyads to thank each other silently, and then to return to real time by once again sounding the seed syllable *AH.*

*And on the way back to real time, as we sound the AH, you who spoke for the Seventh Generation can shake off that role. For the truth is, you belong to the Great Turning too.*

With this particular practice, the processing of it can be almost as rewarding as the ritual itself. Ask for any reflections people would like to share with the whole group. Encourage those who speak up to identify the role they played.

## VARIATIONS

1.  In an earlier form, the ritual was done in two concentric circles; each person in the outer circle sits facing a person in the inner circle. Those in the outer circle are themselves in the present time, and those in the inner circle are future humans of the Seventh Generation. After each spoken encounter, the future ones rise, step back to move one place to the right and sit again. In this way the inner circle moves clockwise while the outer circle stays stationary.

2.  Here's another question to use if you have time. Place it after #1.

    *Ancestor, when did you first realize the Industrial Growth Society was doomed? How did it dawn on you that humans would have to live in a radically different way for complex life-forms to continue?*

### *Field Work on the Great Turning*
### (45 minutes)

Here's a practice to follow after a presentation of the Great Turning and its three dimensions. Combining group discussion and imaginative role-play, it lets us view this transition to a life-sustaining society from the perspective of a future generation. Don't include it in the same workshop with the Wheel of the Great Turning (Chapter 6).

## METHOD

This process assumes that participants are already familiar with the three dimensions of the Great Turning (Chapter 1). It unfolds in two distinct parts.

In **Part One**, participants count off by three and separate into three groups with newsprint, markers and space to talk. Each group is devoted to a different dimension of the Great Turning, and for 15 minutes they bring to mind all the elements of that dimension they are personally acquainted with, and they list them on the newsprint.

**Part Two** begins when the guide calls the groups to come back together with the fruits of their work. Now a dramatic and surprising change occurs. Note: Make sure there's no hint of the shift to future time before this point.

The guide has written on a flip chart or whiteboard the particulars of time and place:

Evermore University [make up a name]
Fall Semester, 21__ [choose a date about a hundred years
in the future]
— Graduate Course: History of the Great Turning

The guide now plays the part of a professor greeting students in the course as they come back together after several weeks of fieldwork. It becomes clear by the professor's remarks that the students' research sought to determine the causes behind the eventual success of humanity's third revolution, colloquially known as the Great Turning. The professor acknowledges how challenging the fieldwork must have been, given that so many records were lost with the collapse of the Industrial Growth Society.

Each research group is represented by a couple of students who proceed to present and discuss the conclusions of their research.

There is great enjoyment as they play the part of future students looking back at this remarkable chapter of human history.

## The Storytellers Convention

### (20–30 minutes)

Our worldview can shift when we stop telling ourselves why something can't happen. By vividly envisioning a hoped-for future, we begin to believe that it is really possible. Enriching this vision with all our senses — imagining colors, shapes, sounds, smells, tastes, facial expressions and the *feel* of this possible future — activates our creative and intuitive faculties.

Research shows that people who approach a problem by imagining it has already been solved tend to be more creative in inventing possible solutions. This *imaginary hindsight* approach can apply to the next 24 hours or to the next century. The Storytellers Convention, created by Chris Johnstone and described in *Active Hope*,[5] uses imaginary hindsight to support people's visions and work for a life-sustaining future.

### METHOD

The guide invites people to imagine traveling through time to a hoped-for future hundreds of years from now. They imagine they are at a gathering of storyteller-historians at this time in the future. In pairs (or groups of three or four), they take turns sharing stories that they might have heard as children in this future time, stories about the Great Turning that started in the early 21st century when human society seemed on the path to collective suicide. "Though things didn't look too promising at first, a widespread awakening occurred, and huge numbers of people rose to the challenge of creating the life-sustaining society familiar to the storytellers now."[6]

After sharing their stories, the group travels back to the present time, carrying with them a deepened sense of the epic adventure we are all part of.

## A Thousand Years of Healing

From whence my hope, I cannot say,
except it grows in the cells of my skin,
in my envelope of mysteries it hums.
In this sheath so akin to the surface of the earth
it whispers. Beneath
the wail and dissonance in the world,
hope's song grows. Until I know
that with this turning
we put a broken age to rest.
We who are alive at such a cusp
now usher in
one thousand years of healing!

Winged ones and four-leggeds,
grasses and mountains and each tree,
all the swimming creatures,
even we, wary two-leggeds
hum, and call and create
the Changing Song. We remake
all our relations. We convert
our minds to the earth. In this turning time
we finally learn to chime and blend,
attune our voices; sing the vision
of the Great Magic we move within.
We begin
the new habit, getting up glad
for a thousand years of healing.

— Susa Silvermarie[7]

**10**

# Going Forth

*Go forth on your journey, for the benefit of the many,*
*for the joy of the many, out of compassion for the welfare,*
*the benefit and joy of all beings.*

— Gautama the Buddha

*Already my gaze is upon the hill, the sunlit one.*
*The way to it, barely begun, lies ahead.*
*So we are grasped by what we have not grasped,*
*full of promise, shining in the distance.*

*It changes us, even if we do not reach it,*
*into something we barely sense, but are;*
*A movement beckons, answering our movement ...*
*But we just feel the wind against us.*

— Rainer Maria Rilke

T HE CULMINATION OF THE WORKSHOP serves as a bridge between the experiences of our work together (described in the
last four chapters) and the daily lives we are about to resume. We
have come to see with new eyes our ineluctable place in the web of

life, our connections with all beings through space and time and the kind of power that is ours for creating a life-sustaining culture. Now we use this new vision to discern more clearly the distinctive role we each can play in the Great Turning.

This chapter offers practices for doing this. Before describing them, let us first look at the Work That Reconnects to be clear about what it provides us — and what it does not. It gives us no dogma or ideology, no panacea for society's ills, no blueprint for resolving the global crisis — not even a certainty that we can act in time to save life on Earth. Such a guarantee, were it possible, would not be likely to summon forth our best efforts — the leap of courage and creativity that is required of us now.

## Discoveries Made So Far in the Spiral

What then can we expect to take with us, as we go forth into the world and our individual lives?

+ A heightened awareness of the suffering and dangers besetting our world with a greater respect for our capacity to face them without dodging, denying or numbing out
+ An upsurge of energy as we unblock feedback loops by accepting our pain for the world, reframing it as compassion
+ A wider sense of identity as a unique and integral part of the living body of Earth
+ A growing appreciation for community — with each other, with our brother-sister species, with our ancestors and future generations. We feel supported by them as well as accountable to them
+ A stronger motivation to join with others in service to life; confidence in the power of our solidarity
+ A fresh sense of the diversity of our gifts and of the many interdependent roles to be played in the Great Turning
+ Hence, gratitude for who we are as individuals, with all our personal strengths and limitations — even our wounds — and for our desire to be of use
+ Commitment to goals extending beyond our individual lifetime; liberation from dependence on immediate, measurable results

> How do we move forward? It's not rocket science. We need to worry less about doing what is more important, and more about doing whatever we can. Those of us who are used to power need to learn to listen as much as we talk, and those with less power need to learn to talk as much as we listen. The truth is that we can't know which act in the present will make the most difference in the future, but we can behave as if everything we do matters ....
>
> — Gloria Steinem

✦ Gladness in being alive now, in this epochal moment on Earth; a sense of the privilege of taking part in the Great Turning

Now, as we approach the end of the workshop, we both digest these gifts of learning and see quite specifically how they can shape our lives and our actions.

## Practices

### Networking

For lasting benefit to workshop participants, be sure to give them opportunities to network with each other — sharing interests, ideas and hopes about actions they are engaged in or would like to engage in for the Great Turning. It is good to allow time for this early on in the workshop, but if you haven't, do it now.

#### METHOD

This is a freewheeling process, often good before a meal when people can continue to talk informally. Begin it by inviting people to stand at random (popcorn style) to name the issues and activities that they are called to. Then everyone can mingle and gather around particular themes.

As an alternative, use sheets of newsprint on the wall. Ask people to post their areas of concern — say, Schools, Factory Farms, Climate Change, Nuclear Waste, GMOS, Homelessness. The posting process itself may result in some groupings. Then people can gather around common concerns, share ideas and information.

⸱⸱⸱

## Communicating Our Concerns and Hopes
### (30–45 minutes)

At each step in our work for the world, we engage with other people. Many do not appear to share our concerns, but because of their relationship to us or their position of responsibility, we'd like to enlist their support — or at least their understanding. It's easy to feel intimidated when we fear that they are opposed to our views. This role-playing exercise, along with the guidelines that follow, helps us to be more confident and skillful.

### METHOD

Have everyone assemble in pairs. Then your instructions cover the following points. *Think of someone with whom you find it hard to talk about your concerns for the world and the actions you want to take. It could be your father or sister, your employer or lover, or even the US President or the Secretary of Defense. Assign that identity to your partner along with some clues as to how to play the role and what responses this person might give. Partners, feel free to ask for clarification, and let your intuition guide you, too.*

Then begin the role-play: *Speakers, tell this person what you see, how you feel and what you feel impelled to do about it. Note any feelings of awkwardness, shame or powerlessness that may arise, and continue nonetheless. Partners respond in your role, keeping your replies fairly brief, so the burden of communication is on the speaker.*

After a few minutes, ask the pairs to reverse roles, the speakers taking on the identity of the persons they have chosen to address, and their partners taking the role of speaker. This reversal of roles is revealing and productive, breaking through our old, automatic assumptions about the person we are addressing. We may experience his confusion and fear; we may see ourselves in a new light. We discover how we tend to lock people into adversarial positions by our presuppositions, projections and our previous history with them. Reversing roles back again, the conversation continues, but now the speaker is more aware of the inner experience of the person being addressed; she often feels freer to be herself.

Generally, two rounds of role-playing take place so that everyone has a chance to practice speaking to a person of their choice. In the general discussion following the role-plays, write up two lists from participants' responses to two questions:

1.  Why is it often so difficult to share our concerns for the world?
2.  What are some guidelines for communicating our view, especially with those we assume to hold a different opinion?

Here are some common difficulties:

+ We don't want to get into an argument, especially with people who are important in our lives.
+ We are afraid of triggering others' anger or fear.
+ We are afraid we don't know enough facts to sustain our views.
+ We are afraid of appearing self-righteous or fanatical.
+ We hesitate to talk about things that evoke strong feelings and opinions, because it's considered bad manners.
+ We don't want to make anyone uncomfortable.
+ We are reluctant to get embroiled in heated and fruitless debates.

In this time, when our collective choices are so critical, how can we discuss our concerns productively? Here are some guidelines:

+ **Beware of making assumptions** about the other person's views because they are a certain age, dressed in a certain way, come from a particular region, class or ethnicity or hold a particular job.
+ **Find common ground before examining differences.** If you begin by ascertaining areas of agreement (e.g. "Nuclear war is possible" or "We need clean air and water for our children"), both parties can trust each other more and proceed to see where their views diverge. Then offering the information that has led to your view can fill a gap in the other's knowledge and lead to reappraisal of old assumptions. A person may simply not know, for example, about

the extent of clearcutting in the Pacific Northwest or the current level of expenditures on nuclear weapons.

+ **Share feelings as well as facts.** Facts are debatable; feelings are not. We can report our own feelings with varying degrees of accuracy and honesty, but they are not open to question. Sharing your feelings invites other people to share theirs as well, moving the conversation away from argument and towards mutual listening.

+ **Share your personal experience.** The facts and figures we cite take on more reality for people when we describe what led us to the views we hold. Personal experience, like feelings, is not open to debate.

+ **Trust the other person's ability to learn and change over time.** Even if the person seems entrenched in a contrary position, change may be stirring within. And you may never know if change has occurred as a result of your discussion, or what other information the person may receive from others to add to yours.

+ **See yourself and the other within the larger context:** your shared humanity, the stresses of the Industrial Growth Society, the long, uneven journey to a life-sustaining culture. This breeds patience and goodwill.

+ **Remember to hold the other person and yourself with compassion,** even when you seem to find no common ground. We can never know what suffering and hardship might underlie another's seemingly intractable position. You can "agree to disagree" with a measure of equanimity.

## Life Map

### (20–30 minutes)

This simple and engrossing process can be counted on to yield a fresh perspective on one's life, with unexpectedly appreciative insights into its valor and purpose.

### METHOD

Instructions from the guide: *Taking pen and paper, draw a map of your life's journey up to now. Let it flow like a stream in a wandering line around the page, from your birth in this lifetime to the present moment. Along the line draw symbols or pictures to convey significant events that enriched or redirected the course of your life and your sense of its purpose. When you get to the present, think of the different trajectories you are considering taking; draw them in dotted lines out from the point of Now, each perhaps with its own icon or image.*

After 15 minutes invite people to share their maps in small groups.

> Our leaders got confused.
> So we are all leaders now.
> They told us there was nothing we could do.
> They were wrong.
> When we tell ourselves
> There's nothing we can do, we are wrong.
>
> ... We're all making the soup
> we're all eating.
> We're all weaving the cloth
> we're all wearing.
>
> — Anne Herbert and Paloma Pavel

## *Imaging Our Power*

### (40 minutes)

Imaging on paper with colors can give us access to intuitive wisdom. Here we allow a subliminal sense of potential to emerge in graphic form. This is especially useful following the previous exercise.

### METHOD

This process is similar to Imaging with Colors in Chapter 7, and it may help to review the description of that exercise. After people have arranged themselves and their paper and colors, suggest something like this:

*Our sense of the power that is in us can be hard to convey in words. Close your eyes and breathe deeply for a moment or two ... then try to sense what your power is like .... Let images and sensations emerge .... Then take your paper and colors and begin to draw how that power feels or appears to you at this moment. Do this quickly, without too much thought.*

After five minutes or so, the drawings are shared in small groups. Some are swirls and shadings of color; some are symbolic (a heart with a sun, a tree with deep roots and many creatures in its branches). One woman drew a river winding through the landscape and in its curly rushing waters were many objects: first nuclear missiles and cooling towers, stick figures of soldiers and hungry children — and then as the river progressed, trees, flowers, birds, musical notes. "My power is not to close myself off any more," she said, "but to be open to the horror and awfulness, to let it all flow through me and to let it change into what I choose to make happen. These tributaries flowing in are all the people who are doing the same thing. So I guess it isn't my river or my power anymore, but everybody's."

> I understood that work was another way of worshipping, that listening and working were one and the same thing.
>
> — Beautiful Painted Arrow

The drawing of one man, an engineer, appeared to be a huge fish net. "I started to draw my anger — see this part here is a gun — but then it started connecting with the anger of others, and then with their needs and then with their hopes. And now I'm not sure which part of the net I am. I am part of it all. I guess that is my power."

## The Sword in the Stone

### (30 minutes)

T.H. White, in *The Sword in the Stone*, tells us the story of King Arthur as a boy. Joanna has recounted this story in workshops because it portrays the dimensions of power available to us as open interconnected systems:

*The wizard Merlin, as Arthur's tutor, schooled the boy in wisdom by turning him into various creatures and had him live, for brief periods, as a falcon, an ant, a wild goose, a badger, a carp in the palace moat.*

*The time came when the new King of All England was to be chosen; it would be he who could draw the sword from the stone. All the famous knights who came to the great tournament went to the churchyard in London where the stone mysteriously stood; they tried mightily to yank out the sword that was embedded in it. Heaving and sweating, they* competed to prove their superior strength. No deal; tug and curse as they might, the sword did not budge. Then the disgruntled knights departed to return to their jousting.

Arthur, who was just a teenager then, lingered behind, went up to the stone to try his own luck. Grasping the sword's handle he pulled with all his strength until he was exhausted and drenched. The sword remained immobile. Glancing around, he saw in the shrubbery surrounding the churchyard the forms of those with whom he had lived and learned. There they were: badger, falcon, ant and the others. As he greeted them with his eyes, he opened again to the powers he had perceived in each of them — industry, cunning, quick boldness, perseverance. Knowing they were with him, he turned back to the stone and, breathing easily, drew out the sword, as smooth as a knife from butter.

After telling the story, lead the group on the following guided journey in your own words, as they sit with their eyes closed.

You have a task to do for the healing our world. Your task may seem impossible to accomplish. Let it be symbolized by the sword in the stone. Feel the grain of the stone — how rough and unyielding it is, how the sword is anchored in it right up to the hilt. No matter how hard you strain and pull, the sword does not budge ....

Just as Arthur looked about in the churchyard, look around your life to see the beings who have been your teachers in some way. Some you may live and work with now. Some may have lived a long time ago, but their qualities do not die; they live on. Let these beings appear in your mind's eye: loved ones, teachers, saints, leaders, animals that have inspired you. Think of the qualities in each that you love and admire, breathe them in ....

These friends are smiling at you now, reminding you of what is available to you now. The courage, the intellect, the goodness and power that poured through their lives can also be yours. Breathing in these strengths, reach for the handle of the sword, slowly, calmly .... Now draw it out. See how the sword answers not to your own separate ego-efforts, but to the power of all beings, as you open to them.

Who appeared in the surrounding bushes of your life and gave you strength to pull the sword from the stone? Who gave you insight and courage? The gifts they received from the web of life are available to you as well.

After the story and the guided journey, people can tell each other about those from whom they draw power.

## Callings and Resources

### (1–1½ hours)

This practice helps each of us clarify our role in the Great Turning, and to focus on a specific path or project. It brings to light the many and often unsuspected resources available; it also identifies immediate steps to take. Because it is done in pairs, it also creates a strong sense of mutual support. Over the years and without fail, we have found that this practice has a strengthening and often lasting effect on all who take part in it.

### METHOD

People work in pairs, taking turns. In response to a series of questions from the guide, one partner speaks while the other serves as scribe, making written notes, perhaps in the speaker's own journal. The speaker can be encouraged to take full advantage of having a scribe, and relax, maybe stretch out to give freer rein to the mind. At the end of each series of questions, the speaker gives the scribe a hand massage, before they reverse roles.

Questions we frequently use are:

1. *If you knew you could not fail, what would you do in service to life on Earth? Here is our chance to pull out the stops and think big, with no ifs or buts getting in the way.*

    An alternative first question is: *If you were liberated from all fear and open to all the power available to you in the web of life, what would you do in service to life on Earth?*

2. *In pursuing this vision, what particular project do you feel called to undertake? It can be a new direction in work you're already doing — or something entirely new. Here's your chance to get specific. Think in terms of what could be accomplished, or well underway, in a year's time.*

3. *What resources, inner and outer, do you now have that will help you do that? Inner resources include talents and strengths of character, as well as knowledge and skills you've acquired. External resources include relationships, contacts and networks you can draw on — not to forget babysitters, rich relatives, computer-savvy friends — as well as your location, employment, real goods and money in the bank.*

4. *Now what resources, inner and outer, will you need to acquire? To follow your calling, what will you need to learn and to get? These can run from assertiveness training, to grants, to contacts within organizations and the support they can give you.*

5. *How might you stop yourself? What obstacles might you throw in your way? We all have familiar patterns of self-doubt and sabotage.*

6. *How will you move through or around with these obstacles?*

7. *What can you do in the next week, no matter how small the step — if only a phone call — that will move you along this path?*

When both partners have scribed the other's responses (and exchanged hand massages), each scribe in turn reads back to the other from the notes they have taken, using the second-person pronoun: *you want to, you have, one way you might stop yourself.* And the other listens as if hearing, at long last, their marching orders from the universe. The written notes are then exchanged so that each can take with them their callings and resources.

## VARIATION

If time is too short for the whole process, skip the scribing. Have people simply note their own responses to each question and then share their answers with another person by announcing firmly: *I am going to ...* or *I will ...* and *I can tap these resources ...* (and similar declarations).

> In time of crisis, we summon up our strength. Then, if we are lucky, we are able to call every resource, every forgotten image that can leap to our quickening, every memory that can make us know our power. And this luck is more than it seems to be: it depends on the long preparation of the self to be used.
>
> — Muriel Rukeyser

## Consultation Groups

### (60 minutes)

As a follow-on to the above exercise, people meet in four-person consultations to get real with their visions and plans. These groups provide feedback and advice and often suggestions about contacts and resources.

### METHOD

Each pair from the Callings and Resources practice now joins with another pair to make a group of four, bringing the notes of their plans.

*You are now provided an unparalleled opportunity. You are offered what money cannot buy: top-flight consultants who are allied with your vision. Take a moment to reflect on the plans you've been hatching. Where can you use some excellent advice? Is it to get clearer on your project and what you can achieve? Is it how to find the resources you need, or how to deal with particular obstacles? You each have 15 minutes. Hone your question(s) carefully in your mind, so that you can speak briefly and give the others time to respond.*

It is hard to bring these groups to a close, so give two minutes advance warning and remind people that they'll have time when the workshop finishes to confer further.

## Corbett

### (45–60 min)

The Work That Reconnects recognizes the intrinsic organizing power of intention. Even in an uncertain world, we can still choose where we put our minds and how we respond to circumstances and events. Justine and Michael Thoms describe *the genius of intention:*

> When you are clear about your intention and at peace with yourself, aligned and moving with purpose in your work, then magic happens. People appear, affinity projects

emerge, support from unimagined quarters suddenly manifests.[1]

In Corbett, our capacity for intention is tested and amplified by hearing from multiple perspectives:

1. the person who holds the intention
2. the voice of Doubt
3. the voice of a human ancestor
4. the voice of a future human

The practice was created near a small town named Corbett in the Columbia Gorge.

## METHOD

People sit in groups of four. They are given some moments of silence for each person to select an important intention they would like to explore further. Then each of the four takes a turn, first describing their intention, and then hearing it addressed by the other three people in the group. Each of the other three speaks in turn from a different perspective. Going clockwise around the circle, these perspectives are: the voice of Doubt, the voice of a human ancestor and the voice of a future human.

Explain that each of these voices is meant to serve the person holding the intention. The voice of Doubt is helpful by bringing up misgivings and fears that could derail or weaken the intention if they are not faced squarely. The ancestral voice brings in the wisdom of the past, and the future human opens vistas of what this intention could mean to coming generations. Each person commenting gets about two minutes to speak, while the intention holder listens silently. In this fashion, every person in the group gets a chance to speak all four voices.

Allow time at the end of each round for the intention holder to reflect on any insights that have arisen, thanking the other voices. Foursomes have found it helpful to assign each perspective to a chair and move to new seats before each round.

### Variation

This practice can also be done in groups of three, in which case the fourth voice, that of the future, is spoken by the person who has spoken as Doubt. The value of this is two-fold: it saves time and it often allows the voice of Doubt to speak more boldly, knowing there will be a chance to take a more encouraging role.

## Clearness Committee

### (45 minutes for each focus person)

The Clearness Committee is a venerable Quaker practice for seeking clarity in important decisions, such as marriage. This method of discernment is based on a two-fold conviction: (1) that each of us has access to inner wisdom and (2) that this inner light can become clear when a group gives its caring, undivided attention and offers questions instead of advice.

Traditionally, the seeker or focus person invites five or six trusted individuals (with as much diversity of relationship to the seeker as possible) and provides them beforehand a written description of the situation or choices he is facing. The Clearness Committee then meets for about three hours, with the possibility of continuing in a second or third meeting in subsequent weeks. One member agrees to serve as clerk (or facilitator), another as recorder — and everyone serves as prayerful listener and channel for clarifying questions.

The essential and defining feature of the Clearness Committee is this: that after the focus person summarizes the issue, members of the committee assist her by asking questions rather than giving advice or problem solving. Honest, caring queries, arising out of prayerful silence, help the focus person to see herself and her situation in a new light and unblock her inner wisdom and authority.

### Workshop Adaptation

In a workshop or intensive of sufficient duration (at least five days) an adaptation of the Clearness Committee process has been very valuable in the Going Forth stage. Here everyone is given the opportunity to be the focus person and seek clarity on a particular issue. The time for each person is necessarily reduced (less than an hour), but this time span has proved sufficient to yield important insights.

The Clearness Committee can also be used in a group that meets regularly over an extended period of time, for everyone in turn or upon request of a group member.

## Method

Block out two sessions of three hours each in the latter half of the workshop, say on two consecutive afternoons. (The work can be done in 2½ hour sessions, but it's a squeeze.) The process requires such keen, sustained attention that back-to-back sessions are tiring.

Divide the participants into groups of five or at most six people each. It is useful in this practice to have people who are partners or work colleagues end up in the same small group.

Each group is given a separate, undisturbed meeting place. In each three-hour session, three people take their turns as focus person or seeker.

Before breaking into groups, take time to explain the process in detail:

+ Acknowledge the Quaker origins of this method and state its purpose.
+ While each of us faces a number of issues, we select just one to bring to the Clearness Committee. The process works best when we specify and delineate a particular issue — even if it is a major one — that calls for some choice or action on our part.
+ Strict confidentiality is to be observed (unless the focus person specifies otherwise).
+ Timing: Each person has 45 minutes as focus person or seeker. Of this allotted time the focus person takes no more than ten minutes to present his particular issue and situation. That leaves 35 minutes for the Clearness-style queries and possible reflections at the close. There will be a ten-minute stretch break before the next person's turn as seeker.

+ Before presenting his issue, the focus person asks another group member to be facilitator (who will serve as timekeeper and process reminder) and yet another to be the scribe (jotting key queries and points, perhaps in the focus person's own notebook).

+ At this point, group members may decide if they wish to listen and respond to the focus person from the perspective of one living in the past, the present or the future. (*I'll be an ancestor this time.*) To include the beings of the three times has been useful in our adaptation of the Clearness Committee, for it opens us to the wider context of our work and some radically different perspectives. (*From the viewpoint of a future being, I would ask you this ...*) These adopted roles are to be held lightly and not weighted with literalness, lest they restrict other questions one may be moved to ask.

+ Both before and after the focus person presents her issue, the group takes some moments of silence. It is a prayerful silence in which we devote our full attention to the seeker. The questions we offer will arise out of that prayerful intention.

+ Make clear, above all, that *questions* are the heart of the Clearness Committee. It requires mindfulness and self-discipline not to fall into old habits of wanting to *fix* and give advice. This means no psychological rescuing, no solutions offered, no stories or wise counsel from our own experience. Only honest, probing, caring questions are called for. Though often challenging, these questions are offered with humility and an attitude of absolute respect.

+ When the queries we offer are actually advice in disguise, (*Have you thought of ...*) or when we lapse into anecdotes from our own lives, the facilitator helps us stick to the Clearness practice. On the other hand, don't hold back on questions just because they may seem off the wall. A query like *What colors do you associate with these job alternatives?* may prompt a rewardingly intuitive response.

+ It is, of course, in the answers the focus person hears himself making that he uncovers his inner wisdom. So his responses should be ample enough to allow for that, yet brief enough to let more questions be asked. Some questions may stir reflections that the focus person finds hard to articulate or wishes to keep to himself. He is always free to refrain from a verbal answer.

- If there is time at the end, group members may wish to speak of the qualities they sense in the focus person and the kind of trust they feel in his capacity to make the right choice and take the right action.

- Sometimes the right line of action becomes immediately clear to the focus person; sometimes it unfolds more gradually, as she continues later to digest the experience of the Clearness process. She is encouraged to trust in this gradual unfolding, but if her intuition strongly prompts her near the end of the session to ask the group for direct advice, she may, of course, do so.

If time permits, consider giving people more opportunity to prepare. This would include a silent time alone, in which they let a key issue/question emerge. And then they might talk briefly in pairs to help themselves name and specify this issue. The Life Map practice can precede the Clearness Committee to help people clarify their questions.

꩜

### Dialoging with Mara to Strengthen Our Resolve
(45–60 minutes)

In Buddhism, there is a hand gesture called the *bhumisparsa mudra*, which means gesture of touching the Earth. It is features in the story of when Gautama, soon to become the Buddha, sat down under the bodhi tree. We can imagine him saying, in effect, *I am not going to get up until I have broken through to the secret of the suffering we cause ourselves and others. Until I wake up to that, I am not going to move.* This infuriated Mara, a mythic figure serving as challenging counterpart to the Buddha. Mara sent demons to frighten Gautama and dancing girls to distract him, but the Buddha-to-be didn't waver. Finally, Mara challenged him outright. *By what right and authority do you think you can solve the mystery of suffering? Just who do you think you are?*

In response to this challenge, Gautama offered no personal credentials, no *curriculum vitae*. He didn't say "I'm the son of a king. I graduated *summa cum laude* from the Yoga Institute or went to

Harvard Business School." He said nothing at all about himself. He simply reached down and touched the Earth, saying in effect, "This is my right to be here; this is my right to seek freedom from endless suffering and inflicting of suffering." It was by the authority of Earth that he sought liberation from suffering, and when he did that, the scriptures say, the Earth roared.

So we can make that gesture too. We can touch the Earth. That act, even if only mental, reminds us of who we are and what we are about, as we confront the global corporate economy. We are here for the sake of life. By the authority of our belonging to Earth from the beginning of time, we are here.

Often as activists, we repress the voices of fear and doubt as well as the voices seducing us into pleasurable distractions. This practice gives us the chance to voice all the seductions, doubts and fears that pull us off course, which are represented by Mara. It gives us practice in standing up to Mara and finding our ground, our authority.

It is good in this practice for the facilitator(s), instead of taking part, to scan the group and be available to help.

## METHOD

Form groups of three. Each person takes a turn as the focus person for 15 minutes, while the other two people are listening allies in this dialogue with Mara. The focus person uses two cushions, sitting on one and facing the other.

> Cushion One is the place of intention/resolve/
> determination
> — Cushion Two is Mara

The focus person starts in the place of resolve, telling the two witnesses of something she intends to put into action on returning home. This could be either a very small plan or a larger project, something close to the heart that the focus person may feel a little fearful of doing. It's good to start with a few moments of centering. *Ground yourself in your body and in Earth. Feel the support of Earth and the whole Earth community. Trust in your life experience. Don't hide your dreams — some of the greatest things people have done have grown from seeds of ideas that might have seemed crazy at the time.*

After stating her intention, the focus person moves onto Cushion Two and becomes Mara, voicing fears, doubts and criticisms (e.g. who are *you* to think you can stand up and do this; you haven't got time; you don't know enough).

Then the focus person moves back to Cushion One and responds to Mara.

*You may need to recenter yourself on the cushion; you don't need to respond to Mara immediately. Find your ground quietly and then speak.*

The dialogue continues for about ten minutes, during which time the allies witnessing this process can help in two ways:

1. At certain points, the focus person may wish one of the allies to act as Mara.
2. At other times, especially if the focus person is finding it difficult to respond to Mara, an ally may move behind her, putting a hand on her shoulder and speak to Mara on her behalf.

The time comes when Mara demands of the focus person: *By what authority are you doing this?* and the focus person replies by touching the earth and saying, with full resolve: *By the authority of Earth, I will ...*

After everyone has had a chance to be focus person, the threesomes talk about their experience, before reconvening in the large group for people to share what they have learned.

> I want to free what waits within me
> So that what no one has dared to wish for
> May for once spring clear ...
> May what I do flow from me like a river,
> No forcing and no holding back.
> — Rainer Maria Rilke

## Bowing to Our Adversaries

(15–20 minutes)

As we go forth in the Great Turning, there are systems and institutions that we will and must challenge. The men and women who serve these structures may appear as our opponents, but they are likely in bondage to our true opponents: institutionalized forms of greed, hatred and delusion. Here is a practice that helps to free us from fear of and ill will.

Buddhist teacher Thich Nhat Hanh encourages his students to express their respect, gratitude and goodwill by the act of bowing — to their elders and teachers, the Buddha Dharma and the spiritual community, their original faith traditions, their ancestors, their home place on the planet. Because some Westerners are uncomfortable with notion of bowing, he calls it Touching the Earth. This particular practice for honoring our adversaries was composed by Caitriona Reed, an ordained member of Thich Nhat Hanh's Order of Interbeing.

## METHOD

Everyone stands with enough room in front of them to kneel and touch the ground with hands and forehead. Or if they prefer, people can simply bow from the waist. If there is an altar or emblem, like an Earth flag, they can be facing it. The guide reads the text aloud, pausing after each paragraph, at which point everyone (guide included) touches the Earth. Let each bow be marked by a bell or gong. Maintain a slow, unhurried pace throughout.

We begin by bowing to the Earth, in gratitude for life itself. Then we bow to the ancestors and teachers we revere, and, after that, to all our companions in the Great Turning. Now the bows to our adversaries begin:

> *You, who destroy the natural world for profit, you show me how much I respect and honor our abundant and beautiful planet home. So I bow to you in gratitude and touch the Earth.*
>
> *You bring forth in me the love I feel for this life-bearing land — its soil, air and waters — and for the community that rises in its defense. Because of the strength with which I resist your actions, I learn how strong my love really is. I bow to you in gratitude and touch the Earth.*
>
> *Because the pain I feel when I witness the pain of the world is no less than your pain — you, who perpetuate destruction*

*and cut yourselves off from the web of life. I bow to you in compassion and touch the Earth.*

*Because the pain of greed, alienation and fear is no less than the pain of sorrow for what is lost, I bow to you in compassion and touch the Earth.*

*For the power of my anger, arising from my passion for justice, I bow to you in gratitude and touch the Earth.*

*Because we all want to be happy, to feel intact and part of a single whole, for that shared longing, I bow to you in compassion and touch the Earth.*

*Because your actions challenge me to see the limits to my own understanding, and free me from holding my view as the only correct one, I bow to you in gratitude and touch the Earth.*

*You who teach me that the mind is a miracle, capable of manifesting as love, as greed, as fear, as clarity or delusion — you who show me what I myself am capable of when I am governed by fear and greed — O great awesome teachers, I bow to you in gratitude and touch the Earth.*

*Understanding that we all belong to the web of life, and with love in my heart, I bow to you and touch the Earth.*

## Creating Study/Action Groups

Study circles have been called the greatest social inventions of the 20th century. Engrossing and fun, they elicit our innate curiosity, raise our sights and widen our horizons, while offering an immediately rewarding experience of community. They uncover our capacity to think cogently about big issues of common concern — a capacity that we may not have suspected we had. They increase our respect for our self and each other, breaking down barriers of isolation and powerlessness. These functions are multiplied when participants, wanting to embody the values that arise, undertake projects together — and the groups become study/action groups. The energy that is unleashed, when we move out to do together what we may have felt inadequate to do alone, can transform our lives and our society.

Participation in study/action groups has given direction to Molly and Joanna's lives. When Joanna's children were in high school, the family met with neighbors to follow a plan of study on macroeconomics: reading selections, taking turns facilitating and eventually coming up with joint projects.[i]

Years later, wanting to learn about the care of radioactive waste, Joanna organized a study/action group with a co-designed curriculum, which Molly soon joined. Because of the subject matter easily led to feelings of hopelessness, we included a psycho-spiritual component in every session, which generated some of our Deep Time practices. The group's work together helped us sustain our motivation and become informed enough to give public talks in the community and testimony in government regulatory hearings. This study/action group generated the Nuclear Guardianship Project; a full description of this group and its adventures appears in Joanna's memoir *Widening Circles*.[2]

## STEPS IN ORGANIZING A STUDY/ACTION GROUP

+ Choose a topic and select a book to study or curriculum to follow. (See Study/Action Groups in the Resource section of this book for curricula.)
+ Study groups using *Coming Back to Life* and/or *Active Hope* work best when they divide each session between cognitive discussion of the material and an interactive process. This is an excellent way to train facilitators in the Work That Reconnects.
+ Determine the number of sessions the group will hold; people feel freer to join a group when they know the duration is limited. The group's meeting can always be extended for those who choose to continue. Also choose the frequency and length of sessions. Weekly or monthly meetings of two hours work well.
+ Issue an invitation (say, by contacting selected friends and/or putting a notice on public bulletin boards). Aim for the optimal

---

[i.] The study and action plan called A Macroanalysis Seminar was created by the Movement for a New Society in the early 1970's, which later launched New Society Publishers.

size of eight to twelve people. Don't ask people to commit before they've come to an introductory session.

+ Select a venue such as your local church, synagogue, mosque, school or community center and, of course, consider meeting in one or more participants' homes.

+ Take time in your first meeting to review guidelines for successful study/action groups and agree on commitments (such as regular attendance, reading and preparation between meetings). Many of the suggestions for guiding the work provided in Chapter 5 are excellent for study/action groups. Other guidelines are included in the manuals and curricula listed in the Resource section.

+ We recommend rotating facilitators, enhancing the group's sense of shared responsibility.

+ Honor the meeting as sacred time and space with a simple ritual at the beginning and end. Light a candle, for example, or take a moment of silence to breathe.

+ Make use of interactive processes to sustain motivation and exercise the moral imagination.

## The Four Abodes

We often use this meditation, described in Chapter 13, in the form of a Milling near the end of a workshop.

## Five Vows

### (15 minutes)

By now each of us in the workshop is in touch with our sincere desire to take part in the Great Turning. In the days and years ahead, however, there will be so many distractions and demands on us that we yearn for a practice to help us stay faithful to this intention of our hearts.

This became clear to Joanna on the last afternoon of a two-week intensive workshop. She was out walking and met a young monk from the Buddhist retreat center hosting the event. "Well," he said, "now I expect on your last day, you'll be giving people vows." Joanna told him that was not something she did. "Pity," he said, "I find in my own life vows so very helpful: they channel my energy to do what I really want to do."

Continuing on her walk, Joanna looked at her hand and thought, "if we're to have vows, they shouldn't number more than the fingers of one hand." Almost immediately the Five Vows came to her.

When she later asked the group what they thought about taking vows, they were enthusiastic. They would soon be scattered far and wide making these vows to one another and to themselves deepened their sense of being linked as a community. Now used by many people around the world, the vows bring a heartening sense of belonging to a widening fellowship of intention.

In some cultures, the term *vow* can sound too religious or authoritarian. So we can choose to refer to them as *commitments* or *intentions*. In any case, they offer an anchor point, reminding us again and again of the purposes we hold dear and the behaviors that help us serve them.

Toward the end of the workshop, the vows are posted on the wall for people to read and consider if they want to take them on. On the last evening or last day, a simple ritual is held. With everyone

### Five Vows

- I vow to myself and to each of you to commit myself daily to the healing of our world and the welfare of all beings.
- I vow to myself and to each of you to live on Earth more lightly and less violently in the food, products and energy I consume.
- I vow to myself and to each of you to draw strength and guidance from the living Earth, the ancestors, the future beings and our brothers and sisters of all species.
- I vow to myself and to each of you to support you in your work for the world, and to ask for help when I need it.
- I vow to myself and to each of you to pursue a daily spiritual practice that clarifies my mind, strengthens my heart and supports me in observing these vows.

standing, the guide recites each vow, asking the people if they wish to take that vow. Those who do, answer "Yes" and recite the vow; then a bell is rung.

## Circle of Blessings

(2–5 minutes per person)

For a circle of participants to express their appreciation and good wishes to each other is a fitting conclusion to a Workshop That Reconnects. We have found two main ways to hold a Circle of Blessings. In the first each participant speaks before being blessed, and in the other there is nothing they need to say.

### METHOD ONE

One at a time, each person steps forward into the circle and declares in a sentence a particular action or path they intend to pursue. The full circle responds by singing the person's name several times and with spontaneous words of affirmation and encouragement. They may stretch out their hands, palms forward, to transmit their regard energetically. In this way, each participant is held in a field of collective appreciation and support.

### METHOD TWO

In a simpler and actually more moving ritual, there are no words from the person stepping into the center. At the outset, the guide suggests to the circle:

> Here's a chance for you to look one at a time at each person in our group and experience the full intensity of your appreciation and regard. Take a moment to relish the uniqueness of each person and the marvel of their readiness to be of service to life on Earth. After a few heartbeats, we'll sing the person's name, over and over, with hands outstretched, palms forward.

## Two Poems for the Road Ahead

As Earth,
working on behalf of Earth,
we trust and are at ease.

Aligning ourselves
with the upwelling vitality
which is bluestem, the
focused intelligence which
is heron,

we are hopeful
in the present moment — a fountain
of sufficiency

— Doug Hitt[3]

God speaks to each of us as he makes us,
then walks with us silently out of the night.
These are the words we dimly hear:
You, sent out beyond your recall,
Go to the limits of your longing.
Embody me.
Flare up like flame
and make big shadows I can move in.
Let everything happen to you: beauty and terror.
Just keep going. No feeling is final.
Don't let yourself lose me.
Nearby is a country they call life.
You will know it by its seriousness.
Give me your hand.

— Rainer Maria Rilke[4]

# 11

## The Work That Reconnects with Children and Teens

*To all the children*
*To the children who swim beneath*
*The waves of the sea, to those who live in*
*The soils of the Earth, to the children of the flowers*
*In the meadows and the trees in the forest, to*

*All those children who roam over the land*
*And the winged ones who fly with the winds,*
*To the human children too, that all the children*

*May go together into the future ....*

— Thomas Berry

MANY ADULTS, ESPECIALLY PARENTS AND TEACHERS, face an agonizing dilemma: how to talk with our children about the Great Unraveling, knowing they will suffer its effects in their lifetimes. We want to shelter them from harsher realities and yet help prepare them for the challenges ahead.

*What can I say to my kids? I want them to be happy, feel safe.*
*I feel guilty somehow — guilty about the kind of world*

217

*we're handing them and deceptive that this is one area I am
not being honest with them about what I know and feel.*

*I don't want to spoil their childhood by bringing up fears
they can do nothing about. But, I wonder, am I protecting
them or myself?*

We want so much to protect our children (and ourselves) that we
often remain silent about our pain for the world and the threats to
the web of life that evoke that pain. But are children all that ignorant
of the mounting dangers we face? Do they really not know?
Kathleen Rude shared her version of this quandary:

> Even though I was an environmental activist in junior high
> and high school, I find that I want to shelter my nieces
> and nephews from the harsh realities of global warming,
> Fukushima, extinction, overpopulation, gmos. I want them
> to have a childhood free of these horror stories. I'm furi-
> ous that they are inheriting a world so messed up (and yes,
> I know, so full of opportunity for creative, heroic, magi-
> cal, collaborative work). I know how important it is to be
> engaged with our world, and yet I want to shield these
> precious ones from the heartache of it. And I wonder how
> can they cope with the environmental and social crap when
> they're dealing with so much in their personal lives. I'm
> taking a look at my reaction and trying to learn from it. It's
> teaching me some empathy for those who have a hard time
> with honoring our pain in the name of wanting to protect
> and shield those we love.[1]

## What Do Children Know and Feel?

Reports from Work That Reconnects facilitators who work with
children and a couple of recent studies indicate the children may
know a lot more about what's happening in the world than adults
think they do. And they often carry strong feelings about it. They may
not know all the details about climate change, for example, but they
know that adults are worried about something called that. Children

pick up feelings of anger, fear and sadness from adults around them, without necessarily knowing what's stirring those feelings.

A UNICEF-UK survey published in 2013 "found that almost three-quarters of young people aged 11–16 are concerned about how climate change will impact on their lives ... [and that] two-thirds of young people were worried about how climate change will affect other children and families in developing countries. Awareness of climate change among the young people was high, with 88% of those surveyed claiming to know at least a little about it and just 1% saying they knew nothing about climate change."[2] Another survey commissioned by Habitat Heroes showed that one out of three preteens fears an Earth apocalypse in his or her lifetime.[3]

We as authors gathered perspectives and practices from many people steeped in the Work That Reconnects who engage with children in various capacities. They all report that children know a great deal about global threats to life, and they are grateful for opportunities to share their feelings with people who accept and respect them. Nearly all children, says one teacher, are aware of apocalyptic scenarios out in the culture: films such as *The Hunger Games*, ads depicting the end of the world, images on television of earthquakes, tsunamis, wildfires and hurricanes.

Children, at least younger ones, generally adopt their parents' point of view about the world, but that doesn't necessarily reassure them. Children raised in fundamentalist Christian homes may hear about The Rapture and worry about what will happen to their friends, teachers or even themselves if they haven't been good enough. Children may fear, if their parents do, that the government is going to come take away their guns, or that they will be overrun by immigrants or whatever group their parents fear or hate.

When children feel despair for the future, they develop fewer defenses than most adults; they are not as numbed and detached. Adults depersonalize the peril, talk in abstract terms about "collateral damage" or "acceptable risks," while children see it in concrete terms: homeless families on the street, dismembered limbs, people drowning or trapped in burning buildings, homes destroyed by bombs, hurricanes or floods.

During the 1970s, in his work with Educators for Social Responsibility, psychiatrist Eric Chivian, interviewed many school children regarding the threat of nuclear war. He described how children dealt with the knowledge of nuclear weapons and possible war at different stages of their development. At the third-grade level, he found a marked sense of confusion, hopelessness and fear of abandonment. Some had frequent nightmares. By fifth-grade, children had more information and felt anger at the stupidity and hypocrisy of the adult world. By seventh grade, this anger turned to cynicism and gallows humor. In high school, the emotional reactions became more complicated, because these teenagers faced critical choices about college, careers and families, but the shadow of The Bomb robbed these choices of reality and meaning. The young people of the seventies began to erect defenses of indifference and defiance.[4] Today, with escalating and multiplying threats to life and health — combined with amplified media exposure — children are likely to experience even greater confusion, fear, anger, cynicism and defiance. Clearly, adult silence, no matter how well motivated, does not serve our children.

Many children, moreover, struggle with serious personal and social problems. They may witness violence almost daily, through media and first-hand: school shootings and lockdowns, drive-by killings, domestic violence, rape, teen suicide, drug and alcohol addiction, homelessness and child abuse. In the midst of all this, they can feel isolated and lonely, especially if no one wants to hear about their fears, anger and grief. When we provide the opportunity for kids to talk about what's in their minds and hearts, we need to listen and accept whatever they share, whether personal or global in scope. Remember there is no purely private suffering — pain arises within the web of life we share. Many so-called private problems, such as domestic violence and child abuse, are triggered and intensified by the stresses inherent in the unraveling of Industrial Growth Society. It's all of a piece.

## The Effects of Silence

Adults' silence on all these threats to safety and well-being, and our desire to carry on business as usual take a high toll on children and adults alike. Silence conveys fatalism, seeming to say that our collective future is out of our hands, and that there's nothing we can do to change it.

Silence can also convey indifference. If parents don't talk about these issues, a child can conclude that they don't care — perhaps even wonder if their parents don't care what might happen to their children.

Silence reinforces repression. Adults' difficulty in communicating in these areas teaches that certain feelings are taboo: feelings like grief, fear, anger and even compassion for the suffering of people and animals. In turn, this repression of feelings can breed cynicism. Teens may begin to wonder whether feelings of anguish over destruction and injustice even exist in many grown-ups. If we do have these feelings, then we are hypocrites for pretending everything is all right. If we really don't have such feelings, we deserve their contempt. They may try to shock us awake, so we see the horror of what we are doing to the Earth and one another. Some forms of music like heavy metal, rap and electronica, with loud volume, heavy beat and angry lyrics, may be manifestations of their fury. At the same time, some rap and hip hop musicians provide powerful outlets for truth-telling and feelings, detailing injustice and oppression.

And of course the toll is wider yet. The rising incidence of drug and alcohol abuse, crime, suicide and screen addiction among teenagers and even children is sad evidence of the erosion of meaning. A sense of alienation, both from family and future, is pervasive, manifesting not only in anti-social and self-destructive behaviors, but less visibly in the loss of the capacity to make meaningful choices and commitments.

America Worden, a colleague in the Work That Reconnects and teacher at a Waldorf School, sent us this poem by one of her students. Sixteen-year-old Molly Lockwood wrote it in response to the dissonance she felt after a discussion in civics about knowing that we all need to stop driving, and no one stopping, or even starting to stop:

### Loud Silence

Loud and clear the words unspoken,
Crystal silence still unbroken.
Blank the stares on every face,
Underneath them, strong distaste.

In every heart's a silent riot
Burning need to smash the quiet.
Yet the words remain unsaid,
Blaring silence still is fed.

The kindling piles ever higher ...
who will speak and light the fire?[5]

## Suggestions for Overcoming the Fear and the Silence

What can we do to break the silence and meet our children on the level of their own deep responses? Sadly, given the destructive processes already unleashed, we parents and teachers cannot make the world a safe place for our children. Even if we stopped all fossil fuel use today, climate disruption will continue to unfold for decades, maybe centuries. In a world so full of death and destruction, how can we nurture the little ones' sense of safety and security as they develop their sense of self? What do older children and teens need from us and how can we best support them?

Here are some suggestions, drawn from our own life experience and from our colleagues who work with children and teens. No doubt many of our readers could add to our list.

**Take joy in life with them, especially in nature.** First and foremost, help your children ground themselves in nature by taking them into natural settings as much as possible (and leave your cell phone behind). Take time to watch a snail, admire a flower, hug a tree. Help children overcome the *nature phobia* resulting from enslavement to television and electronic devices and recover their innate connection with the natural world. Share your own sense of the sacredness and beauty of the web of life. In a similar way, gardening together builds practical, empowering skills while witnessing first hand the miracle of life.

We can also share our delight in music and art (especially the homegrown variety) and treasures of our spiritual traditions.

**Know and honor your own feelings.** Identify for yourself your own fear, anger and sorrow for the world. While we want to be honest and open with our children, we don't want to use our conversations with them to vent our own feelings. Attend a Work That Reconnects workshop or organize a peer group where you can use the approach and practices of this book. In a group or alone, take time to talk with the child within yourself; feel your inner child's fears and learn what he or she needs from your adult self.

**Invite children to share their feelings and knowledge.** Begin by asking open questions, such as "What troubles you about the world today?" or by briefly sharing your own feelings about an item in the news; then ask about their feelings. Talk about an action you are engaged in, why you are doing it, and then ask how they feel about it.

**Give your complete attention.** Once you have broached the subject, don't rush off on an errand or preoccupy yourself with another activity. Ignore your cell phone and computer. Take time, even for silence. But don't force the issue. Children have the right not to hear or talk about scary things and usually have an innate sense of what they are ready to deal with. Do not assume children are oblivious or unconcerned if at a given moment they are not ready to talk about it.

**Listen deeply without intervention.** Resist the temptation to interrupt or tell them everything is OK. When we listen deeply to them, they begin to overcome feelings of powerlessness and isolation. Physical contact is reassuring, if not overdone: "Come sit next to me; I'd like to hear about that."

**Help children affirm and define their feelings.** What remains unspoken and unacknowledged is more frightening than a danger we can talk about together. Many children and adults do not know what they are feeling before they express it. Help children put their vague apprehensions into words or images, even act them out. At the same time, don't think you must relieve your children of their emotional pain. Just sharing will help relieve their fear of the feelings — and your fear as well.

**Acknowledge what you don't know.** Children will ask questions you can't answer. Remember that questions are often veiled statements about concerns and fears. Invite children to express the concern behind the question — that may help them more than any answer you can give. Your job is to help the child explore questions and feelings, not necessarily to provide answers. So whether or not you have an answer, you can simply say, "I've wondered about that, too. What do you imagine might happen? How do you feel about that?" Or, when appropriate, "What do you think we might do about that?"

**Support them in taking action in their own right.** We all feel empowered when we act on behalf of our world. Children and teens are no different. They feel validated when we take their ideas seriously and help them find immediate, practical ways of putting these ideas into action. Encourage them to draw or write their imaginings and to share them with one another. Then be ready to help if a project emerges.

There are many ways that children can work for the Great Turning, especially hands-on within in their own community. Many children love environmental cleanups in nearby parks and natural areas, because they can see tangible results in the bags of debris collected and in the litter-free landscape they leave behind.

Other possibilities: Write letters to the editor of local papers and to local, state and national officials. Make posters and join rallies. Volunteer for local organizations, helping with mailings, making phone calls, running errands. Organize or join a children's action group to discuss, learn, leaflet, march and raise money for a cause in a variety of ways from bake sales to car washes.

Any of these actions can provide a strong and meaningful sense of peer support and community, so children no longer feel isolated, fearful and powerless. Taking part in the Great Turning builds self-respect and confidence.

**Show them you care by your own actions.** Children model themselves on their parents, either by imitation or rebellion. And, because children regard their parents as powerful, they tend to feel safer when they see their parents working to make things better. As much as they may need a safe cocoon when they are very young, older children need a community of shared values and adventures. Vivienne Verdon-Roe tells a story about a second-grade class she attended during the Cold War, in which all but one of the children said they expected a nuclear war to occur. When the remaining child was asked why he was so confident of the future, he answered, "Because my mother and father go to meetings to stop nuclear war."

## Using the Work That Reconnects

The Work That Reconnects offers children and teens opportunities to prepare themselves for the Great Unraveling and the Great Turning. Through the Work, they can:

+ Experience and understand Earth as a living presence, sensing their interconnectedness with all life-forms.
+ Gain a lively awareness of the Great Turning and the many heroes working for the sake of life on Earth.
+ Come to trust and share their feelings, ideas and intuition.
+ Generate imagination and courage to face the unknown. These are needed to make educational and career choices in a culture losing its direction.
+ Find joy and compassion working with others on behalf of life.
+ Discover their unique gifts to bring to the Great Turning.
+ Connect to a deepened sense of purpose in taking action on behalf of Earth.

### Generation Waking Up

We are the middle children of History, coming of age at the crossroads of civilization, a generation rising between an old world dying and a new world being born. We are the "make-it or break-it" generation, the "all-or-nothing" generation, the crucible through which civilization must pass or crash.[6]

This is how Joshua Gorman described the call he heard that defined his mission to rally high school and college-age young people for the Great Turning. Generation Waking Up's website explains:

Our generation's calling is clear: to create a thriving, just, sustainable world that works for all, we must take bold and systemic action to transform our whole society. Generation Waking Up is a response to this call, a campaign created by our generation to rally all that is needed to take this movement to scale.[7]

Joshua approached Joanna in 2009, wanting to incorporate the Work That Reconnects into this initiative, and the first workshop with her took place in 2010. Others followed in 2011 that were exclusively for youth. Joanna found the young people were especially mobilized by climate change issues and that they welcomed the emotional and spiritual support of the Work That Reconnects, as well as its open interactive nature.

## Practices for Children and Teens

The growing field of environmental education and nature awareness offers many relevant activities; see the Resources section at the end of the book. The practices described here relate directly to the Spiral of the Work That Reconnects.

**One Caveat:** In our culture, teachers are expected to stand in front of a class delivering facts and asking questions, with students expected to listen and respond. Often there is a right answer or preferred response to the teacher's question. This format might be appropriate when explaining a math problem, but not for the Work That Reconnects. When we aim to help people (including children) uncover and express their feelings and thoughts, it is best not to ask for responses in a large group. Instead, give ample opportunities for children to talk in two's and three's. A Talking Circle can also be used. Prompts can be general: *Take a few minutes to talk with your partner/group about this experience.* When holding a group discussion, ask simply, *Does anyone have something to share about this experience?* rather than *How did this feel?* Especially in rituals, allow children and teens to have their own experience — and to share only what they want to share afterwards.

### Mothers and Daughters Follow the Spiral

The following story from Eva Schilcher in South Germany illustrates how the Spiral as a whole can be used for a one-day retreat. Here it's for mothers and daughters:

> Twice a year over the last decade a group of 10 to 14 mothers and girls (ages 8–17) enjoy an orchestrated full day in

nature for dancing, singing, painting, massage and good food. Their day follows the Spiral, beginning with celebration of the beauty of Earth and her countless life-forms. Open Sentences help prompt the sharing of pain for the world, which is often expressed then in movement and dance. In a recent gathering, the Harvesting the Gifts of the Ancestors brought a sense of the great lineage of mothers and grandmothers through the ages. And the Going Forth took the form of a circle of prayers for mothers and daughters around the world — to which the young ones expressed their wishes for the mothers present, such as "Take time for rest and pleasure and healing touch" and "Listen to your own needs without judgment." [8]

<hr />

## *Talking Circle*[9]

The Talking Circle is one of the most ancient and powerful communication tools. The process is very simple. A group sits in a circle. An object is chosen to be the *talking stick* which is passed around the circle. Whoever holds the stick or object — and no one else — has the right to speak. No one may interrupt and no one may speak out of turn. Anyone who wishes to respond to what another has said must wait until the talking stick arrives. People are also free to pass the stick on without speaking. There is no cross talk. What is said in the circle stays in the circle.

An important aspect of the talking circle is that it provides a place for each child or teen to be witnessed. Very often in our daily lives, a few extroverted people dominate the discourse. The circle evens that out. It gives time for shy or quieter people to speak and for extroverts to listen. It allows time for emotions to settle and insights to arise.

The Talking Circle can be used for any and all of the stages of the Spiral and focus on any issue or theme. Children and teens need to have established a basic comfort level with each other and with the facilitator for the circle to succeed. Teens especially are often reluctant to open up to each other. So it may help to hold an initial circle for basic introductions, and ask a neutral question about where they've lived or schools they've attended. A Talking Circle focused on gratitude (without necessarily calling it that) can help build a sense of common ground and comfort.

## Gratitude

Gratitude practices come easily to children and can include many nature-related activities. Megan Toben of Pickards Mountain Eco-Institute in North Carolina has written:

> When I use the Work That Reconnects with children, I incorporate lots of sensory awareness exercises, mostly from Joseph Cornell's *Sharing Nature with Children*. Of course, as Thomas Berry said, "Children have a natural bond of intimacy with every living thing." We believe this to be true, but we also see a drastic atrophying of the senses in today's media-saturated, sensory-bombarded childhoods. So Joseph's simple practices like blindfolded walks, expanding circles of awareness and deep listening are fun and nurturing for kids (and adults, actually!).[10]

The following practices from Chapter 6 work well with children and teens, with minor adaptations in wording:

+ Becoming Present through Breath, Movement, Sound and Silence
+ Open Sentences on Gratitude

    Use fewer sentences, maybe sentences #1, 4 and 5. Let the partners take turns responding to each open sentence.

+ Gratitude Rounds
+ Mirror Walk

Piglet noticed that even though he had a very small heart, it could hold a rather large amount of gratitude.

— A.A. Milne

## *The Human Camera*[11]

(variation of Mirror Walk)

This practice can be used with even very young children, in which case each little one should be paired with an adult or older child. One person is the photographer and the other is the camera. The photographers guide their cameras, who keep their eyes closed. The photographers search for beautiful and interesting photos, then point their camera's shutters (eyes) at the object or scene they want to "shoot" and press the shutter button to take the photo.

The photographer "presses the shutter button" by tapping the camera's shoulder once to open the camera's shutters. After three to five seconds, two taps tells the camera to close the shutters. Try creative shots: different angles, close ups or panorama shots. While taking photos, it's best to talk as little as possible. Give photographers about ten minutes to take at least three photos.

Then the pairs switch roles. When everyone is finished, have each child draw a favorite photo they took as the camera on an index card. Share the photos in a group; for older children or teens, have them debrief in these small groups. Some debrief questions might include:

+ What did you notice?
+ Which did you like better, being the human camera or the photographer?
+ What will you remember the most?

## Honoring Our Pain For The World

This stage of the Spiral brings special challenges when working with children. Here we really have to address the question of how to protect our children's basic security and safety (at the base of Maslow's hierarchy of needs) while being truthful with them about the state of the world. Megan Toben has asked, "What is developmentally appropriate information regarding the various crises for different age groups?" and answered in this way:

> I've certainly tempered the industrial growth story quite
> a lot for little ones. Mostly what we say is that humans

haven't been taking care of the Earth in the best ways, and now we're realizing it and changing our practices so that we are doing better. The kids usually have a pretty good sense of this, mostly through media themes (Wall-E, Avatar, Ferngully, Captain Planet, etc.) and want to be a part of the shift.[12]

Most of the practices for Honoring Our Pain (Chapter 7) are helpful with minor adaptations, offering children and teens the opportunity to safely express the feelings and concerns they already carry within them. These include:

+ Open Sentences on Honoring Our Pain (variation below)
+ The Milling (variations below)
+ Reporting to Chief Seattle
+ Cairn of Mourning
+ Truth Mandala (see stories below)
+ Bowl of Tears
+ Imaging with Colors and Clay

## Open Sentences

While teaching high-school, Molly used a variety of Open Sentences as writing prompts, asking the students to write each sentence and complete it, with any thoughts and feelings that followed. Afterwards, students paired up and shared what they had written.

## Milling with Open Sentences[13]

### (high-school students)

Many teenagers have trouble looking at each other in silence, so practices such as the Milling can be adapted to feel less awkward. Remember always to point out that people don't have to make direct eye contact, but simply be aware of the person before them, closing their eyes if they wish.

Pam Wood uses Open Sentences when leading a Milling with teens. The practice begins as in Chapter 7, with appropriate references to their life experiences, e.g. a high school campus at lunch hour, worrying about final projects or exams. In the one-on-one encounters, pairs sit down and take turns responding to an Open Sentence. Afterwards the facilitator guides them in a silent reflection similar to those in Chapter 7. Then the Milling resumes, and new pairs form to share feelings and thoughts through another Open Sentence.

Facilitators can choose among the Open Sentences in Chapters 6 or 7, or compose their own. Here are the prompts that Pam uses:

1. *Share a recent experience when you felt a strong sense of connection to life and felt really glad to be alive.*
2. *Share a recent experience when you felt troubled about something happening to the world. It can be an incident, a news item, a dream, something on TV. No need to get into the issues; just try to share your feelings about it.*
3. *One way I help take care of our world is …*

If you sense that the reflection about the hand in the Milling might be too uncomfortable for your group, you can have people explore their own hands.

⬥⬥⬥

### Two Stories of the Truth Mandala with Children

These stories of using the Truth Mandala with children demonstrate how objects can help children share feelings about anything on their minds and hearts. The first, from Elizabeth Koelsch-Inderst, a social worker in Germany, involves a very small group of boys.

> I did the Truth Mandala in the woods with three boys whose family is in my care. We gathered sticks, stones, leaves and berries, and I explained how we do it: *We say what makes us sad, express our anger, talk about our fears and whatever else is on our mind.* We also agreed that after each one spoke we would say, "We'll help you."
>
> After some hesitation and giggling at the beginning, each boy went into the Mandala.

**C.** is sad because he has no friends. He picks up the stick and is about to cry when he says, "Mama hits me. I'm so mad at her."

**D.** says "I still wet my bed without knowing I'm doing it. I'm so ashamed."

And **P.** the youngest says, "Papa promised me a cat I could take care of and talk to. And I never got my cat. I'm so sad."

**D.** goes again into the middle and he says he gets really scared at night and can't sleep when everything is all dark.

**C.** also returns to the middle and says that he's a bad boy and stupid.

We ended the Truth Mandala together; the children cleaned up the sticks, leaves and stones. We then thought about how we would help each other deal with the various issues that had come up. We spoke about courage and joy, and about our hopes. Although we hadn't solved our problems, we emerged from the woods laughing and in wonderful spirits.

Since that afternoon the children have been more open with me and speak about what's on their minds. It's almost as if we four had experienced a mystery together in the woods.[14]

Eva Schilcher, dance and ecotherapist, also from Germany, relates a story of a Truth Mandala she conducted with 12 kids, nine and ten years old, along with their teachers in an after-school program.

The teachers in this after-school program had been changed four times within a year without explanation or a chance to say good-bye. When two new teachers arrived to take charge, the children reacted with resistance, rejection, disrespect and aggression. Everyone was at a loss as to how to handle the situation.

To this new team I suggested a Truth Mandala to give the children a chance to express and understand their emotions, while at the same time letting the adults acknowledge their own distress.

The children were alert and attentive as I explained the ritual. Many strong emotions surfaced, expressing pain in their personal lives, such as moving from another city or country, losing friends and beloved caregivers, along with anger at schools and teachers, with also some anxiety about the new team. Sometimes the anger tipped over into sadness. It all bubbled and boiled like a cook pot on the stove. Some wanted to talk and be heard over and over again. Then came laughter and also some uncertainty. I had to remember the rule that we never know how the Truth Mandala will end. Unfortunately the time was limited (by the scheduled hour for homework), so we ended the ritual with the possibility that the children could speak their feelings later and also write them down. Afterwards they made a poster with their recommendations for the future.

The next day the majority of the group was far more relaxed. Children and teachers could see each other in a fresh way, and they interacted with more ease and respect in the following weeks and months — and have continued to grow together for this last half year.[15]

A Truth Mandala focused on social and environmental issues may be best used with youth in middle and high school. With this age group, Pam Woods suggests passing each object around the circle, giving everyone the opportunity to speak in turn about their grief, anger, fears and numbness, or to simply sit in silence with that feeling before passing the object on.

### Boom Chicka Boom with Feelings
(10 minutes)

This practice is a playful way to let our bodies express the emotions that arise as we learn about problems in the world today. Acknowledge that feelings often come up when we look at the problems in today's world, and that we sometimes avoid looking at them because we don't want to feel them. However, we can use the energy from those feelings to fuel our work for the world.

## Method

With everyone standing up, lead Boom Chicka Boom, a familiar camp song. After each line, everyone repeats it rhythmically.

> *I said a Boom Chicka Boom*
> *I said a Boom Chicka Boom*
> *I said a Boom Chicka Rocka Chicka Rocka Chicka Boom*
> *Uh huh*
> *Oh yeah*
> *One more time _____ style*

You might want to play with a few silly styles first like hiccup style or underwater style. When the group is warmed up, move on to these styles: sad, angry, despairing, guilty, excited, powerful and any others you've heard from the group. Keep the original words, "I said boom chicka boom," but exaggerate the feelings in your voice, face and body and have the group repeat after you. Really go for the feelings. Let yourself feel the anger and the sorrow while you lead it.

When you're done, have them all take a deep breath and shake their bodies out.

This can be followed by one of the more solemn practices from Chapter 7 (Honoring Our Pain). The Bowl of Tears works especially well.

## Seeing With New Eyes

Among the many practices in Chapters 8 and 9 that help us see with new eyes are several that can be used and adapted for youth:

+ The Systems Game
+ Riddle of the Commons Game
+ When I Made a Difference
+ Widening Circles
+ Council of All Beings

+ Open Sentences on Time
+ The Evolutionary Gifts of the Animals
+ Audio Recording to the Future
+ Letter from the Future
+ The Seventh Generation
+ The Storytellers Convention

In addition, our colleagues have contributed ideas for new practices and adaptations of some of the above.

## The Web of Life

(10 minutes)

In a silent circle, people toss balls of yarn to one another, looping the yarn loosely around their wrists before tossing it to the next person. They toss the balls randomly, without any particular pattern, to people anywhere in the circle. Once the web is complete, the leader can make observations like the following:

> *All of existence is an interconnected web, and we are part of it. Notice how strong it is when we're all holding our strand. Notice how what happens in one place affects the whole web. Notice what happens to the web if one strand is hurt or weakened.*
>
> *Some people only care about people who are like them or the places near them. This web shows why we care about people who are like us and people who are different from us. It is why we need to care about the places on earth near us and far from us. We need all kinds of different people, different kinds of life, for the web to be strong. Our destiny is interconnected with the destiny of all people and all forms of life on our planet.*

## Our Life As Gaia[16]

(15–20 minutes)

Sheri Prud'homme uses this meditation with children in a church summer camp. She has someone keep a steady heart-beat on a drum throughout.

Come back with me into a story we all share, a story whose rhythm beats in us still. The story belongs to each of us and to all of us, like the beat of this drum, like the heartbeat of the living universe.

With the heartbeat of the drum we hear the rhythm that underlies all our days and everything we do. Throughout our sleeping, through all our playing, working and loving, our heart has been beating steadily. That steady inner sound has been with us all the way. And so it can take us back now, back through our lives, back through our birth. In our birth mother's womb there was that same sound, that same beat, as we floated in the fluid right under her heart.

Let that beat take us back farther still. Let's go back, back far beyond our beginning in this body, back to the first flaring forth of energy and light. There we were, traveling out with the speed of light, though space and time, in great swirls of gas and dancing particles. Ten billion years later, one of the more beautiful swirls split off from its blazing sun — the sun we feel now on our faces — and became the shape we know as Planet Earth.

At first all was volcanic flames and steaming rains, and the bones of the Earth, called tectonic plates, shifted slowly, pushing into one another. To the heartbeat of this drum you can imagine you are the fire of those early volcanoes, the strength of those tectonic plates. Then we became life in the water as single-celled creatures, and then as fish. We lived in the water with our gills and fins. The salt from those early seas still flows in our sweat and tears.

And the age of the dinosaurs we carry with us, too. When did we appear as mammals? If the entire life of Planet Earth was collapsed into 24 hours, mammals appeared only 30 minutes ago. And when did we become human? Only one second ago. Humans are a very, very new species on Planet Earth.

For a long time we humans lived in small groups in Africa. Can you imagine you remember? We don't have the speed of the other animals or their claws or fangs, but we have our remarkable hands. Our thumbs can move separately from our *other four fingers, and we can shape tools and weapons. And we have in our throats and frontal lobs of our brains the capacities for speech. Grunts and shouts turn into language. Those days and nights on the edge of the forests, as we weave baskets and stories around our fires, make up the longest chapter of our human experience.*

*Then, in small tribes, we begin branching out. We move all across Planet Earth. We learn to survive in the cold and hunt mammoth, and we learn the powers of the plants and trees. Only a little while ago in Planet Earth time, humans begin to farm crops and raise animals to eat. We build great cities. Major religions are created. There is born a man named Buddha, and shortly after another named Jesus, and a while after that, Mohammed.*

*What we now think of as our world, with its machines and computers, is so new that if you take the whole time humans have been here and see it as 24 hours, the world we know today has been here much less than a second.*

*With the heartbeat of the drum travel through the lives your great-grandparents and your grandparents, through the lives of your parents to the moment you were just ready to be born. Take their strength and their love. Your parents offered you a great gift: your own life to live. New parents may have come to you early in your life or you may have kept your birth parents.*

*Move, now, through the years of your own life. Accept the gifts of your experience, own your joys and your sorrows, your unique and precious self.*

*Come now to this moment and stop (drum stops). You are on the edge of time. You cannot see clearly the way ahead or imagine what will be asked of you. But you will carry with you the knowledge that it is a blessing you were born. When you go out from here, listen to the drumbeat (drum beat starts again). You will hear it in your heart. And as you hear it, remember that it is the heartbeat of the universe as well, and of Planet Earth and your larger self.*

꧁꧂

## *The Robot Game*

(20–30 minutes)

A slightly slapstick illustration of the mechanistic worldview we're leaving behind us in the Great Turning, the Robot Game is fun to use toward the end of a day's session, when no more serious work is expected.

### METHOD

Form groups of three, two of which are identified as robots. The robots can only walk straight ahead, like a machine without a steering wheel. They cannot change direction when they reach an obstacle — a wall, a person or another solid object; but like a motor that can't turn itself off, they keep on moving their legs and arms in place. Stuck in the *on* position like a positive feedback loop, they are unable to stop chugging away, with danger of overheating and collapse.

The third person, the manager, is charged with keeping these mechanisms from running amok, and the only way to do this is by changing their direction of movement. This is achieved by tapping the robots on the nose: a tap on the left nostril to turn them to the right, and a tap on the right nostril to go left.

The game starts with the two robots standing back to back. At a signal from the guide, the manager sets the two mechanisms in motion by tapping the tips of their noses simultaneously. Off they go in opposite directions, and their manager has to be alert and quick to keep them from stalling at an obstacle and burning out. The game is over when the guide blows a whistle or when a lot of the robots are overheated. By this time everyone knows something about the limits of a machine — or is too weak from laughter to care.

## *The Council of All Beings in a School Setting*

Anna Mae Grimm, social studies teacher, and Kathleen Rude, Work That Reconnects facilitator, developed a quarter project for high school freshman as part of a World History curriculum at Mequon High School, Mequon, WI. The project included a research paper on the species that each student would speak for, mask making, an orientation to the Great Turning and in-class Council of All Beings.

## Going Forth

As in previous stages of the Spiral, many of the practices in Chapter 10 can be adapted to work with children and teens:

+ Life Map (for teens)
+ Imaging Our Power
+ The Sword in the Stone
+ Callings and Resources (for teens)
+ Circle of Blessings

We suggest a few more practices here, some which can used with adults as well. Before the practices, the facilitator might post a list of local organizations and events that would welcome youth participation, introducing it by saying, *Did you know that ...?*

### Open Sentences for Going Forth

(20–30 minutes)

Open Sentences such as the following can be used to open up this stage or as the main event in a short workshop. Responses can be written and shared in pairs or with the whole group.

+ Something I learned today about the web of life is ...
+ Something I can do every day to help life on the Earth is ...
+ Something I can do with other people to be part of the Great Turning is ...

### Starfish Story and Ritual[17]

Pass out starfish-shaped pieces of heavy card stock or cardboard. Then tell the Starfish Story as follows (rather than reading it). Allow some time for the group members to talk about its meaning for them.

## THE STARFISH STORY
### (ADAPTED FROM "THE STAR THROWER" BY LOREN EISELEY[18])

*Once upon a time, there was a wise man who used to go to the ocean to do his writing. He had a habit of walking on the beach before he began his work.*

*One day, as he was walking along the shore, he looked down the beach and saw a person moving in an unusual way — bending down and then reaching up in an arc. Was it a dancer? He walked faster to catch up.*

*As he got closer, he saw person was a boy. He was not dancing at all. The boy was reaching down to the shore, picking up small objects and throwing them into the ocean.*

*The man came closer still and called out "Good morning! May I ask what it is that you are doing?"*

*The boy paused, looked up, and replied "Throwing starfish into the ocean."*

*"Why are you throwing starfish into the ocean?" asked the somewhat startled wise man.*

*To this, boy replied, "The sun is up, and the tide is going out. If I don't throw them in, they'll die."*

*Upon hearing this, the wise man commented, "But, do you not realize that there are miles and miles of beach and there are starfish all along every mile? You can't possibly make a difference!"*

*At this, the boy bent down, picked up yet another starfish and threw it into the ocean. As it met the water, he said, "It made a difference for that one."*

After telling the story, designate an area that is the beach and an expanse that is the ocean. Have each child write or draw a picture on their starfish to represent one thing they already do or will do for the Great Turning. When everyone is ready, each child says a few words about what they wrote on their starfish and then throws it back in the ocean. Each time, everyone says together: "We made a difference for that one!"

## *The Galactic Council*

(middle and high school — 1 to 2 hours)

This engaging activity helps teens gain a new perspective on human behaviors threatening life and well-being on Earth today. As they report to the Galactic Council about challenges facing us on Earth and watch the reports of others, they gain a larger view of what's happening in our world. Dramatizing a problem brings its reality home to us and also the possibilities for change.

### METHOD

The guide announces that we are about to receive a visit from the Galactic Council. Having heard about grave problems facing life on Earth, the Council wants a report from young people and requests that they act it out, because officials tend to blur the issues with statistics and abstract words.

First, the group brainstorms the general themes that need to be addressed, such as Climate Change, War, Species Extinctions, Overpopulation, Inequality or Prejudice. The guide helps the group combine and prioritize their chosen issues according to the number of participants. Then teams of four or more form, each team choosing a different topic to dramatize.

The teams have 15 minutes to an hour to prepare an enactment of their topic. When the whole group reconvenes, each team takes a turn presenting their skit, which should not exceed ten minutes. All the others act as the Galactic Council — as indeed they can, because we are all members of the galaxy.

The whole group can then share feelings and insights from the experience.

❧

## *Planning Actions*

(teens on up — 1–2 hours)

This three-part exercise shows how a group can work powerfully together, moving from a general goal to steps for immediate and concrete actions.

## METHOD

The process unfolds in three stages.

### 1. ENVISIONING GOALS

### (30 minutes)

List on newsprint categories of interest to the group such as: schools, health, food, transportation, habitat restoration. From this list, the group selects one of the topics to work on in the Great Turning. Remind them that they don't need any expertise, for it is the amateurs who often bring the most novel and ingenious ideas.

First, in silence, each person dreams a bit and then jots on paper notions of an optimal way this particular aspect of society might function (five minutes). Then they take turns sharing their ideas with the group, which then chooses the four or five most appealing ideas (15 minutes).

### 2. PROGRESSIVE BRAINSTORM

### (15 minutes)

Having pondered these ideas, the whole group chooses one it wishes to focus on. That is written as a goal at the top of a large sheet of newsprint and the group begins to brainstorm: what would be needed to reach this goal?

Review the rules for brainstorming:

1. Don't censor, explain or defend your ideas.
2. Don't evaluate or criticize the ideas of others.
3. Save discussion until afterwards.

After four or five minutes, the group chooses one of the ideas that has arisen and brainstorms the conditions this more specific goal would necessitate. This process continues in four to five minute rounds until the goals are quite specific — by specific, we mean something that a teen could conceivably do in the next 24 hours. From the distant goal, the group has moved to immediate steps.

For example, take the goal of clean air. What conditions would free us from air pollution? These are listed in round one of the brainstorm. The group then chooses one of the ideas, say "reduce the use of automobiles." This is written at the top of another piece of newsprint and the group moves quickly into a second brainstorm on what we would need to do to reduce the use of automobiles. Many ideas surface here, too: mandatory carpools, blocked streets, public bicycles, new forms of mass transit. Again, one of these is chosen and brainstormed further as to how it might be implemented. The process continues until concrete actions are suggested that can be immediately implemented, e.g. a door-to-door canvas to enlist support for a cooperative bicycle delivery system. At this point, the group moves into the third stage of the exercise.

### 3. Role-play

Now that the group has an immediate (though still hypothetical) action to undertake, how will we obtain the resources and cooperation needed? How will we enlist people? What types of persons or situations present a particular challenge? Role-playing such encounters helps us move beyond the blocks we often feel at this juncture that keep some of our finest ideas trapped in the world of dreams.

In the example above, the group has decided to organize a cooperative delivery system by bicycle, and for that purpose teams will call on everyone in the community to elicit their support and involvement. We role-play conversations between team members and senior citizens, the owner of a bicycle store or an official in the Highway Department. After a while, in mid-conversation, we reverse roles, team members becoming the people addressed and vice versa.

The exercise is as instructive as it is entertaining. It forces us to discover how well we can think on our feet, what we need to know and say in order to be convincing. Moreover, reversing roles in mid-conversation gives us insight into the thoughts and feelings of the people whose support we are trying to enlist. It breaks us out of polarized we-they thinking, helps us to identify with others and enhances our confidence and effectiveness.

Perhaps the question is not "what should we tell the children?" so much as "what can the children tell us — and one another?" As we work with children, let's be open to what they can teach us — and themselves — as much as what we can teach them. After all, the Latin root of education is *educare*, "to draw forth the innate potential thereof." The Work That Reconnects is based on this understanding; it can help everyone, young and old alike, bring forth our innate wisdom.

**12**

# Learning with Communities of Color

## Part One

*I add my breath to your breath*
*that our days may be long on this Earth*
*that the days of our people be long*
*that we shall be as one person*
*that we finish our roads together ...*

— Laguna Pueblo prayer

by Joanna Macy

WHEN I GAVE WORKSHOPS IN THE GLOBAL SOUTH, I saw how easily local people responded to the Work That Reconnects and made it their own, often more quickly than North Americans and Europeans. So, I hardly imagined the Work That Reconnects could be taken as reserved "For Whites Only," but I came to see why it might seem that way to people of color in my own country. For, through my years of offering the Work That Reconnects in North America, almost all the people who came to my workshops have been white. Since workshop fees, especially at longer residential intensives, can be a problem for some, I raised funds for scholarships.

245

> The human species, led by white Europeans and Euro-Americans, has been on a 500-year-long rampage of conquering, plundering, exploiting and polluting the earth — as well as killing the indigenous communities that stood in the way. But the game is up. The technical and scientific forces that created a life of unparalleled luxury — as well as unrivaled military and economic power for a small, global elite — are the forces that now doom us.
>
> — Chris Hedges

But still, the people of color who came have generally been so few as to seem like a token presence — and they seldom returned to continue with us and make it different. I mourned the loss of the gifts they could bring to the unfolding of the work, knowing that without their perspectives, their stories and stark honesty, this work would not fulfill the promise of its name.

A fresh response to this quandary arose in 2011, when my assistant Anne Symens-Bucher and I realized that we could take the same approach with people of color as we were already doing with men and young people.

Over the years participants in the Work That Reconnects had been predominantly (and not surprisingly) middle-class, middle-aged white women. Several men with a strong history in the work and egged on by Dan Walters of Boise, Idaho, grew so tired of being far outnumbered that they decided to organize male-only workshops in order to draw more brothers to the Work That Reconnects. Starting in 2007, asking Anne to help with the logistics and me to be the teacher (and the only woman allowed), they pulled off three successive men's retreats. These have generated ongoing men's groups and may well have contributed to a more even gender balance in other workshops.

After Joshua Gorman launched Generation Waking Up, he wanted to bring the Work That Reconnects to the youth movement he was organizing. The first such event in 2010 was intergenerational at the request of the sponsoring retreat center, but subsequent four- and five-day workshops were exclusively for young people, and these sessions were charged with their vitality.

Meanwhile, a long-cherished dream of Anne and her husband Terry Symens-Bucher was materializing: Canticle Farm. Now, in

2014, in its fifth year, this intentional community set in a marginalized neighborhood of East Oakland, is inspired by the life of St. Francis and the Work That Reconnects. Canticle Farm describes itself as "a platform for the Great Turning: one heart, one home, one block at a time." Its activities draw on the theory and practice of the Work That Reconnects and include farm work days, sharing permaculture know-how and a hearty lunch; weekly gifting to neighbors of gleaned organic fruit and vegetables; a program for local youth; open liturgies on Sunday; Friday evening gatherings of receptive silence, readings and a vegan supper — and alongside all that, an occasional day-long or weekend of the Work That Reconnects.

For some time now Anne had been keeping track of the people of color who had shown up at our workshops and now added those drawn into the widening circles of Canticle Farm. Before long we took the next step and decided to offer workshops that would be *only* for young activists of color and that would train them to become facilitators of the Work That Reconnects in their own communities.

By winter solstice of 2012, that idea had become a reality: the first experimental group of trainees was underway and would continue biweekly for some three months. A second cohort began a year later, in February 2014, with a third one lining up to start that fall. So, at the date of this writing, there is one completed cohort to report on, and of that I can offer some of my own experience of what we did together and what I learned.

### Getting Started

The invitations to take part in the initial venture drew some 16 activists of color, mostly in their twenties, with four of them residing at Canticle Farm. This first cohort, assembled in late 2012, comprised seven Latino-Americans, six African-Americans and three Asian-Americans (of South Indian, Pakistani and Philippino descent). With such variety of culture and hue, it was clear that *of color* meant one thing only: not Euro-American or European-identified. That definition signals a potent commonality that all the participants shared: not belonging to the culture that has brought us the Industrial Growth Society.

It was decided from the start to retain that distinction and include no white people. There was, of course, the necessary exception of myself, since they wanted the root teacher of the Work That Reconnects. I was aware from the start of the rare privilege of my being able to take part.

Our initial schedule called for one full weekend (Friday evening to Sunday afternoon) and then, at fortnightly intervals, four all-day Saturdays, to which we later added another three. This first course was offered within the gift economy, with no money received by either the host community or the teacher, and participants agreeing to contribute to the work by paying it forward.

### Honoring Our Ancestors

Two African-Americans in the group, Adelaja and Ratasha, were already quite familiar with the Work That Reconnects, so I asked them to take the lead in planning the opening weekend. The start was strong and energizing: participants introduced themselves by their community of color. The warmth and readiness in the room showed we were already moving into the Spiral of the work. Adelaja made that explicit, as he described the stations of the Spiral and led us in open sentences on gratitude. As the evening closed, we invited everyone to return in the morning with an object that was special to them for representing their ancestral lineage.

The next day we sat first in threes, so that each of us would have more time showing the object we had brought — a necklace, an old photograph, a badge, a feathered rattle. Only after a good half-hour did we gather in an open circle in front of the low corner table prepared as an altar. Then randomly, one at a time, when we were ready, we each rose to present our object to the whole group and place it on the altar. I had expected this process to be fairly swift, but the group's rapt attention to each object opened up stories, weaving a spell that slowed the pace of time.

As I look back and reflect on that morning of reverence and tears, I think of how gratitude for the ancestors can decolonize the mind. And I remember my year with the Sarvodaya movement in Sri Lanka. A non-governmental, Buddhist-inspired, community development movement, Sarvodaya was spreading to thousands of villages, and I wanted to learn its organizing methods. As a nation, Sri Lanka had gained its independence, but those in Sarvodaya knew that the people would not find their true freedom so long as they bore the psychic imprint of 450 years of colonial rule — a subliminal sense of unworthiness and cultural inferiority that led them to imitate their former masters in dress, manner and speech. To decolonize their mind, Sarvodaya made every effort to nourish collective self-esteem and pride, calling people to wake up to the strength and beauty of their ancient indigenous culture.

As was evident that first full day with our first cohort, honoring the ancestors can pierce gratitude with pain. The poignant convergence of thankfulness and anguish was noted at the time in an email message from Adelaja, as he wrote of the need "to ground in self-gratitude and cultural gratitude in order to gain the capacity to see how we perpetuate and participate in systems of oppression." And he added, "I believe that grounding in gratitude for who we are and where we are from is key to helping us create safe spaces for ourselves and others."[1]

### The Immensity of the Pain

We had entered the second stage of the Spiral before we knew it. For Honoring Our Pain for the world I'd planned to teach some intermediate warm-ups like the Milling, but the group was ready for a full-tilt ritual. Adelaja wanted to experience the old Despair Ritual he'd read about, where there is a lot of movement and simultaneous expression, so we embarked on that. (Some weeks later we did the Truth Mandala as well.)

I don't know how to convey the intensity of that despair ritual, and how it felt to be in it. I was hearing and witnessing degrees of anger and grief exceeding any I can recall. It was like being in the midst of a storm, shaking with it, awed by it. At the same time I felt honored to be allowed to be there, exposed to the elements, exposed to story after story, one outcry after the other, against the grinding degradation encountered in schools and offices, riding or driving or walking on the street.

Salina, whose immigrant parents had taken her as a child to march with the California farmworkers, gave vent to her pain as a school teacher. Again and again in the ritual process, she cried out over the self-mutilation, drug abuse and violence of her teenage students; the sullen, mean desperation of her new class of first graders and the stultifying indifference of school administrators and staff. She wrote:

> It was contrary to my life experience to sit in a circle of people who honored my pain for the world, who held loving space for my heart broken by broken schools. I felt seen and heard in a way I never imagined possible .... I was amazed that not only did the circle have the capacity to hold experiences I had cloaked in shame, I discovered that I had the capacity to show all parts of me, including the parts I thought were unlovable, unforgivable. It was this work that healed me. I could walk the Earth speaking out my experience in its fullness, without hiding some pieces or masking myself.[2]

## How the Pain of People of Color is Pathologized

From my first fierce onslaughts of despair for our world, I learned how such experiences are dismissed by the dominant culture: the status quo protects itself by reducing them to symptoms of neurosis. As examined in Chapter 2, our pain for the world gets viewed in terms of a personal pathology, rather than as a reason for reassessment and change. This pattern tends to shame and silence the individual. It fosters a fear-driven, obedient citizenry while promoting a medical model for treatment, in profitable service to the pharmaceutical industry.

For people of color, the pathologizing of their distress is especially widespread, burdening them with drug treatments and the stigma of mental illness. To help people involved free themselves from this trap, mental health advocates Sharon Kuehn and Joanna Aguirre are bringing an ecological framework to mental health recovery. They assert that much of the distress that is diagnosed as individual mental illness has its roots in collective dysfunction, radical uncertainty and "denial of concerns for the future of the human race." By bringing the Work that Reconnects into mental health and wellness programs, they hope to demonstrate that "identifying with a purpose larger than ourselves decreases internalized stigma and increases a sense of connection, belonging and personal responsibility." They say that, "Our choice to 'come back to life' as persons who have been diagnosed with mental health issues is exactly what is needed for the Great Turning to succeed right here and now."[3]

After our despair ritual that first day together, we took a spell just sitting around in silence. I'd put colors, pencils and paper in the middle of the floor, and as we lounged there, some of us began to draw. Sitting to the side against the wall, Aries, a black woman in her 20s, was writing nonstop. Later, after we looked at each other's drawings, she read us what she'd written:

### Honoring My Pain

by Aries Jordan

Don't try and fix it
Let me feel my pain
I refuse to be numb
Don't tranquilize me when I have a psychotic break
I have been propping myself up for years
Popping pills to make the nightmares go away
Smiling to keep from crying ...

Let me feel the pain I have hid behind my degrees and educational pursuits
Because the world told me I was not good enough
Don't try and fix it
Let me breathe through it
Because I have been holding my breath for what seems like years

Don't tell me I am overreacting
And give me your proverbs on forgiveness

Let me feel it, it won't kill me
I was told once you have to feel it to heal it
But I have been cruise controlling on numb
Too afraid that if I came to grips with the truth
My truth and our truth
That you will lose faith in me ...

Let my tears fall like a waterfall into the Earth ...
Let me be wild with emotion
As I work through my guilt and shame
The burdens placed on me
That never belonged to me

Let me cry for my ancestors who died with grief
Let me wail on behalf of the abused men and women
Who were told "not to make a sound"
Let me cry for my nation
And many nations under god
I am human
I am alive ...

Let me honor my pain
And don't you dare try and fix it
Because really you're afraid that you will lose it
If I don't stop
My pain is your pain
My grief is your grief
Let me feel it so that I can move forward.[4]

## Seeing the Industrial Growth Society with New Eyes

Historical connections that I had earlier glimpsed came back into focus now. In those early weeks of the first cohort, I pulled from my bookshelves a slim volume I barely remembered reading. Written back in 1944 by Trinidadian scholar Eric Williams before he became his nation's prime minister, *Capitalism and Slavery* described how the Atlantic slave trade essentially financed the industrial revolution.

The trade was triangular: merchants of Bristol and Liverpool bartered trade goods and guns for people on the West African coast, then sailed to the Americas to sell their enslaved Africans and from there took cargoes of sugar, rum, cotton and other plantation products back to England. The staggering wealth accruing to traders and bankers was invested in the mills, mines and technologies that made Britain, and soon other European nations, the world-shaping powers of the industrial age.

Growth and global reach were built in from the start through the ever-expanding need for raw materials and markets. In the process people and land become commodities to buy and sell. Africans sold into slavery were not the only ones to be commodified, but all of nature and in the last analysis all of us. Now we are seeing this commodification in an extreme form, as land grabs for mining and drilling intensify around the world, pushing Indigenous peoples and other subsistence farmers off their land without recompense or legal recourse, and turning their homes into toxic wastelands.

I recognized more clearly now how capitalism's early enmeshment with slavery continues to this day in my own country. The so-called War on Drugs, heavily focusing on people of color, imposing draconian convictions for nonviolent offenses, has led to mass incarcerations. The US is now the planet's top-ranking jailor with 25% of the world's prison population; 60% of these men and women are people of color. Meanwhile, privatized prisons are becoming increasingly profitable to their corporate owners, for the goods produced by prison labor come at a fraction of the labor costs of even sweatshops overseas.

For African-Americans, even those in positions of authority and professional prestige, the legacy of slavery continues invisibly, in the mind. It has recently been termed Post Traumatic Slave Syndrome. Showing how trauma has been passed from generation to generation, organizational consultant Monika Moss has pointed out:

> First it was slavery; then Reconstruction, voter disenfranchisement, land displacement, Jim Crow and segregation; then Vietnam, integration, the war on drugs and the

prison-industrial complex. This is not to speak of welfare reform and the dismantling of civil rights in the name of the war on terrorism. In addition to all of these are the individual and family traumas caused by lynchings, rape, false arrest and imprisonment, sharecropping, Black Codes and other forms of bondage.[5]

Joy Degruy-Leary, author of the book *Post Traumatic Slave Syndrome*, has argued that survival techniques developed during slavery have been carried into the present even when they are no longer needed and to the detriment of the Black community. "There was never a period of time," she wrote, "when Africans in this nation were given the permission or the wherewithal to heal from our injury, so the trauma has continued."[6] I find myself wondering how the Work That Reconnects can be part of that healing.

## Time for a Deep Cultural Awakening

In the course of this adventure I have become more aware of how, as an academically trained white woman, I can be blind to ways that my assumptions, language and behavior may disregard people of color. This is painful for me to acknowledge, but I have learned that there is a whole world of experience and reflection on bridging cultural differences that is there for us to draw upon.

To make the Work That Reconnects available within communities of color is clearly worthwhile, but in order to change the larger culture, it is equally if not more important to raise the consciousness of whites and help free them from the soul-constricting prisons of ethnic and racial privilege. Grassroots resources to this end include Unlearning Racism programs and the new White Awake workshops that adapt the approach and follow the Spiral of the Work That Reconnects. Launched collaboratively by colleagues in North Carolina and Washington DC, White

> To come of age in America as a white person is to be educated into ignorance. It is to be culturally shaped to not know and not want to know the actual context in which you live.
>
> — Rebecca Parker

Awake offers a program and website to "develop race awareness for the benefit of all."[7]

Through members of the first cohort, I came into contact with Patricia St. Onge. Of Mohawk and Quebecois descent, she is a consultant to seminaries and nonprofit organizations in how to work creatively across cultural boundaries. She is the lead author of a remarkably helpful book in this field called *Embracing Cultural Competency*.[8] Familiar with the Work That Reconnects, she is bringing her skills to our second People of Color (POC) cohort at Canticle Farm, weaving a Deep Culture component into each of our weekend sessions. I am delighted that she has contributed to this book.

## Part Two

by Patricia St. Onge

### *Walking Toward the Work That Reconnects*

The year 2013 was significant in my development as a citizen of the world. Early in the year, as I participated in the Interfaith Tent at Occupy/Decolonize Oakland, I heard Rev. Phil Lawson eloquently remind us that the Western, and particularly US frame of reference for identity is often "I am; therefore, we are," and that indigenous worldviews frame it as "we are, therefore I am." Phil's words were inspirational for me and pushed me to think more deeply about what it means to find our identity in the community(ies) to which we belong. It reminded me in a pithy way that, as we enter into deep culture work, it's important to understand and be able to articulate our own cultural location in relationship to the larger "we," which is an ever-expanding community.

In March, I had the honor of speaking at the Oakland International Women's Day event. After the public conversation, a young woman, Ratasha Huff, came to me with tears in her eyes. She told me that what I'd said had given her some clarity about what she'd felt she needed to make Joanna Macy's work more resonant for her. This was the beginning of a wonderful adventure; she introduced me to Joanna. Out of that meeting came a shared commitment to find a way to bring the deep culture work that I'd laid out in *Embracing*

*Cultural Competency* to the first cohort of People of Color (POC) who had gone through the Work That Reconnects trainings with Joanna at Canticle Farm. During the next few months, I had the wonderful experience of sharing with the first POC cohort some of the deep culture work that I've been doing for many years. Together we looked at how the two are complementary.

As many have done before me, I fell in love with Joanna: her warm heart, her brilliant intellect and her generous spirit. I'm learning so much from her, and I have the sense that she values what I'm bringing to our work together. Our growing affection for each other feels both new and very old. I am honored to have the opportunity to continue working with her.

I attended a few of Joanna's workshops and read her books. The Work That Reconnects is deeply resonant for me. One of the rich Aha! moments for me was when she explained about Heraclitus and Parmenides — how their views of reality were so different.[i] It helped me understand why I've felt for a long time that if one thing could change in order to shift things, it would be that we'd come to understand how deeply connected we are to one another and to our Mother, the Earth. In fact, at workshops (during icebreaker time), when asked "if you were a superhero, what super power would you have?" I often answered "I'd have the power to help people see and feel how we're all connected." The more I learned about the Work and looked at it through a deep culture lens, I saw that in relationship to each other, our frames create a pattern in the connections between things — an expression of Heraclitus' understanding of reality. I sensed immediately that a deeper study of the Work That Reconnects, with attention to deep culture, could strengthen my understanding of both and give deeper meaning to each. I hoped it might do that for the cohort as well. As we explored together, it became clear that it was indeed the case.

---

[i.] Parmenides and Heraclitus, pre-Socratic Greek philosophers, presented contrasting views of reality. In the Parmenidean understanding, all substance derives from one immutable essence which does not and cannot change, whereas, in the Heraclitean, all is in dynamic process, subject to continual flux and change.

## Deep Culture as a Lens

Our capacity to understand deep culture is situated both in the mind and in the heart. Like the Work That Reconnects, it is more an experience than an intellectual exercise. It is rooted in an understanding that we are all cultural beings. Our cultural identities inform how we move in the world, whether consciously or not. Some of us have more immediate access to our cultural identity and therefore, find it easy to identify and articulate our cultural location. Some of us have lost it under the pressure of assimilation; others had it stolen from us by force, through colonization, conquest and slavery. All of us, to varying degrees, are so deeply embedded in the dominant culture that, like fish in water, we often don't recognize it for what it is.

What are the elements of deep culture? Some of this may be familiar to you as a reader; for some it may be new thinking. This is a brief overview, not a comprehensive look at deep culture. Even before we begin an exploration, we need to create a safe space; a space where people can explore the fullness of who we are, in all of its brilliance and messiness. We create safety by creating shared agreements for how we want to be with each other as individuals and as a collective. If you've ever been in a workshop of any kind, you're probably familiar with the process of creating ground rules or common agreements. *Use I statements, step up, step back* are a couple of examples. I invite people to think about a time when they felt like they really belonged. What were the elements present there? Then we build our common agreements as part of a process for nurturing belonging. Some agreements that have emerged from that process include: *Listen with our hearts as well as our minds* and *Recognize that we are all here with concern for each other and the world.*

Secondly, we develop shared definitions of words that can easily be misinterpreted and create misunderstanding. Words like privilege, racism, oppression, power, inclusion and exclusion can be charged for us, depending on our histories. By deciding what we mean by them as we work together, we eliminate much of the tension that arises from thinking we're talking about the same things but actually talking past each other. For example, one of the early teams I worked with on this deep culture approach arrived at the following definition of culture:

> Culture is the behaviors, norms, attitudes and assumptions that inform a group of people who are joined by common myths, life ways, values and worldviews. It forms the group's context based on shared knowledge, understandings and experience, both above and below the surface of consciousness.[9]

If you can imagine an iceberg, floating in a body of water, the part that is above the surface really represents only 10% of the actual mass of the iceberg. So it is with culture. The elements that are easily identifiable, like language, dance, music, food, dress, etc. represent the external expressions of culture. Below the surface are countless elements that we generally don't think of as culture. Things like ordering of time, conversation patterns in various social contexts, patterns of handling emotions, eye contact behaviors, notions of leadership and approaches to problem solving are also elements of culture, but they often reside below the surface of our consciousness. This is why we call them *deep culture*. Not recognizing these as elements of culture can lead us to assume that someone who has different understanding and experience is just wrong. When they aren't recognized as elements of culture, the dominant patterns, behaviors and assumptions become *normative*. By looking at culture in a deeper way, we cultivate awareness and appreciation for the more subtle influences on ourselves and on other people. One of the early lessons that surfaced for me became a kind of mantra: *Different is just different, not better or worse.* Though not universally true, it is true often enough that it helps me loosen my grip on my own experience, making room for others to share their experience without the burden of my judgment.

Another place that needs our attention, if we're to do deep culture work, is the historical and current forms and experiences of oppression. Most of us know the broad strokes of US history. We also know the narrative of American/US exceptionalism; the fact that we call ourselves America, which is also the name of all the countries in this hemisphere is a great example of our inflated sense of ourselves. Our stated narrative says that we're a nation of liberty and justice for all. Our lived experience is that we are founded on the legacy of conquest, slavery and misogyny. It's not exceptional that we got our start using the free labor of stolen people working the stolen land.

My family's consulting practice is called Seven Generations Consulting. We chose that name because of the core principle within our Haudenosaunee culture and other worldviews that remind us that we stand on the shoulders of the generations who've come before us, and that the choices and decisions we make today will have an impact for seven generations. The residual effects of hegemony, conquest and slavery are very much alive in our world and in our bones today in the US. So too, is the legacy of resistance and resilience. In much the same way, the work of the Great Turning will last for generations to come. For these reasons, I found the Deep Time work in the Work That Reconnects so compelling. During one workshop, I received this message from my grandson's great, great, great grandson that was both real and very moving to me:

Dear Tota,

I am Emilio X. I am the constellation of stars in the soles of my great, great, great grandfather's feet. We are many; we are strong. We know about Orenda, we have developed the technology to undo many of the problems that were created in the generations before us. We're creating different problems and solving them more quickly because the one lesson we learned from you and the generations in between, and that we carry in our bones, is the very real understanding and experience that we're all connected. So now, when one part of our Mother, including we humans, is hurting, we all feel it. That was the big awareness. We've created systems and communities through which we are reminded. We're not always happy, but we're always aware. Our media remind us. Our structures are designed in ways that manifest it. Our rituals embody it. So, stop worrying so much. We appreciate what you're doing, and we know that it feels very stressful. I will tell you that making time for the relationships is as important as anything else you do. We're standing on your shoulders. We love you. Thanks for honoring your ancestors so that we might honor you.

Another aspect of deep culture work is that it requires of us that we co-create any process. *Nothing about us without us* is a phrase that has long held significance for groups in struggle for equity and justice. Communities most impacted by policies and institutional actions must have a voice in determining those policies and actions. This notion has been at the root of political struggle for generations, from Eastern European campaigns for political integrity in the 16th century, through the civil and human rights struggles of the mid-20th, to the disability rights and immigration reform struggles in the late 20th century. The commitment to self-determination by groups who have been and continue to be marginalized is a key element in shifting power dynamics. As Joanna reminds us, in a Parmenidean world, power looks like domination, power over, with winners and losers needed to make it work. When we know we're all connected, power looks like energy; like what is required to start an engine. Martin Luther King said that "power without love is reckless and abusive, and love without power is sentimental and anemic. Power at its best is love implementing the demands of justice, and justice at its best is power correcting everything that stands against love."[10]

The more I learn about the Work That Reconnects, the more I appreciate the essence of it as a universally important way of being in the world. Each element of the Spiral presents opportunities to provide greater access for people from all cultural backgrounds, including, but not exclusively related to race. Gender, sexual and gender identity, class and age are all access points. Our cultural location with respect to all aspects of culture informs how we experience the world and the Work That Reconnects. Because much of my work is done in the US, for me, race is the fault line through which all forms of oppression get filtered. In my experience and observation, oppression based on gender, sexual orientation and disability have racial components to them.

## Weaving the Threads Together
### GRATITUDE

In a deep culture context, the Work That Reconnects becomes accessible to more communities. Because it's a framework, we can find the stories and practices in our own traditions that point to the invitation to the Great Turning. I share stories from my own tradition with an invitation for the reader to find the stories in your own traditions that make the Work come alive and have meaning in your own context. For example, as we explore gratitude on the Spiral of the Great Turning, it resonates because one of the bedrock experiences of the Haudenosaunee is that of gratitude. Before we do anything, we speak the *Ohen:ton Karihwatehkwen*/The Words Before All Else. We express deep gratitude for every aspect of life. This is an element of our culture that is embedded in our way of being. By doing the work that reconnects through the lens of culture, we encourage participants to find the place in their own stories where gratitude is a central element of life.

As we explore the systems thinking that shapes the Work That Reconnects, we invite folks to find the stories in their own traditions that point to the same truths that European and Euro-American systems thinkers surfaced in their studies. As I heard Joanna talking about the notion that reality is the energetic connections between beings and that what we experience as reality is a series of patterns that are formed by the energy that moves everything, my heart sang. In Mohawk, we call that energy *Orenda*; the thread that moves among all beings and between the worlds of earth and spirit. It's all one system!

Many communities have prophecies like the Shambhala Warrior, people and/or beings who forged pathways toward peace making. In my tradition, we learn about the Great Peacemaker whose message transformed relationships and institutions among previously warring nations and formed the Confederacy of the Five Nations, on which the US colonies based their own Confederacy. So many cultures have stories of strength, unity and compassion. By offering the Work That Reconnects in a culturally-based way, people from historically marginalized communities, in fact *all* communities can find the stories from their own traditions that invite them into and point the way to the Great Turning more easily.

## Honoring our Pain for the World

As we broaden the stories that point to the Work That Reconnects, communities of color can be a resource for communities of privilege — and not just the "teach us how to be good allies" kind of resource. While every community and cultural group has suffered natural disasters and significant measures of injustice, there is something about the experience of Native American, African-American and other communities of color that can be instructive for all of us, regardless of our racial and ethnic background. Indigenous communities experienced near annihilation at the hands of the settlers and the diseases they brought to this land over the last 520+ years. Native people have already been in the place that all of us are today; looking into the face of complete destruction. People who were enslaved and their descendants have the experience of being taken out of their world, stripped of their identity as members of deep and rich cultural communities and being made to believe they were/are less important and valuable than others. An important piece of the marginalizing of communities is to tell them that they've made no significant contributions to humanity. This is the reality for many communities of color.

These experiences of oppression and the resistance and the resilience of their responses have created antibodies to suffering that can be instructive as we all develop deeper levels of resilience and resistance to the current threat of global annihilation. All of us have that wisdom in us; for those whose ancestors were focused on colonization, conquest and enslavement, it's a bit harder to access.

## Seeing with New Eyes

Our Mother, the Earth, is at risk of being overwhelmed by our disregard for her well-being. Most Indigenous people I know recognize that we are not destroying her; we are destroying ourselves. When she's really at risk of dying, she will shake us loose. In the context of the Work That Reconnects, that gives us motivation to do what our life is calling us to in order to repair the harm we've done. The deep culture work provides a pathway that allows us to answer that call — in ways that are authentic and culturally based. If/when we're paying attention to culture, it increases the likelihood that we will engage with cultural humility and not in ways of misappropriation. A restorative approach helps me not to rush to blame those in power, but rather to ask: what is the harm being done and what needs to be done to repair the harm? I find this very liberating. It makes room in my thinking and in my heart even for those who are leading the destruction of our environment. How can we hold each other accountable in proportion to our responsibility for doing harm, while recognizing that we all need to be involved in repairing the harm in proportion to our understanding of the solutions? We're all in this together. This is the *new eyes* that I learn from the Work That Reconnects. I realize that in many ways, they are really very old eyes; we're regaining sight.

## GOING FORTH

By working together and sharing leadership in the Work That Reconnects, we all can reintegrate our ancestral wisdom even as we heal our ancestral trauma. Finally, when everyone is at the table, the conversation is much deeper and richer. Going forth is a collective process that has significant meaning for all of us. Joanna set the tone for this early on in the work. While it is a significant piece of her life's work, she has never "owned" it. She invites everyone who understands the work of the Great Turning to engage in it. I so appreciate that about her. I would add an invitation to engage in the work in ways that acknowledge and affirm that we all, in all of our beautiful diversity, have much to learn from each other. We may find that the Great Turning is, in some ways, a Returning to some very old, life-sustaining ways as well as a Turning toward new expressions and new emergent life-sustaining societies. It is important work; work on which we can bet our lives ... and that of our Mother.

## Part Three

by Adelaja Simon, Adrián Villaseñor Galarza and
Andrés Thomas Conteris

*Joanna invited participants in her trainings for people of color to respond
to two questions:*

1. *From your experience, what do you think the Work That Reconnects
   can most significantly contribute to communities of color?*
2. *And what do you think that people of color most significantly contribute to the Work That Reconnects?*

*She received the three responses that follow.*

### Adelaja Simon

*Adelaja Simon is a Haitian Nigerian Black US-er and Work That
Reconnects facilitator.*

I think that the Work That Reconnects can most contribute a
much-needed framing and container for personal experience growing up in this time of crisis and opportunity. In hearing about the
Spiral for the first time, I traced my own life experiences within its
frame. I have been able to look at some very difficult experiences of
racism and classism, knowing that they have shaped the person that
I know and love today. It has helped me to see that I am not alone in
my struggle, and that, when held through a conscious framework, we
can see the gifts in our individual and collective struggles.

People of color most significantly contribute to the Work That
Reconnects a felt sense of the structural impacts of the Industrial
Growth Society in the human realm. There is a grounding in our
humanness in this country — through sharing about the worldwide legacy of oppression — that I have experienced in working
with other POC [people of color] folks. This grounding has opened a
doorway into seeing myself as part of the larger network of humans
— and through that, as an integral member in the body of Earth. I
had found it much easier to connect to the other-than-human world
than to humans. In opening up this doorway, I have been able to

hold myself with more compassion, and that compassion spreads out to all humans.

There is also the closeness to cultural heritage that POC folks carry. If held carefully, this closeness can begin to stir up the longing that lives in each of us to connect with our individual history and family lineage as our true window into our collective history and healing.

I would also like to highlight that it is important to work with our own communities in facilitating cultural change. I have often heard in movements for social change the phrase, "We need more people of color here." I believe that the opposite may be more helpful, "What is it in me or in this system that is excluding or non-inviting to folks of color?"

### Adrián Villaseñor Galarza

*Adrián Villaseñor Galarza, Ph.D., is Mexican from Guadalajara and a Work That Reconnects facilitator in Mexico and US.*

From my experience, I believe that the Work That Reconnects can be a powerful catalyst of flourishing change in communities of color. This is partly because of the Work's invitation to see beyond the confines of the industrial system, reconnect with life's true forces and fall in love with each other. Communities of color have a long history of repression and subjugation, making the compassionate re-empowerment ignited by the Work That Reconnects all the more crucial for engaged action in our periled days. Given the historical development of communities of color, there's a widespread intergenerational trauma interwoven with repressed anger and fear that can be healthily transformed and unleashed via the Work That Reconnects for the benefit of the Earth community. In fact, this pent-up energy within communities of color might be crucial in the creation of a better future for all.

I believe that the key contribution of communities of color to the Work That Reconnectsis an opening to the multiplicity of voices that make up the chorus of humanity. The voice of the repressed and the wounding of the Earth are latent in communities of color. One criticism that may be offered to the Work That Reconnects — along with a large number of amazing proposals for self-growth and sustainable action born in an industrialized context — is the potential disconnect with the everyday realities of most people in the planet. Celebrating and including people of color in the Work That Reconnects begins healing this gap while greatly enriching the Work itself. New exercises, perspectives and practical applications may emerge from the inclusion of the historically repressed. In other words, people of color have the potential to make the Work That Reconnects applicable to a broader audience and take it to fresh heights.

### Andrés Thomas Conteris

*Andrés Thomas Conteris is a US-Latino human rights activist and founder of Democracy Now in Spanish.*

At a macro level, the Work That Reconnects looks deeply into how Industrial Growth Society eviscerates the life-support system on Earth while at the same time provides concrete tools to shift toward a life-sustaining civilization. Given the history of dominance by white supremacy in Western culture, communities of color feel the evisceration in a particularly acute fashion: genocide of indigenous nations, human trafficking/slave trade, forced labor, deportation of immigrants, disproportionate mass incarceration and more. The shift toward becoming a life-affirming species in the midst of the death cycle can only take place by constellating the soulfulness conjured by those who have been most marginalized, especially women and people of color. The Work that Reconnects offers techniques and resources that serve to fortify those who have been subordinated because of their gender/race/ethnicity. The synergy at play compels the Work itself to become more authentic when the experiences of communities of color are truly honored.

## Part Four: Sharing the Work That Reconnects with First Nations

by Andrea Avila
*Andrea Avila is an art therapist from Mexico.*

First Nations people in Canada have endured abuse for many years. Their land was stolen and their children were put in residential schools where 50% of them died. As a result, today many First

Nations people feel hopeless, have PTSD and experience complicated grief.

Seven years ago in 2006, I began to work as an educator and art therapist for and with Indigenous people in Canada. I was hired to create programs for youth and to train people in art-based approaches for working with the youth. I was aware that most people working with youth had vicarious trauma and were experiencing burnout. They often expressed a lack of trust in the effect their work would have on the youth.

The Work That Reconnects offered me specific tools for showing the interdependence we have with each other and with the universe, aligning my work with indigenous epistemologies and decolonizing methodologies. Following Joanna's teachings, I was able to share my view of the extraordinary moment we are presently living on Earth and invite them to see the importance of the role we are all playing in the Great Turning.

I have used most of the activities and rituals in *Coming Back to Life* with the people I work with, and I have found three to be particularly useful in my work with First Nations:

1. The Cairn of Mourning Ritual, which I use when confronting the grief from residential schools
2. Imaging Our Power, when working with youth
3. The Double Circle [now called Seventh Generation Practice] to bring awareness of the power of lineage

As an art therapist I have adapted many of Joanna's ideas into visual metaphors that I use in my private practice and also with groups in workshops. Her book *Active Hope* has given me not only the opportunity to understand the Work That Reconnects more deeply, but also to make a journey of self-transformation, awakening and love, which I hope to share with people I work with.

## 13

# Meditations for the Great Turning

*Meditation is to be aware of what is going on — in our
bodies, in our feelings, in our minds, and in the world ....
Life is both dreadful and wonderful. To practice meditation
is to be in touch with both aspects. Please do not think
we have to be solemn to meditate. In fact, to meditate well,
we have to smile a lot.*

— Thich Nhat Hanh

To heal our society, our psyches must heal as well.
Haunted by the desperate needs of our time and beset by
more commitments than we can easily carry, we may wonder how
to find the time and energy for spiritual disciplines. Few of us feel
free to take to the cloister or meditation cushion to seek personal
transformation.

We do not need to withdraw from the world or spend long hours
in solitary prayer or meditation to begin to wake up to the spiritual
powers within us. The activities and encounters of our daily lives can
serve as the occasion for that kind of discovery. Here are seven practices that help, transcribed as Joanna has offered them in workshops.

Because they are useful in our ongoing lives as well, we present them here in this concluding chapter.

Some of these meditations — on death, loving-kindness, compassion, mutual power and mutual recognition — happen to be adapted from the Buddhist tradition. As part of our planetary heritage, they belong to us all. No belief system is necessary, only a readiness to attend to the immediacy of your own experience. They will be most useful if read slowly with a quiet mind (a few deep breaths will help).

When you read them aloud for others or record them, pause often to let silence happen and imagery unfold. The purpose is not to direct people's minds so much as to evoke and suggest.

> We lie in the lap of immense intelligence, which makes us receivers of its truth and organs of its activities.
>
> — R.W. Emerson

## The Web of Life

Workshop participants often enjoy lying down while being guided in this meditation.

*Relax your body as fully as you can .... Feel your breathing in your lungs, abdomen ... how it glides in and out .... The oxygen ignites each cell, stirs it awake as it burns in the metabolism of life .... Extend your awareness deep within to feel this energy ....*

*It is all around you, too ... sustaining all the bodies in this room ... weaving us into the web of life.*

*Imagine you can see interlacing currents, like threads of light .... See how they connect us and extend beyond this room, this moment .... Experience the great multiplicity of strands ... formed by countless relationships, woven of the work and food, the laughter and tears you've shared with others .... They shape what you are ... they hold you in place .... Sense those interwoven threads, rest into them.*

*The web sustains your bones and blood and skin, concocted so intricately out of the food you have eaten ... out of grains, vegetables, fruit,* nuts .... *The soil that yields the grain for your bread, the boughs of the tree that bear apples for you* .... *The hands that plow, sow, reap, gather ... they all are of your body now* ...

*Back through time this web extends ... mothers, fathers, great-grand-mothers and great-grandfathers ... giving you your coloring and features ... your gestures, your tone of voice* .... *The web extends back through countless generations, through numberless ancestors we share ... all the way back to those with gills and wings* .... *For it is of star stuff evolving that we all are made in the flowing of time ... We are each a jewel in this vast net, that called us into being ... each of us an irreplaceable gem, sparkling with awareness, reflecting the world* .... *Sound of gull crying over the sea, sight of mountain rising ... colors of sunrise ... scents of pine and loam ... the excitement of a new idea ... the melody of a half-forgotten song.*

*There is pain, too, coming in along the strands of the web ... a friend with cancer ... an oil spill coating the beach ... an Iraqi mother weeping for her lost children* .... *Do not shut them out, they live in the web of this planet-time* .... *Open to these sorrows, breathe them in, so the channels may stay open for the flow of energy and life and change* .... *If we block the pain, we block the joy as well* .... *There is power in the flowing of this fluid net, love that has enriched us, and love that we give* .... *Feel the caring and love that flow through you* ....

*Open to the pulsing of the web, its murmurs, whispers, tugs* .... *Through that vast network all forms arose, intelligence arose* .... *It shaped you as it shaped the mockingbird and the deep-diving trout* .... *You are of it ... of it, even to the terrors we've unleashed now* .... *Open to it all, unafraid, relaxed, alert* .... *We are the universe knowing itself.*

*To all our brothers and sisters we open now ... in this time of great hardship. We go now through a dark place, but we do not go alone* .... *And we do not go without our own timeless knowledge of the dark* .... *We come from it, it is behind our eyes ... and we will look into it, togeth-er, until the dark itself is clear ... and home* .... *There is nowhere you can go where you're not held in the web that sustains us all.*

*Still sensing these connections through space and time, we stir and stretch now, open our eyes* ....

### Gaia Meditation[1]

This simple spoken meditation, composed by John Seed and Joanna, guides us into precise and close identification with the elements and with the evolving life-forms of Earth. This meditation is often done in pairs, with people contemplating one another while listening to the words.

*What are you? What am I? Intersecting cycles of water, earth, air and fire — that's what I am, that's what you are.*

*WATER — blood, lymph, mucus, sweat, tears, inner oceans tugged by the moon, tides within and tides without. Streaming fluids floating our cells, washing and nourishing through endless riverways of gut and vein and capillary. Moisture pouring in through and out of you, of me, in the vast poem of the hydrological cycle. You are that. I am that.*

*EARTH — Matter made from rock and soil. It too is pulled by the moon as the magma circulates through the planet heart and roots suck molecules into biology. Earth pours through us, replacing each cell in the body every seven years. Ashes to ashes, dust to dust, we ingest, incorporate and excrete the earth, are made from earth. I am that. You are that.*

*AIR — the gaseous realm, the atmosphere, the planet's membrane. The inhale and the exhale. Breathing out carbon dioxide to the trees and breathing in their fresh exudations. Oxygen kissing each cell awake, molecules moving in constant metabolism, interpenetrating. That dance of the air cycle, breathing the universe in and out again, is what you are, is what I am.*

*FIRE — Fire from our sun that fuels all life, drawing up plants and raising the waters to the sky to fall again replenishing. The inner furnace of your metabolism burns with the fire that first sent matter/energy flaring out through space and time. This is the same fire as the lightning that flashed into the primordial soup, catalyzing the birth of organic life.*

*You were there, I was there, for each cell of our bodies is descended in an unbroken chain from that event through the desire of atom for molecule, of molecule for cell, of cell for organism. In that spawning of forms, death was born, born simultaneously with sex, before we divided from the plant realm. So in our sexuality we can feel ancient stirrings that connect us with plant as well as animal life. We come from them, an unbroken chain — through fish learning to walk the land, scales turning to wings, through migrations in the ages of life.*

*We have been but recently in human form. If Earth's whole history were compressed into 24 hours beginning at midnight, organic life would begin only at 5 PM ... mammals emerge at 11:30 PM ... and from amongst them at only seconds to midnight, our species.*

*In our long planetary journey we have taken far more ancient forms than these we now wear. Some of these forms we remember in our mother's womb, take on vestigial tails and gills, grow fins that turn to hands.*

*Countless times in that journey we died to old forms, let go of old ways, allowing new ones to emerge. But nothing is ever lost. Though forms pass, all returns. Each worn-out cell consumed, recycled ... through mosses, leeches, birds of prey ....*

*Think to your next death. Give your flesh and bones back into the cycle. Surrender. Love the plump worms you will become. Launder your weary being through the fountain of life.*

*Beholding you, I behold as well all the different creatures that compose you — the mitochondria in the cells, the intestinal bacteria, the life teeming on the surface of the skin. The great symbiosis that is you. The incredible coordination and cooperation of countless beings. You are that, too, just as your body is part of a much larger symbiosis, living in wider reciprocities. Be conscious of that give-and-take when you move among trees. Breathe your carbon dioxide to a leaf and sense it breathing fresh oxygen back to you.*

*Remember again and again the old cycles of partnership. Draw on them in this time of trouble. By your very nature and the journey you have made, there is in you deep knowing of belonging. Draw on it now in this time of fear. You have earth-bred wisdom of your interexistence with all that is. Take courage and power in it now, that we may help each other awaken in this time of peril.*

<hr>

## Death Meditation

Most spiritual paths begin by recognizing the impermanence of human life. Medieval Christians honored this in the mystery play of *Everyman*. Don Juan, the Yaqui sorcerer, taught that the enlightened warrior walks with death at his shoulder. To confront and accept the inevitability of our dying release us from triviality and free us to live boldly.

An initial meditation on the Buddhist path involves reflection on the twofold fact that: "death is certain" and "the time of death is uncertain." In our world today, nuclear weaponry, serving in a sense as a spiritual teacher, does that meditation for us, for it tells us that we can die together at any moment, without warning. When we allow the reality of that possibility to become conscious, it is painful; but it also jolts us awake to life's preciousness, heightening our awareness of the beauty and uniqueness of each object and each being.

*Look at the person you encounter (stranger or friend). Let the realization arise in you that this person lives on an endangered planet. He or she may die in a nuclear war or from the poisons spreading through our world. Observe that face, unique, vulnerable .... Those eyes still can see; they are not empty sockets ... the skin is still intact .... Become aware of your desire that this person be spared such suffering; feel the strength of that desire .... Keep breathing ....*

*Also let the possibility arise in your consciousness that this may be the person who is with you when you die ... that face the last you see ... that hand the last you touch .... It might reach out to help you then, to comfort, to give water .... Open to the caring and connection that arise in you ....*

❧

## Loving-Kindness

Loving-kindness, or *metta*, is the first of the four Abodes of the Buddha, also known as the *Brahmaviharas*. Meditation to arouse and sustain loving-kindness is a staple of the Sarvodaya Shramadana Movement for community development in Sri Lanka and is accorded minutes of silence at the outset of every meeting. Village workers find that it develops motivation for service and overcomes feelings of inadequacy and hostility.

Joanna first received instruction in this meditation from Sister Karma Khechog Palmo, a nun in the Tibetan Buddhist tradition. Here is a version that she has adapted for use in the West:

*Close your eyes and begin to relax, exhaling to expel tension. Now center in on the normal flow of the breath, letting go of all extraneous thoughts as you passively watch the breathing-in and breathing-out ....*

*Now call to mind someone you love very dearly .... In your mind's eye see the face of that beloved one ... silently speak her or his name .... Feel your love for this being, like a current of energy coming through you.... Now let yourself experience how much you want this person to be freed from fear, how intensely you desire that this person be released from greed and ill will, from confusion and sorrow and all the causes of suffering .... That very desire is the great loving-kindness ....*

*Continue to feel that warm flow coming through the heart; see in your mind's eye those with whom you share your daily life, the people you live and work with: family, close friends, colleagues .... Let them appear around you. Behold them one by one, silently speaking their names ... and direct to each in turn that same current of loving-kindness, undiluted .... Among these beings may be some with whom you are uncomfortable or in conflict. With those especially, experience your desire that each be free from fear, from hatred, free from greed and ignorance and all the causes of suffering ....*

*Now in wider concentric circles, allow your relatives and acquaintances to appear .... Let the beam of loving-kindness play on them as well, pausing on the faces that appear in your mind's eye. With them as well, experience how much you want their freedom from greed, fear, hatred and confusion, how much you want all beings to be happy ....*

*Beyond them, in concentric circles that are wider yet, appear now all beings with whom you share this planet-time. Though you have not met, your lives are interconnected in ways you do not know. To these beings as well, direct the same powerful current of loving-kindness. Experience your desire and your intention that each awaken from fear and hatred, from greed and confusion ... that all beings be released from suffering ....*

*As in the ancient Buddhist meditation, we direct the loving-kindness now to all the hungry ghosts, the restless spirits that roam in suffering, still prey to fear and confusion. May they find rest .... May they rest in the great loving-kindness and in the deep peace it brings....*

*By the power of our imagination let us move out now beyond our planet, out into the universe, into other solar systems, other galaxies, other Buddha-fields. The current of loving-kindness is not affected by physical distances, and we direct it now, as if aiming a beam of light, to all centers of conscious life …. To all sentient beings everywhere we direct our heartfelt wish that they too be free of fear and greed, of hatred and confusion and the causes of suffering …. May all beings be happy….*

*Now, from out in the interstellar distances, turn and behold your own planet, your home …. See it suspended there in the blackness of space, like a jewel turning in the light of its sun …. That living blue green planet laced with swirls of white is the source of all you are, all you've ever known and cherished …. Feel how intensely you desire that it survive the mounting dangers and wounds of this time. Direct toward it the strong current of your love and prayers for its healing ….*

*Slowly approach this planet now, drawing nearer, nearer, returning to this very part of it, this region, this place …. And as you enter this place, behold the being you know best of all … the person you've been given to be in this lifetime …. You know this person's need for love and strong desire to do the right thing …. Let the face of this being, your own face, appear before you …. Speak the name you are called in love …. And experience, with that same strong current of loving-kindness, how deeply you desire that this being be free from fear, released from greed and hatred, liberated from ignorance and confusion and all the causes of suffering …. The great loving-kindness linking you to all beings is now directed to your own self … know now the fullness of it.*

## Breathing Through

Basic to most spiritual traditions is the recognition that we are not separate, isolated entities, but integral and organic parts of the vast web of life. We can open to the pain of the world in confidence that it can neither shatter nor isolate us, for we are not objects that can break. We are resilient patterns within a vaster web of knowing.

Because we have been conditioned to view ourselves as separate, competitive and thus fragile entities, we need to relearn this kind of resilience. One way is to practice simple openness, as in this exercise of Breathing Through, adapted from an ancient Buddhist meditation for developing compassion.

*Closing your eyes, focus attention on your breathing. Don't try to breathe any special way, slow or long. Just watch the breathing as it happens, in and out. Note the accompanying sensations at the nostrils or upper lip, in the chest or abdomen. Stay passive and alert, like a cat by a mouse hole ....*

*As you watch the breath, note that it happens by itself, without your will, without your deciding each time to inhale or exhale .... It's as though you're being breathed — being breathed by life .... Just as everyone in this room, in this city, in this planet now, is being breathed by life, sustained in a vast living breathing web ....*

*Now visualize your breath as a stream or ribbon of air. See it flow up through your nose, down through your windpipe and into your lungs. Now from your lungs, take it through your heart. Picture it flowing through your heart and out to reconnect with the larger web of life. Let the breath-stream, as it passes through you and through your heart, appear as one loop within that vast web, connecting you with it ....*

*Now open your awareness to the suffering that is present in the world. Drop for now all defenses and open to your knowledge of that suffering. Let it come as concretely as you can ... images of your fellow-beings in pain and need, in fear and isolation, in prisons, hospitals, tenements, refugee camps .... No need to strain for these images; they are present to you by virtue of our interbeing. Relax and just let them surface ... the vast and countless hardships of our fellow humans, and of our animal brothers and sisters as well, as they swim the seas and fly the air of this planet ....*

*Now breathe in the pain like granules on the stream of air, up through your nose, down through your trachea, lungs and heart — and out again into the world net .... You are asked to do nothing for now, but let it pass through your heart .... Be sure that stream flows through and out again; don't hang on to the pain .... Surrender it for now to the healing resources of life's vast web ....*

*With Shantideva, the Buddhist saint, we can say, "Let all sorrows ripen in me." We help them ripen by passing them through our hearts ... making good rich compost out of all that grief ... so we can learn from it, enhancing our larger, collective knowing ....*

*If no images or feelings arise and there is only blankness, gray and numb, breathe that through also. That numbness is a very real part of our world ....*

*And if what surfaces is not the pain of other beings so much as your own personal suffering, breathe that through, too. Your own anguish is an integral part of the grief of our world, and arises with it ....*

*Should you feel an ache in the chest, a pressure in the rib cage, as if the heart would break, that is all right. Your heart is not an object that can break .... But if it were, they say the heart that breaks open can hold the whole universe. Your heart is that large. Trust it. Keep breathing ....*

Breathing through, once we learn it, becomes useful in daily life in the many situations that confront us with painful information. By breathing through the bad news, rather than bracing ourselves against it, we can let it strengthen our sense of belonging in the larger web of being. It helps us remain alert and open, whether reading the news, receiving criticism or simply being present to a person who is suffering.

For activists and those dealing most directly with the problems of our time, the practice helps prevent burnout. It reminds us that both our pain and our power arise from our interconnectness, and it offers a healing measure of humility. For when we accept our world's pain as the price of our caring, it naturally flows into action, without drama or self-righteousness.

❧

## The Great Ball of Merit

Compassion, which we generally understand as grief in the grief of others, is but one side of the coin. The other side is joy in the joy of others — which Buddhists call *mudita*. To the extent that we allow ourselves to identify with the sufferings of others, we can identify with their strengths as well, building a sense of adequacy and resilience. We face a time of great challenge that demands of us more commitment, endurance and courage than we can dredge up out of our individual supply. We can learn to draw on the other neurons in the neural net. We can see them with gladness as a present resource, like money in the bank.

This practice is adapted from the "Meditation of Jubilation and Transformation" written down two thousands years ago at the outset of the Mahayana Buddhist tradition. You can find the original version in Chapter 6 of *The Perfection of Wisdom in Eight Thousand Lines.*[2] We find it very useful today in two forms. The first one, which we use in workshops, is closer to the ancient practice. As you guide the meditation, remember to make the hand gestures.

> Realize that for every ongoing war and religious outrage and environmental devastation and bogus Iraqi attack plan, there are a thousand counter-balancing acts of staggering generosity and humanity and art and beauty happening all over the world, right now, on a breathtaking scale, from flower box to cathedral.
>
> — Mark Morford

*Relax and close your eyes. Open your awareness to all the beings who share with you this planet-time ... in this town ... in this country ... and in other lands .... In your mind's eye, behold their multitudes .... Now let your awareness open wider yet to encompass all beings who ever lived ... of all species and creeds and walks of life, rich, poor, kings and beggars, saints and sinners .... See the vast vistas of these fellow-beings stretching into the distance like successive mountain ranges ....*

*Now consider that in each of these innumerable lives some act of merit was performed. No matter how stunted or deprived the life, there was a gesture of generosity, a gift of love, an act of valor or self-sacrifice ... on the battlefield, or in the workplace, hospital or home .... From these beings in their endless multitudes arose actions of courage, kindness, of teaching and healing. Let yourself see these manifold and immeasurable acts of merit....*

*Now imagine you can sweep together these acts of merit ... sweep them into a pile in front of you .... Use your hands .... Pile them up .... Pile them into a heap, viewing it with gladness and gratitude ... Now pat them into a ball .... It is the Great Ball of Merit .... Hold it now and weigh it in your hands .... Rejoice in it, knowing that no act of goodness is ever lost. It remains ever and always a present resource ... a means for the transformation of life .... So now, with jubilation and gratitude, you turn that great ball ... turn it over ... over ... into the healing of our world.*

As we can learn from contemporary science and visualize in the holographic model of reality, our lives interpenetrate. In the fluid tapestry of space-time, there is at root no distinction between self and other. The acts and intentions of others are like seeds that can germinate and bear fruit through our own lives, as we take them into awareness and dedicate — or turn over — that awareness into the grace that empowers us all. Gautama, Jesus, Dorothy Day, Gandhi, Martin Luther King, Wangari Maathai, Nelson Mandela and countless heroes of our time — all can be part of our Ball of Merit, from which we can draw inspiration and strength. Other traditions feature notions similar to this, such as the Treasury of Merit in the Catholic Church.

The second, more workaday version of the Ball of Merit meditation helps us open to the powers in ordinary people around us. It is in direct contrast to the commonly accepted, patriarchal notion of power as something personally owned and exerted over others. The exercise enriches our attention to all we meet in our daily life, to view them with fresh openness and curiosity as to how they can enhance our Ball of Merit. We can play this inner game with someone opposite us on the bus or across the bargaining table. It is especially useful when dealing with a person with whom we are in conflict.

We can silently ask:

> *What does this person add to my Great Ball of Merit? What gifts of intellect can enrich our common store? What reserves of stubborn endurance can she or he offer? What flights of fancy or powers of love lurk behind those eyes? What kindness or courage hides in those lips, what healing in those hands?*

Then, as with the Breathing Through exercise, we open ourselves to these strengths, inhaling our awareness of them, relishing their presence.

Too often we let our perceptions of the powers of others make us feel inadequate. Alongside an eloquent colleague, we can feel inarticulate; in the presence of an athlete, we can feel weak and clumsy; so we can come to resent both ourselves and the other person.  In contrast, the practice of the Great Ball of Merit delivers us from comparison and envy. The gifts and good fortunes of others appear not as competing challenges, but as resources we can take pleasure in. We can learn to play detective, spying out treasures for the enhancement of life from even the unlikeliest material. Like air and sun and water, they form part of our common good.

In addition to releasing us from the mental cramp of envy, this practice offers two other rewards. One is pleasure in our own acuity, as our merit-detecting ability improves. The second is the response of others who, though ignorant of the game we are playing, sense something in our manner that invites them to disclose more of the person they can be.

༺ঌৠ঳༻

## The Four Abodes

also known as Learning to See Each Other

This meditative practice is adapted from the Buddhist *Brahmaviharas*, or Heavenly Abodes — sometimes called the Four Immeasurables — which are loving-kindness, compassion, joy in the joy of others and equanimity. It helps us to truly see each other and experience our intrinsic connectivity.

We offer it in workshops as a guided meditation, either as a Milling with four different partners or with people sitting in pairs facing each other. At its close, we encourage people to use it as they go about their daily lives. It is an excellent antidote to boredom, when our eye falls on another person, say on the subway, or waiting in a check-out line. It charges that idle moment with beauty and discovery. It also is useful when dealing with people whom we are tempted to dislike or disregard; it breaks open our accustomed ways of viewing them. When used as a meditation-in-action, one does not, of course, gaze long and deeply upon the other as in the guided exercise. A casual glance is enough.

In many cultural settings, it is considered rude to look directly into another's eyes. Even in the US, sustained eye contact can provoke embarrassment. Be sure you don't imply that participants should do this, but rather invite them to become aware of the full presence of the other. They might even face each other with their eyes closed, mentally picturing the other's face, and from time to time opening their eyes to refresh their memory.

Here are some words you can use for guiding this practice after you've started the Milling:

*Stop now in front of another person and take their hand in yours. Rest into your breathing. Before you is a human of planet Earth. The opportunity to behold the uniqueness of this particular being is given to you now ....*

*To enter the first abode, open your awareness to the gifts and strengths in this being .... Though you can only guess at them, there are behind those eyes unmeasured reserves of courage and intelligence ... of patience, endurance, wit and wisdom .... There are gifts that even this person is unaware of having .... Consider what these powers and potentials could do for the healing of our world, if believed and acted on .... As you consider that, experience your desire that this person be free from fear ... free from greed ... from hatred and confusion and from all the causes of suffering .... As you feel how much you genuinely want this, know that what you are experiencing is the great loving-kindness .... It is such good medicine for our world.*

*You may bow to this person, take your leave in any way that feels right, and go back to milling.*

*Finding yourself in front of another person, take both their hands in yours. Again, open your awareness to the unique, unrepeatable human being before you, as we enter the second abode. Now let yourself open to the pain that is in this person's life. As in all human lives, there are sorrows in this one. Though you can only guess at them, there are disappointments and failures, losses and loneliness and abuse .... There are hurts that this person may never have told to another human being .... Now you cannot take that pain away, but you* **can** *choose to be with it. As you sense your readiness to be with another's suffering, know that what you are experiencing is the great compassion. It is excellent for the healing of our world ....*

*Again we bow and take our leave in any way that feels right, and after more milling find ourselves in front of yet another person.*

*Entering the third abode, put your palms together at shoulder height. As you behold the person before you, consider how good it would be to work together ... on a joint project, toward a common goal, perhaps something big .... Think what it would be like to plan and plot and conspire together, take risks ... discover each other's strengths in working together ... celebrating the successes along the way, consoling each other over the setbacks, forgiving each other when you mess up ... and simply being there for each other .... As you open to that possibility, you open to the great wealth, the power in each other's powers, the joy in each other's joy ....*

*Again we bow and take our leave in any way that feels right, and after more milling find ourselves in front of a fourth person.*

*Now entering the fourth and last abode, let your awareness drop deep within you like a stone, sinking below the level of what words can express ... to the deep flows of relationship that interweave our lives through space and time, through myriad encounters and countless forms .... See the being before you as if seeing the face of one who, at another time, another place, was your lover or your enemy, your parent or your child .... And now you meet again on this brink of time, almost as if by appointment ... and you know that your lives are as inextricably interwoven as nerve cells in the mind of a great being .... Out of that web you cannot fall ... no stupidity, failure or cowardice can ever sever you from that living web. For that is what you are .... Rest in that knowing. Rest in the Great Peace .... Out of it we can act, we can risk everything ... and let each encounter be a homecoming to our true nature .... Indeed it is so.*

Let us close with the same suggestion that often closes our workshops. It is a practice that is a corollary to the earlier death meditation, in which we recognize how threatened now is each person we meet:

*Look at the next person you see ... a neighbor, child, co-worker, bus driver, or your own face in the mirror. Regard him or her with the recognition that:*

*In this person are gifts for the healing of our world, powers that can redound to the joy of all beings.*

## Two Litanies

These litanies can be used in a workshop where a centering ritual is needed. For example, "We Have Forgotten Who We Are" can be used before or following intense practices in Honoring Our Pain or transitioning to Seeing With New Eyes. "We Journey Together" is good at the outset of a workshop and also as part of Going Forth.

They are usually done as responsive readings, with the guide reading the major sections and the rest of the group responding according to the script. A meditation bell might be rung after each group response.

## We Have Forgotten Who We Are

### (from the UN Environmental Sabbath[3])

*We have forgotten who we are.*
*We have forgotten who we are.*
We have alienated ourselves from the unfolding of the cosmos.
We have become estranged from the movements of the earth.
We have turned our backs on the cycles of life.
*We have forgotten who we are.*
We have sought only our own security.
We have exploited simply for our own ends.
We have distorted our knowledge.
We have abused our power.
*We have forgotten who we are.*
Now the land is barren.
And the waters are poisoned.
And the air is polluted.
*We have forgotten who we are.*
Now the forests are dying.
And the creatures are disappearing.
And humans are despairing.
*We have forgotten who we are.*
We ask forgiveness.
We ask for the gift of remembering.
We ask for the strength to change.
*We have forgotten who we are.*

❁ ❁ ❁

## We Journey Together

| Leader: | Response: |
|---|---|
| In the face of growing darkness | *We journey together* |
| In the face of ecological decline | *We journey together* |
| In the face of social upheaval | *We journey together* |
| In the face of growing uncertainty | *We journey together* |

**All:** *In the face of growing darkness, we journey together toward the light.*

| Leader: | Response: |
|---|---|
| As we search for glimpses of truth | *We journey together* |
| As we search for signs of possibility | *We journey together* |
| As we search for heralds of a new era | *We journey together* |
| As we search for angels of hope | *We journey together* |

**All:** *As we search for glimpses of truth, we journey together toward new levels of meaning.*

| Leader: | Response: |
|---|---|
| As we build our world out of chaos | *We journey together* |
| As we build our world out of shatter illusions of superiority | *We journey together* |
| As we build our world out of our inadequate Institutions | *We journey together* |
| As we build our world out of our unfair sharing of resources | *We journey together* |

**All:** *As we build our world out of chaos, we journey together toward a new era of justice.*

| Leader: | Response: |
|---|---|
| As the universe unfolds | *We journey together* |
| As the universe unfolds through spontaneous communion | *We journey together* |
| As the universe unfolds through new levels of meaning | *We journey together* |
| As the universe unfolds through new forms of life | *We journey together* |

**All:** *As the universe unfolds, we journey together in God's[i] great becoming.*[4]

---

[i.] Here you may want to omit "God" or use "the Great Turning" instead.

## Appendix A: Chief Seattle's Message

CHIEF SEALTH, OR SEATTLE AS HE IS NOW KNOWN, delivered a speech in his native Duwamish to his tribal assembly in the Pacific Northwest in 1854. Notes on the speech were jotted down by one Dr. Henry Smith, who emphasized that his own English, which reflects the usage of his time — including the use of the generic male which may or may not have been found in the original — was inadequate to render the beauty of Sealth's imagery and thought.

The version we now have was in fact recreated from Dr. Smith's jottings by film scriptwriter Ted Perry in 1970. We abridged his version for the purposes of this practice while still retaining its stirring evocation of Native American reverence for the natural world.

The Great Chief in Washington sends word that he wishes to buy our land ....

How can you buy or sell the sky, the warmth of the land? This idea is strange to us.

If we do not own the freshness of the air and the sparkle of the water, how can you buy them?

Every part of this earth is sacred to my people. Every shining pine needle, every shady shore, every mist in the dark woods, every clearing and humming insect is holy in the memory and experience of my people. The sap which courses through the trees carries the memories of the red man ....

We are part of the earth, and it is part of us ....

So, when the Great Chief in Washington sends word that he wishes to buy our land, he asks much of us.

The Great Chief sends word he will reserve us a place so that we can live comfortably to ourselves. He will be our father and we will be his children.

So we will consider your offer to buy our land. But it will not be easy. For this land is sacred to us.

The shining water that moves in the streams and rivers is not just water but the blood of our ancestors. If we sell you our land, you must remember that it is sacred, and you must teach your children that it is sacred and that each ghostly reflection in the clear water of the lake tells of events and memories in the life of my people. The water's murmur is the voice of my father's father.

The rivers are our brothers, they quench our thirst. The rivers carry our canoes and feed our children. If we sell you our land, you must remember, and teach your children, that the rivers are our brothers — and yours, and you must henceforth give the rivers the kindness you would give any brother ....

The air is precious to the red man, for all things share the same breath — the beast, the tree, the man, they all share the same breath. The white man does not seem to notice the air he breathes ....

So we will consider your offer to buy the land. If we decide to accept, I will make one condition: the white man must treat the beasts of this land as his brothers ....

What is man without the beasts? If all the beasts were gone, men would die from a great loneliness of spirit. For whatever happens to the beasts soon happens to the man. All things are connected.

You must teach your children that the ground beneath their feet is the ashes of our grandfathers. So that they will respect the land, tell your children that the earth is rich with the lives of our kin. Teach your children what we have taught our children, that the earth is our mother. Whatever befalls the earth befalls the sons of the earth ....

This we know. The earth does not belong to man; man belongs to the earth. This we know. All things are connected like the blood which unites one family. All things are connected.

Whatever befalls the earth befalls the sons of the earth. Man does not weave the web of life, he is merely a strand in it. Whatever he does to the web, he does to himself ….

So if we sell you our land, love it as we've loved it. Care for it as we've cared for it. Hold in your mind the memory of the land as it is when you take it. And with all your strength, with all your mind, with all your heart, preserve it for your children and love it ….

## Appendix B: The Bestiary by Joanna Macy

Short-tailed albatross
    Whooping crane
        Gray wolf
            Woodland caribou
                Hawksbill sea turtle
                    Rhinoceros

THE LISTS OF ENDANGERED SPECIES GROW LONGER EVERY YEAR. With too many names to hold in our minds, how do we honor the passing of life? What funerals or farewells are appropriate?

Reed warbler
    Swallowtail butterfly
        Bighorn sheep
            Indian python
                Howler monkey
                    Sperm whale
                        Blue whale

Dive me deep, brother whale, in this time we have left. Deep in our mother ocean where once I swam, gilled and finned. The salt from those early seas still runs in my tears. Tears aren't enough any-more. Give me a song, a song for a sadness too vast for my heart, for a rage too wild for my throat..

Giant sable antelope
    Wyoming toad
        Polar bear
           Grizzly bear
                Brown bear
                    Bactrian camel
                        Nile crocodile
                            Chinese alligator

Ooze me, alligator, in the mud whence I came. Belly me slow in the rich primordial soup, cradle of our molecules. Let me wallow again, before we drain your swamp and pave it over.

Gray bat
    Ocelot
        Pocket mouse
           Sockeye salmon
                Hawaiian goose
                    Audouin's gull

Quick, lift off. Sweep me high over the coast and out, farther out. Don't land here. Oil spills coat the beach, rocks, sea. I cannot spread my wings glued with tar. Fly me from what we have done, fly me far.

Golden parakeet
    West African ostrich
        Florida panther
           Galapagos penguin
                Imperial pheasant
                    Mexican prairie dog

Hide me in a hedgerow, badger. Can't you find one? Dig me a tunnel through leaf mold and roots, under the trees that once de-fined our fields. My heart is bulldozed and plowed over. Burrow me a labyrinth deeper than longing.

Thick-billed parrot
  Blue pike
    Snow leopard
      Molokai thrush
        California condor
          Lotus blue butterfly

Crawl me out of here, caterpillar. Spin me a cocoon. Wind me to sleep in a shroud of silk, where in patience my bones will dissolve. I'll wait as long as all creation if only it will come again — and I take wing.

Atlantic Ridley sea turtle
  Coho salmon
    Helmeted hornbill
      Marine otter
        Humpback whale
          Steller sea lion
            Monk seal

Swim me out beyond the ice floes, mama. Where are you? Boots squeeze my ribs, clubs drum my fur, the white world goes black with the taste of my blood.

Gibbon
  Sand gazelle
    Cheetah
      Chinchilla
        Asian elephant
          African elephant

Sway me slowly through the jungle. There still must be jungle somewhere. My heart drips with green secrets. Hose me down by the waterhole; there is buckshot in my hide. Tell me old stories while you can remember.

Desert tortoise
  Crested ibis
    Hook-billed kite

Mountain zebra
Tibetan antelope
Andrew's frigatebird

In the time when his world, like ours, was ending, Noah had a list of the animals, too. We picture him standing by the gangplank, calling their names, checking them off on his scroll. Now we also are checking them off.

Ivory-billed woodpecker
Indus river dolphin
West Indian manatee
Wood stork

We reenact Noah's ancient drama, but in reverse, like a film running backwards, the animals exiting.

Ferret
Gorilla
Tiger
Wolf

Your tracks are growing fainter. Wait. Wait. This is a hard time. Don't leave us alone in a world we have wrecked.

# Appendix C: Ethics and Declarations of Rights

ERE ARE DOCUMENTS AND WEB LINKS of major initiatives for the Great Turning that are close to Joanna's and Molly's hearts, having been the focus of our activism for many years and nourishing of Deep Time work. The Nuclear Guardianship Ethic appears in its entirety; we briefly introduce the other Declarations and refer the reader to relevant websites.

## Nuclear Guardianship Ethic
### (created 1990, revised July 2011)

The Guardianship Ethic grew out of the study/action group on nuclear waste that met regularly with Joanna and Fran Macy from 1988 to 1994. Their work together produced the Nuclear Guardianship slideshow, the room-size nuclear waste map of the United States, testimony at regulatory hearings of the DOE, three issues of the *Nuclear Guardianship Forum* (a freely distributed tabloid publication) and Deep Time exercises such as the Seventh Generation Practice. For narrative description of this group and its work, see Joanna's memoir, *Widening Circles*.[1]

1. Each generation shall endeavor to preserve the foundations of life and well-being for those who come after. To produce and

abandon substances that damage following generations is morally unacceptable.

2. Given the extreme toxicity and longevity of radioactive materials, their production must cease. The development of safe, renewable energy sources and non-violent means of conflict resolution are essential to the health and survival of life on Earth. Radioactive materials are not to be regarded as an economic or military resource.

3. We accept responsibility for the radioactive materials mined and produced for our alleged benefit.

4. Future generations have the right to know about their nuclear legacy and the dangers it brings.

5. Future generations have the right to protect themselves from these dangers. Therefore, it is our responsibility to pass on the information they will need, such as the nature and effects of radiation, and methods for monitoring and containing it. We acknowledge that deep burial of radioactive materials precludes these possibilities and risks widespread contamination.

6. Transport of radioactive materials, with its inevitable risks of accidents and spills, should be undertaken only when storage conditions at the site of production pose a greater hazard than transportation.

7. Research and development of technologies for the least hazardous long-term treatment and placement of nuclear materials should receive high priority in public attention and funding.

8. Education of the public about the character, source and containment of radioactive materials is essential for the health of present and future generations. This education should promote understanding of the interconnectedness of all life-forms and a grasp of the extraordinary time spans for which containment is required.

9. The formation of policies for managing radioactive materials requires full participation of the public. For this purpose, the public must have ready access to complete and comprehensible information.

10. The vigilance necessary for ongoing containment of radioactive materials requires a moral commitment. This commitment is

within our capacity and can be developed and sustained by drawing on the cultural and spiritual resources of our human heritage.

*The Nuclear Guardianship Ethic is proposed as an evolving expression of values to guide decision-making on the management of radioactive materials.*[2]

## Declaration of the Rights of Nature/Mother Earth

By recognizing the Rights of Nature, we shift from the dominion-over mentality and redefine our rightful place as part of the larger Earth Community.[3]

In 2008, Equador became the first nation to include the Rights of Nature in its Constitution as well as explicit recognition of celebrating Nature, or *Pachamama* (Mother Earth), as vital to our existence.[4]

In 2009, the United Nations General Assembly proclaimed April 22 as International Mother Earth Day, acknowledging that Earth and its ecosystems are our common home and that it is necessary to promote Harmony with Nature in order to achieve a just balance among the economic, social and environmental needs of present and future generations.[5]

In April 2010, 32,000 people from around the world attended the World's People's Conference on Climate Change and the Rights of Mother Earth in Cochabamba, Bolivia. They proclaimed the Universal Declaration of the Rights of Mother Earth.[6]

## Declaration of Rights of Future Generations and Bill of Responsibility for Present Generations

by Molly Brown

Towering red rock mesas welcomed some 150 women and more than a dozen men to the high desert town of Moab, Utah at the end of September 2012 for the first *Women's Congress for Future Generations*. People came from 23 states, Canada and Russia to help create a Declaration of the Rights of Future Generations. I was grateful that I could participate, traveling there by train with nine other women from Northern California.

Why consider the rights of future generations and the responsibilities of present generations to uphold these rights? To quote the Congress program:

> All bodies — from human bodies and bodies of water to the welfare of the body politic — bear the imprint of the ways in which this generation, and previous generations, handled nuclear technologies, mining, war, pollution, industrial farming and the fossil fuels at the center of our economy. Future Generations will inherit the consequences of what has been released, buried, leveled, left behind, and squandered without full consideration of long-term consequences. The needs of Future Generations for clean air and water, fertile soil and raw materials have rarely factored into decisions about how we plan and organize our society today.[7]

Participants in the Congress believed that we humans must acknowledge these consequences as well as the responsibilities of present generations to protect Future Generations of all species from further harm. The Declaration we drafted and will continue to craft and disseminate — with the help of many other hearts and minds — can serve to awaken and educate our communities so that we humans will consider the effects of our choices on Future Generations, including all members of the Earth community. This document could be adopted as a resolution or ordinance by local towns and counties and/or by our state governments, to inform their decision-making processes.[8]

# Appendix D: Bodywork and Movement and Using the Spiral in Writing Workshops

## Bringing Bodywork and Movement into the Work That Reconnects

by Barbara Hundshammer, dance therapist, Germany[1]

IN FACILITATING THE WORK THAT RECONNECTS I have found bodywork and movement to be of immense benefit. To list these benefits I can say that embodiment of the work through motion and sensory awareness:

1. Brings relaxation. Participants get comfortable with themselves, their bodies, the group and the room — and nonverbal connection is created.
2. Strengthens presence, attention and mindfulness as an important basis for the Work That Reconnects.
3. Integrates mind, heart *and* body — so that the learning process is deepened and anchored on a cellular level.
4. Offers recreation and "digesting" between more verbal and theoretical parts.
5. Supports the sensing and expressing of emotions.

6. Deepens and integrates the exercises of the Work That Reconnects.
7. Helps keep us from getting fixated or stuck on particular emotions, thoughts or details.
8. Dramatizes the connection between our bodies and nature: caring for our bodies also means caring for the Earth.

To give you some impressions of my work, I will introduce the *Spiral on the Body*, an approach where I assign five body resources to the stages of the Spiral of the Work That Reconnects. I owe these resources, which participants of my workshops find helpful and enjoyable, to my teacher Susan Harper. Her bodywork, named Continuum Montage, is beautifully synergistic with the Work That Reconnects.[2]

These five Resources of Being are always available to the body and do not require any leadership, any equipment or training process. I always introduce them at the beginning of a workshop, along with the Spiral of the Work That Reconnects, so that participants can revisit them at any time and see which one they currently may need. The five body resources are sensousness, gravity, fluidity, breath and space.

### Stage One: Gratitude
### Body Resource: Sensuousness

*Sensuousness* — as the ability to sense, feel and be alive in a living body — leads directly to *gratitude*.

When I am aware of more body sensations, I am able to inhabit more of my organism. Sensations are the way life is speaking to me. Before verbal language, we employ the language of sensations. To have the ability to see, to listen, to smell, to taste, to touch and to sense can awaken our gratitude and connect us with the intelligence of the self-organizing potential of life. "There is an intimate reciprocity to the senses; as we touch the bark of a tree, we feel the tree touching us .... The senses, that is, are the primary way that the earth has of informing our thoughts and of guiding our actions."[3] All body exercises that enliven our senses and deepen sensory awareness are useful in this stage of the Spiral.

## EXERCISE FOR STAGE ONE:
## I SHOW SOMETHING BEAUTIFUL TO MY PARTNER

This exercise was originated by my honored teacher Gisela Adam, a German pioneer of dance therapy. People divide into pairs and decide to be A or B. Partner A has the task of showing something beautiful to her partner. This should be done without speaking, via pantomime, gestures, body language and touch. The beautiful exists in the imagination and can be a place, activity, animal or treasure. Partner A should describe this wonderful item in a detailed and lively way so that both partners can discover and experience this thing. Partner A can take the other's hand or board an aeroplane or swim across a river to reach the wonderful something. Allow about ten minutes for this part of the exercise. When each pair has returned, partner B tells partner A what she thinks has been shown to her. Partner A unravels the mystery.

Then they change roles. The exercise provides joy, creativity, childlike curiosity, connectivity, laughter, relaxation and presence. It offers a wonderful foundation for experiencing gratitude.

### Stage Two: Honoring Our Pain for the World

Body Resource: Gravity

When we establish a broader body awareness and a deepening of our senses, we feel both more joy and more pain. This is a precondition for perceiving our pain for the world. But our culture does not support us in learning how to ground our bodies. Being able to relate to gravity and to bond with it is crucial for our relationship to the ground, the place and the Earth. In stage two of the Spiral of the Work That Reconnects, I use grounding body exercises and the experience of *being deeply rooted* to support participants in perceiving the Earth's pain, as well as to prepare them for exercises that *honor our pain for the world.*

Even just the thought of honoring their pain often causes participants to worry about becoming overwhelmed by their grief, and they therefore try to hold themselves back. Having established a reliable relationship with gravity allows people to ground intense emotions and to uphold a feeling of being *carried by the earth.*

Bodywork is generally very helpful in this stage of the spiral, because it gives our grief, anger and fear an embodied expression. "Cognitive information about the crises we face, or even about our psychological responses to them, is insufficient. We can only free ourselves from our fears of the pain ... when we allow ourselves to experience these feelings."[4]

After an intensive process, such as the Truth Mandala, I make sure that participants can integrate their experience through movement *before* talking about it. A mindful walk in nature is good, as are other methods of digestion, such as lying down and holding different body parts or releasing body tensions by pressing them into the ground. Thus people can reconnect with their bodies and experience that even after heavy emotions they do not feel lost. This usually leads in an organic way directly to the next stage.

### EXERCISE FOR STAGE TWO: GROUNDING PROCESS

This exercise takes some time to really explore each body position (about 45 minutes). It provides a good preparation for honoring our pain for the Earth or a helpful integration after an intensive process of despair work.

> *Lie down on your back on a mat or blanket; relax and focus on your breath. Be aware of the tides of your breathing. Let all tensions and emotions release themselves into gravity.*
>
> *Imagine tiny roots from the back of your body extending into the ground and taking in fresh, raw, primal Earth energy. Roll onto your side, continue to plant roots into the ground and take in energy. Remain aware of your inhaling and exhaling.*
>
> *Come into a ventral position. Extend your roots from the front side of your body into the Earth and allow yourself to be nourished by Earth energy.*
>
> *Come into a quadruped position. Feel the support of gravity by pressing your hands, feet and other body parts into the floor.*
>
> *Sit up and ground yourself via roots that reach from your pelvic floor into the Earth.*

*Stand up and plant roots from your feet into the Earth. Extend your roots throughout the soil until they meet the roots of the other persons in the room. Imagine the picture of huge redwood trees holding each other up via their root systems.*

*Slowly start walking across the room, still feeling the rootedness, the nourishment of the Earth and the connection to the other people. Be aware of your breath and notice any changes.*

## Stage Three: Seeing with New Eyes

### BODY RESOURCES: FLUIDITY AND BREATH

After having gone through pain, we are open for new perspectives: stage three of the spiral is a shift in perception and opens us to interconnectedness, as well as the theoretical foundations of systems theory. In the words of Joanna Macy: "We are open, living systems like all life on Earth and as such, streams of matter, energy and information run through us, keeping us alive. We are made of change; we do not need to protect ourselves against change, because change is our nature."[5]

What better teacher than our body and its *fluidity*: the manifold streams of movement on cellular, molecular and biochemical levels that are running through us!

Movement is information. Just as we move ourselves, we are informed by ourselves. What would it be like if we were to explore movements that are precultural and more biologically based? Wave motions, flowing, gliding, spiraling, movements of rivers and sea animals, but also growth movements of a plant or the wave-like dance of grass in the wind, allow us to experience our bodies as open systems. Furthermore, sequences that direct the focus on new, playful, unexpected, spontaneous movements enforce *seeing with new eyes*. Simple suggestions like balancing on one foot provide the physical experience of feedback loops and illustrate the huge capacity of our bodies to change.

In free movements, the body has the ability to self-correct. The same dynamics apply when thoughts or emotions become persistent or rigid. Even the most challenging emotional upset is more manageable when it naturally moves and changes. If we allow ourselves to move like water in unpatterned, natural ways, the self-regulating, self-healing potential can be more fully expressed.[6]

The mutability of our body is also shown in *breath*. "In each breath we change density and re-form ... at least 17,000 times each day ...."[7] Breathing connects us moreover with the whole life process: with human beings, plants, animals, the atmosphere and even with past and future generations. They all share the same air — therefore I relate the resource of breath to this stage of the Spiral and particularly to the exercises of Deep Time.

### EXERCISE FOR STAGE THREE: ROBOTS AND RUBBER PEOPLE

Divide the room into two halves (a rope or a cord can define the midline). One half is space for the robots — linear, angular, mechanical, rigid, structured and sequential movements like a machine or robot. The other half is the space for the rubber people — flowing, free and flexible movements without direction, as if you were composed of elastic. Invite the group to explore both extremes through dancing and moving and to switch sides several times. The passage from one side to the other should be noticed carefully. You can use music.[8]

This exercise illustrates the wide range of our body's mutability and adaptability and provides a lively and funny experience of its fluid capacity. People's experiences with both movement sets should be reflected upon verbally afterwards. It is important not to judge; both extremes belong to our body's capabilities, but each will lead to exhaustion if continued for an extended time.

### Stage Four: Going Forth
### Body Resource: Space

Having experienced the fluid capacity and mutability of our bodies, the next stage of the Spiral is *going forth*. New spaces have opened internally and externally, and we can enter these spaces. Therefore I assign the body resource of *space* to the fourth stage of the Spiral. Establishing inner space and orienting in surrounding space enable us to move into every direction. New perspectives and new movements need to be manifested. How can we turn our visions, our intentions and our goals into reality? The field of movement provides many suggestions: we can express our strength and enthusiasm in movement; we can explore going forth with different forms of walking or integrate body exercises for our feet.

Movement is also a good way to prepare transition into daily life. I often facilitate circle dances in this part of the spiral. They offer the opportunity to collect the group energy, to celebrate gratitude and joy and/or to close the workshop harmoniously.

### EXERCISE FOR STAGE FOUR: NOW — VISION — TRANSITION

This movement process provides an interesting combination with Callings and Resources, either as a physical preparation before or an embodied integration after this exercise. It needs a sufficiently large room and people who are to some degree experienced in body perception.

Without music: Invite your participants to express in movement and dance their actual situation, their *now*, including how they are doing, what their lives feel like, what they would like to change.

After about five minutes, ask them to pause and spontaneously find a gesture/short movement that expresses and symbolizes their individual now. Then invite the participants to bring their *visions* into movement and dance — what they want to manifest in their lives, their dreams, goals, their intentions for the Great Turning. Encourage them to allow unlimited, uncensored visions, as if they could realize them through dancing. Again, ask them to pause and to find a gesture/movement that expresses their vision.

In the third round, people are invited to explore the transition between the first and second movements — the passage from *now* to *vision* — and to discover a symbolic gesture/movement. It does not need to be a logical or elaborate piece, but rather a gesture/movement that emerges from one's deeper body wisdom and creativity. Allow people to deepen and repeat this last gesture/movement for integration. As a conclusion, the particular transition movements can be presented to the group.

In conclusion, I would like to stress that movement and body exercises offer many possibilities and benefits in the context of Work

That Reconnects; nevertheless they should be applied carefully! People do not like to be forced to move or dance. Consciously reaching into their own bodies is unfamiliar for many people. As a guide, you should feel comfortable with bodywork yourself — and choose with care the appropriate practices for your group. Even if these exercises might look very simple, they are strong deepeners, and you should be aware of their possible impacts.

Even so, I encourage you to open the Work That Reconnects to the broader field of movement. I invite you to experience on your own how you and others are moved and inspired by embodied Work That Reconnects. I heartily invite everybody to share any comments, feedback and experiences with me!

## REFERENCES

Abram, David. *The Spell of the Sensuous: Perception and Language in a More-Than-Human World*. Pantheon, 1996.

Clinebell, Howard. *Ecotherapy: Healing Ourselves, Healing the Earth*. Augsburg Fortress, 1996.

Gintis, Bonnie. *Engaging the Movement of Life: Exploring Health and Embodiment Through Osteopathy and Continuum*. North Atlantic, 2007.

Hartley, Linda. *Wisdom of the Body Moving: An Introduction to Body-Mind Centering*. North Atlantic, 1995.

Macy, Joanna and Molly Young Brown. *Coming Back to Life: Practices to Reconnect Our Lives, Our World*. New Society, 1998.

Macy, Joanna and Chris Johnstone. *Active Hope: How to Face the Mess We're in without Going Crazy*. New World, 2012.

Olsen, Andrea. *Body and Earth: An Experiential Guide*. Middlebury, 2002.

## Using the Spiral in Writing Workshops

by Louise Dunlap, writing teacher, USA

As I dropped deeper into the Work That Reconnects, it naturally merged with the way I teach writing. After many years in universities especially with graduate students who have social justice and environmental interests, I had learned that the struggle to write — in all its complexity — arises from the domination model imposed through schooling and the other institutions that surround us. Strength and power in writing — even very technical and strategic writing — come from tapping our truest feelings, formulating deeper analyses and reaching out to audiences with empathy. And these are best cultivated in communities of sharing.

The Work That Reconnects, techniques expanded my toolkit for building this kind of community among silenced writers — both students and the many ordinary citizens who want to lend their voices to the Great Turning. Each course (and each session) now begin with *Gratitude*. Using open sentences in partners has been a great way to do what popular educators call "creating safety," while awakening the empowering energy of gratitude at the same time. Or, to get people writing after briefer introductions, I use open sentences focusing on gratitude as free-writing prompts, inviting people to write about what makes them grateful for a particular ancestor or to be alive in these times. (*Free-writing* or spontaneous writing is key to nurturing fluency, self-confidence and eloquence among reluctant writers.) I love inventing original gratitude prompts that come out of my own daily life or experiences my students have mentioned.

*Honoring our Pain for the World* is central in a writing course. Perhaps the single greatest factor in writing blocks is people's fear of what will happen if they tell the whole truth about a challenging topic or show feelings that are seen as weaknesses in the wider world. As soon as I experienced the honesty and eloquence of a Truth Mandala, I knew it belonged in a writing course — followed by plenty of time to write. Sometimes I offer the full version, but often I need to adapt to situations where ritual is not part of classroom culture. Once I moved us to a to a different location and once, when space was limited, I drew the four quadrants on the chalkboard and treated the process as a brainstorm. That night a student passionate about climate change expressed for the first time how she felt about learning that we have passed the tipping point.

The project of *Seeing With New Eyes* is similar to the main teaching of the writing course — that our problems stem from an entire culture that silences our voices and requires systemic change. In the

writing workshop we can recognize this and create our own culture
— based on interconnection, not judgment or top-down critique.
And we can use new discoveries in communication to figure out how
a truth that emerged in protected ritual space can be moved out into
the wider world (perhaps in different form) to shift consciousness,
create new institutions or strengthen holding actions. To help us
imagine how audiences react to our words, I adapt Corbett — with
people in small groups reading their key ideas and hearing responses
from an *ally*, a *doubting reader* (sometimes I make this an adversary) and either a future being or one from the nonhuman world.
In one workshop I watched a woman from South Sudan change her
whole plan for writing about women in peace struggles. The exercise
helped her envision a different audience from the adversarial one she
had imagined. Now she saw that her ideas could really do some good
if she wrote about them for women's groups already active on the
ground.

The *Going Forth* is always important in a writing workshop because our time together only scratches the surface of underlying
habits of silence, and most people want to develop a writing practice
that is sustainable in the long term. My students have thanked me
for setting aside time for a full round of Goals and Resources. I do
this in partners, using as many of the questions as there is time for
and encouraging people to check in together in a month's time. I add
a question about which practices people want to include in their own
writing lives going forward. I'm always thrilled when they decide to
make free-writing on gratitude a daily thing or to start their own
version of a non-judgmental feedback group — these practices in
themselves help reverse the Industrial Growth Society's patterns of
silencing.

Each time I teach, I find more uses for the wonderful ideas and
practices of the spiral and leave my students with more energy for
transforming our world.

— Louise Dunlap is author of *Undoing the Silence*.[9]

# Endnotes

## CHAPTER 1

1. Lester Brown. [online]. [cited July 9, 2014]. [online]. cap-lmu. de/fgz/portals/sustainability/definitions.php.
2. From a poster by Paul Cienfuegos, regional leader of the Community Rights movement. See Community Environmental Legal Defense Fund website. CELDF.org and Paul Cienfuegos. com, both [online]. [cited June 8, 2014].
3. Robinson Jeffers. "The Tower Beyond Tragedy." Tim Hunt, ed. *The Collected Poetry of Robinson Jeffers*, Vol. 1 1920–1928. Stanford, 1988, p. 177.

## CHAPTER 2

1. Shakespeare. *Hamlet*. Act 3, scene 1.
2. Peter Marin. *Freedom and Its Discontents: Reflections on Four Decades of American Moral Experience*. Steerforth, 1995, p. 131.
3. David Orr. "Speed." *The Nature of Design: Ecology, Culture, and Human Intention*. Oxford, 2004, p. 45.
4. Willian Ernest Henley. "Invictus." Arthur Quiller-Couch, ed. *The Oxford Book of English Verse, 1250–1900*. Oxford, 1902, p. 1019.

5. Dr. Robert Murphy, personal communication.

6. Zhiwa Woodbury. "Planetary Hospice — Rebirthing Planet Earth." [online]. [cited June 11, 2014]. workthatreconnects.org/wp-content/uploads/2014/03/Planetary-Hospice.pdf.

7. Anita Barrows. "Psalm." *We Are The Hunger.* Unpublished manuscript, 1998.

## Chapter 3

1. Gregory Bateson. *Steps to an Ecology of Mind: A Revolutionary Approach to Man's Understanding of Himself.* Chandler, 1972, p. 462.

2. Ludwig von Bertalanffy. *General Systems Theory.* Braziller, 1968, p. 12.

3. Bateson, *Steps to an Ecology of Mind,* p. 476.

3a. Norbert Wiener. *The Human Use of Human Beings.* Avon, 1967, p. 130.

4. John Seed, Joanna Macy, Pat Fleming, Arne Naess. *Thinking Like a Mountain: Towards a Council of All Beings.* New Society, 1988, p. 35.

5. Ibid., p. 36.

6. Ibid., p. 20.

7. Llewellyn Vaughan-Lee. *Darkening of the Light: Witnessing the End of an Era.* Golden Sufi Center, 2013.

8. Rabbi Arthur Waskow. "Move Our Money, Protect Our Planet: God, Earth, & Strategy." Shalom Center, February 6, 2014. [online]. [cited June 13, 2014]. theshalomcenter.org/content/move-our-money-protect-our-planet-god-earth-strategy.

9. Ervin Laszlo. *Introduction to Systems Philosophy: Toward a New Paradigm of Contemporary Thought.* Gordon and Breach, 1972, p. 170.

10. Bateson. *Steps to an Ecology of Mind,* p. 319.

11. Kazimierz Dabrowski. *Positive Disintegration.* Little Brown, 1964.

12. Paul Hawken. *Blessed Unrest: How the Largest Social Movement in History Is Restoring Grace, Justice, and Beauty to the World.* Viking, 2007, p. 142.

13. Ibid, pp. 143–144.
14. Unpublished text composed in 1990 by Joanna Macy in collaboration with German colleagues in the Work That Reconnects.

## Chapter 4

1. Ranier Maria Rilke, trans. Joanna Macy and Anita Barrows. *Rilke's Book of Hours: Love Poems to God*. Riverhead, 1996, I, 51.
2. Joanna Macy. *Despair and Personal Power in the Nuclear Age*. New Society, 1983.
3. Joanna Macy and Molly Brown. *Coming Back to Life: Practices to Reconect Our Lives, Our World*. New Society, 1998.
4. Joanna Macy. *World As Lover, World as Self: Courage for Global Justice and Ecological Renewal*, rev. ed. Parallax, 2007.
5. Joanna Macy. *Widening Circles: A Memoir*. New Society, 2001.
6. Joanna Macy and Chris Johnstone. *Active Hope: How to Face the Mess We're in Without Going Crazy*. New World, 2012.

## Chapter 5

1. Doug Hitt, personal communication, March 2014.

## Chapter 6

1. Here's the link for the full story of Joanna and Fran's work in Novozybkov: "The Story of the Elm Dance." Joanna Macy website. [online]. [cited June 17, 2014]. joannamacy.net/theelmdance/55-thestoryoftheelmdance.html.

## Chapter 7

1. Thanks to Kathleen Rude for this variation.
2. Jack Belden. *China Shakes the World*. Monthly Review, 1970, pp. 487–8.
3. Carolyn McDade. *My Heart is Moved*. Carolyn McDade Music, CD, 2007. [online]. [cited June 18, 2014]. carolynmcdademusic.com/heart.html.
4. Adrienne Rich. "My Heart is Moved" from *The Dream of a Common Language: Poems 1974–1977*. Norton, 1978.

## Chapter 8

1. Edward Conze, trans. *The Perfection of Wisdom in Eight Thousand Lines*. Four Seasons, 1973.
2. Adapted from: Julian Edney. "The Nuts Game: A Concise Commons Dilemma Analog." *Environmental Psychology and Nonverbal Behavior*, Vol. 3 (1979), pp. 252–254. [online]. [cited June 19, 2014]. g-r-e-e-d.com/Nuts Game.htm.
3. Bill Johnston. "I Take to Myself." Reprinted with permission of the author.
4. For a narrative of a Council of All Beings, see Seed et al. *Thinking Like A Mountain, pp. 79–90.*
5. *Alberto Ríos. "Who Has Need, I Stand with You." Orion Magazine* (online), May/June 2010. © Alberto Ríos. Used with permission.

## Chapter 9

1. Robert J. Lifton. *The Broken Connection*. Simon and Schuster, 1979, p. 338.
2. Not previously published.
3. Vangelis. *Ignatio*. Barclay/Polygram CD (reissue) #813 042-2, 1990. [online]. [cited June 23, 2014]. amazon.com/Ignacio-Vangelis/dp/B000001F4D.
4. Rosalie Bertell. Personal communication, c. 1991.
5. Macy and Johnstone, *Active Hope*, p. 173.
6. Ibid.
7. Published with permission of Susa Silvermarie. ReVisionary's View website, susasilvermarie.com.

## Chapter 10

1. Justine Willis Toms and Michael Toms. "The Native Genius of Intention" in *True Work: Doing What You Love and Loving What You Do*. Harmony, 1998, p. 112.
2. Macy, *Widening Circles*.
3. Doug Hitt. Unpublished poem, 2008. Used with permission.
4. Rilke, trans. Macy and Barrows, *Rilke's Book of Hours*, I, 59, p. 119.

## Chapter 11

1. Kathleen Rude, Work That Reconnects facilitator. Email to authors, March 2014.
2. Unicef UK website. "Poll: British children concerned by effects of climate change." April 17, 2013. [online]. [cited June 26, 2014]. unicef. org.uk/Latest/News/British-Children-deeply-concerned-by-effects-of-climate-change-/.
3. Suzy Becker. "Helping Little People Cope with the World's Big Problems." *The Center Post,* The Rowe Center, (Fall/Winter 2013–14), p. 15. [online]. [cited June 26, 2014]. rowecenter.org/upload/docs/ROWE-CPFall&Winter2013.pdf.
4. Chivian E. et al. "American and Soviet Teenagers' Concerns about Nuclear War and the Future." *The New England Journal of Medicine,* Vol. 319 #7 (1988), pp. 407–413.
5. Unpublished poem by Molly Lockwood, used with permission.
6. Generation Waking Up website. "Our Story." [online]. [cited June 26, 2014]. generationwakingup.org/about/story.
7. Ibid.
8. Eva Schilcher. Email to authors, February 2014.
9. Suggested by Robert Croonquist in "From Hero to Human," an unpublished manuscript.
10. Megan Toben of Pickards Mountain Eco-Institute in North Carolina. Email to authors, March, 2014.
11. Adapted by Pam Wood from Joseph Cornell. *Sharing Nature with Children II.* Dawn, 1999.
12. Toben, email to authors.
13. Created by Pam Wood.
14. Elizabeth Koelsch-Inderst. Email to authors, February 2014.
15. Schilcher, email to authors.
16. Adapted by Sheri Prud'homme from Seed et al, *Thinking Like a Mountain,* p. 57.
17. Thanks to Sheri Prud'homme for this story and ritual.
18. This story can be found in: Loren Eiseley. *The Unexpected Universe.* Harvest, 1972 or Loren Eiseley. *The Star Thrower.* Harvest, 1979.

## Chapter 12

1. Adelaja Simon. Email to author, February 2013.
2. Salina Espinosa-Secthko. Letter to author, 2014.
3. Sharon Kuehn and Joanna Aguirre. "Reconnect! An Ecological Framework for Social Inclusion, Wellness and Sustainable Communities." Teaching poster from Wellness Recovery Educators.
4. Aries Jordan. Quoted with permission of author. Published on her website: journey2womanhood.tumblr.com/page/3.
5. Monica K. Moss. "Meaning making is the challenge of cultural competency" in Patricia St. Onge et al. *Embracing Cultural Competency: A Roadmap for Nonprofit Capacity Builders.* Fieldstone Alliance, 2009, p. 49.
6. Joy Degruy-Leary. *Post Traumatic Slave Syndrome: America's Legacy of Enduring Injury and Healing.* Uptone, 2005, p. 49.
7. White Awake website. [online]. [cited June 28, 2014]. whiteawake. org.
8. St. Onge, *Embracing Cultural Competency.*
9. Author's notes from the People of Color Caucus at the Alliance for Nonprofit Management Annual Conference in Houston Texas, 2003.
10. Martin Luther King Jr. "Where Do We Go From Here?" Speech delivered at the 11th Annual SCLC Convention, Atlanta, Georgia, August 1967. [online]. [cited July 11, 2014]. http://mlk-kpp01. stanford.edu/index.php/encyclopedia/documentsentry/ where_do_we_go_from_here_delivered_at_the_11th_annual_ sclc_convention/.

## Chapter 13

1. John Seed and Joanna Macy. From Seed et al. *Thinking Like a Mountain,* pp. 41–43.
2. Conze, trans. *The Perfection of Wisdom in Eight Thousand Lines.*
3. "UN Environmental Sabbath Program" in Elizabeth Roberts and Elias Amidon, eds. *Earth Prayers From Around the World: 365 Prayers, Poems, and Invocations for Honoring the Earth.* Harper, 1991, pp. 70–71.

4. Rev. Daniel Martin. "We Journey Together" in Elizabeth Roberts and Elias Amidon, eds. *Prayers for a Thousand Years*. Harper, 2010, pp. 246–7.

## APPENDIX C

1. Macy, *Widening Circles*, Chapter 23 "The Poison Fire."
2. Joanna Macy. "Nuclear Guardianship Ethic." [online]. [cited July 1, 2014]. joannamacy.net/nuclear-guardianship-ethic.html.
3. Global Alliance for the Rights of Nature. [online]. [cited July 1, 2014]. TheRightsofNature.org; Rights of Mother Earth. [online].. [cited July 1, 2014]. rightsofmotherearth.com.
4. Rights of Mother Earth. "Ecuador Rights of Nature." [online]. [cited July 1, 2014]. rightsofmotherearth.com/ecuador-rights-nature/.
5. United Nations. *Harmony with Nature*. [online]. [cited July 1, 2014]. harmonywithnatureun.org.
6. Global Alliance for the Rights of Nature. *Universal Declaration of Rights of Mother Earth*. [online]. [cited July 1, 2014]. http://therightsofnature.org/universal-declaration/.
7. Taken from the initial program for the first Congress held in Moab in September 2012.
8. For current versions of the Declaration and supplementary material, please see these websites: Future First. FutureFirst.us; Women's Congress for Future Generations. "Living Draft of the Declaration of the Rights Held by Future Generations." wcffg. org/declarationfortherightsoffuturegenerations.cfm; Northern California Circle of the Women's Congress for Future Generations. norcalwcffg.blogspot.com/; Toward a Declaration of the Rights Held by Future Generations. "Resources." celebratewcffg.wordpress.com/resources-2/; Science and Environmental Health Network. "Guardianship of Future Generations." sehn.org/guardianship-of-future-generations/. All citations [online]. [cited July 1, 2014].

## APPENDIX D

1. Barbara Hundshammer. email: bahu@zibko.de, website: zibko. de.

2. Susan Harper. Continuum Montage. [online]. [cited July 1, 2014]. continuummontage.com.

3. David Abram. *The Spell of the Sensuous: Perception and Language in a More-Than-Human World.* Pantheon, 1996, p. 268.

4. Joanna Macy and Molly Young Brown. *Coming Back to Life: Practices to Reconnect Our Lives, Our World.* New Society, 1998, p. 59.

5. Joanna Macy, oral recording, 2009.

6. Bonnie Gintis. *Engaging the Movement of Life: Exploring Health and Embodiment Through Osteopathy and Continuum.* North Atlantic, 2007, p. 132.

7. Ibid., p. 23.

8. For example: Andreas Vollenweider. *Dancing with the Lion.* Audio CD. Sony, 2009, track 2 "Dancing with The Lion."

9. Louise Dunlap. *Undoing the Silence: Six Tools for Social Change Writing.* New Village Press, 2007. website: undoingsilence.org. [online]. [cited July 2, 2014].

# Resources

## The Work That Reconnects

Macy, Joanna and Chris Johnstone. *Active Hope: How to Face the Mess We're in without Going Crazy.* New World, 2012.[i]

Macy, Joanna and Norbert Gahbler. *Pass It On: Five Stories That Can Change the World.* Parallax, 2010.[i]

Reason, Peter and Melanie Newman, eds. Foreword by Joanna Macy. *Stories of the Great Turning.* Vala, 2013.

Seed, John, Joanna Macy, Pat Fleming and Arne Naess. *Thinking Like a Mountain: Towards a Council of All Beings.* New Society, 1988.

## Websites

Work That Reconnects network: WorkThatReconnects.org

Active Hope: ActiveHope.info

Great Turning Times newsletter: www.facilitationforlifeonearth.org/great-turning-times.html

---

[i.] Available in translation. Check workthatreconnects.org or JoannaMacy.net for languages and ordering information.

Songs for the Great Turning: songsfortheGreatTurning.net

JoannaMacytrainingvideos:univ-great-turning.org/study-areas-by-person/joanna-macy/

Vimeo Channel: vimeo.com/channels/workthatreconnects

Facilitation for Life on Earth, UK: facilitationforlifeonearth.org/
Roseaux Dansants, France: Roseaux-Dansants.org

Society for Applied Deep Ecology, Germany: holoninstitut.de;
tiefenoekologie.de

Terr'Eveille, Belgium: terreveille.be

Interhelp Network: interhelpnetwork.org

The Cooperative University of the Great Turning: univ-great-turning.
org

Joanna Macy's website: JoannaMacy.net

Molly Brown's website: MollyYoungBrown.com

## TRANSFORMING THE FOUNDATIONS OF OUR COMMON LIFE

Alexander, Michelle. *The New Jim Crow: Mass Incarceration in the Age of Colorblindness.* New Press, 2012.

Alperovitz, Gar. *America Beyond Capitalism: Reclaiming Our Wealth, Our Liberty, & Our Democracy.* 2nd ed. Democracy Collaborative & Dollars and Sense, 2011.

Benyus, Janine M. *Biomimicry: Innovations Inspired by Nature.* Harper, 1997.

Brown, Ellen Hodgson, JD. *The Web of Debt: The Shocking Truth about Our Money System and How We Can Break Free,* 5th ed. Third Millenium, 2012.

Brown, Lester. *Full Planet, Empty Plates: The New Geopolitics of Food Scarcity.* Norton, 2012.

Crozier-Hogle, Lois and Darryl Babe Wilson, J. Leibold, ed. *Surviving in Two Worlds: Contemporary Native American Voices.* University of Texas, 1997.

Cullinan, Cormac. *Wild Law: A Manifesto for Earth Justice,* 2nd ed. Chalsea Green, 2011.

Dawson, Jonathan, Ross Jackson and Helena Norberg-Hodge, eds. *Gaian Economics: Living Well with Planetary Limits.* Permanent Publications, 2010.

Douglass, James W. *JFK and the Unspeakable: Why He Died and Why It Matters.* Touchstone, 2010.

Dreier, Peter. *The 100 Greatest Americans of the 20th Century: A Social Justice Hall of Fame.* Nation, 2012.

Eisenstein, Charles. *Sacred Economics: Money, Gift, and Society in the Age of Transition.* Evolver, 2011.

Gershon, David. *Social Change 2.0: A Blueprint for Reinventing Our World.* High Point, 2009.

Greenwald, Glenn. *No Place to Hide: Edward Snowden, the NSA, and the US Security State.* Metropolitan, 2014.

Hawken, Paul. *Blessed Unrest: How the Largest Movement in the World Came into Being and Why No One Saw It Coming.* Viking, 2007.

Heinberg, Richard. *The End of Growth: Adapting to Our New Economic Reality.* New Society, 2011.

Heinberg, Richard and Daniel Lerch, eds. *Post Carbon Reader: Managing the 21st Century's Sustainability Crises.* Post Carbon Institute, 2010.

Hopkins, Rob. *Transition Handbook: From Oil Dependency to Local Resilience.* Green Books, 2008.

Hopkins, Rob. *The Power of Just Doing Stuff: How Local Action Can Change the World.* Green Books, 2014.

Johnstone, Chris. *Find Your Power: A Toolkit for Resilience and Positive Change.* Permanent Publications, 2010.

Klein, Naomi. *The Shock Doctrine: The Rise of Disaster Capitalism.* Penguin, 2007.

Korten, David. *When Corporations Rule the World,* 2nd ed. Berrett-Koehler, 2001.

Korten, David. *The Great Turning: From Empire to Earth Community.* Kumarian Press, 2006

Kropotkin, Peter. *Mutual Aid: A Factor of Evolution.* 1902, reprint Forgotten Books, 2008.

Jensen, Robert. *We're All Apocalyptic Now: On the Responsibilities of Teaching, Preaching, Reporting, Writing, and Speaking Out.* Monkey Wrench, 2013.

Jensen, Robert. *The Heart of Whiteness: Confronting Race, Racism, and White Privilege.* City Lights Books, 2005.

Litfin, Karen T. *Ecovillages: Lessons for Sustainable Community*. Polity, 2014.

Mandela, Nelson. *A Long Walk to Freedom: The Autobiography of Nelson Mandela*. Little Brown, 1995.

Mander, Jerry. *The Capitalism Papers: Fatal Flaws of an Obsolete System*. Counterpoint, 2012.

Mander, Jerry. *In the Absence of the Sacred: The Failure of Technology & the Survival of the Indian Nations*. Sierra Club, 1991.

McKibben, Bill. *Eaarth: Making a Life on a Tough New Planet*. Times, 2010.

Moser, Suzanne C. "Getting Real About It: Meeting the Psychological and Social Demands of a World is Distress" in Deborah R. Gallagher, ed. *Environmental Leadership: A Reference Handbook*, Sage, 2012.

Orr, David. *Earth in Mind: On Education, Environment, and the Human Prospect*. Island, 2004.

Parker, Rebecca. "Not Somewhere Else, But Here" in Marjorie Bowens-Wheatley and Nancy Palmer Jones, eds. *Soul Work: Anti-Racist Theologies in Dialogue*. Skinner House, 2002.

Patel, Raj. *Stuffed and Starved: The Hidden Battle for the World Food System*, 2nd ed. Melville House, 2012.

Pavel, M. Paloma, ed. *Breakthrough Communities: Sustainability and Justice in the Next American Metropolis*. Massachusetts Institute of Technology, 2009.

Peavey, Fran. *By Life's Grace: Musings on the Essence of Social Change*. New Society, 1993.

Reich, Robert. *Beyond Outrage: What has Gone Wrong with Our Economy and Our Democracy, and How to Fix It*. Vintage, 2012.

Robbins, John and Ocean Robbins. *Voices of the Food Revolution: You Can Heal Your Body and Your World with Food!* Conari, 2013.

Shiva, Vandana. *Making Peace with the Earth: Beyond Resource, Land and Food Wars*. St. Martin's Press, 2012.

Solnit, Rebecca. *A Paradise Built in Hell: The Extraordinary Communities That Arise in Disaster*. Penguin, 2010.

Steingraber, Sandra. *Raising Elijah: Protecting Our Children in an Age of Environment Crisis*. Da Capo Press, 2013.

St. Onge, Patricia et al. *Embracing Cultural Competency: A Roadmap for Nonprofit Capacity Builders*. Fieldstone Alliance, 2009.

Wheatley, Margaret and Deborah Frieze. *Walk Out Walk On: A Learning Journey into Communities Daring to Live the Future Now*. Berrett-Koehler, 2011.

Worldwatch Institute. *State of the World, 2013: Is Sustainability Still Possible?* Worldwatch Institute, 2013.

### JOURNALS, ORGANIZATIONS AND WEBSITES

Beyond Nuclear: beyondnuclear.org

Bioneers: bioneers.org

Community Environmental Legal Defense Fund: CELDF.org

Climate Parents: climateparents.org

Dahr Jamail's monthly "Climate Disruption Dispatches" for Truth-out.org: DahrJamail.net

The Earth Charter Initiative: earthcharterinaction.org

Earth Island Journal, Earth Island Institute: earthisland.org

Earth Law Center: EarthLawCenter.org

Ecological Options Network: eon3.net

Eradicating Ecocide Global Initiative: eradicatingecocide.com

Fairewinds Energy Education: fairewinds.org

Findhorn Foundation, Scotland: findhorn.org

Global Exchange: globalexchange.org

Institute for Energy and Environmental Research: ieer.org

Living Economies Forum with David Korten: Livingeconomiesforum.org

Mothers for Peace: mothersforpeace.org

The Nation magazine: thenation.com

New Society Publishers: newsociety.com

Nuclear Guardianship Library: www.NoNukes.org: univ-great-turning.org/nuclear-guardianship

Nuclear Information and Resource Service: nirs.org

ONEarth Magazine: Environmental Health, Science, and Policy: onearth.com

100Fires bookstore, "Extraordinary books for a healthy planet": 100Fires.com

Orion magazine: orionmagazine.org
Permaculture Magazine: permaculture.co.uk
Positive Futures Network & YES! Magazine: yesmagazine.org
Positive News: positivenewsus.org
Post Carbon Institute: postcarbon.org
Science and Environmental Health Network: sehn.org
Survival International: survivalinternational.org
Dr.Vandana Shiva: navdanya.org
Transition Towns: transitionnetwork.org, transitionus.org
Waging Nonviolence: wagingnonviolence.org
Women's Earth Alliance: womensearthalliance.org
Worldwatch Institute: worldwatch.org

## SHIFT IN PERCEPTION AND VALUES

Abram, David. *The Spell of the Sensuous: Perception and Language in a More-Than-Human World.* Pantheon, 1996.

Akwesasne Notes. *Basic Call to Consciousness.* Native Voices, 1991.

Baker, Carolyn. *Sacred Demise: Walking the Spiritual Path of Industrial Civilization's Collapse.* iUniverse, 2009.

Berry, Thomas. *Evening Thoughts: Reflecting on Earth As Sacred Community.* Sierra Club, 2006.

Brown, Molly Young. *Growing Whole: Self-Realization for the Great Turning.* Psychosynthesis Press, 2009.

Buzzel, Linda and Craig Chalquist. *Ecotherapy: Healing with Nature in Mind.* Sierra Club, 2009.

Fox, Matthew. *The Coming of the Cosmic Christ: The Healing of Mother Earth and the Birth of a Global Renaissance.* Harper, 1988.

Fox, Matthew. *Original Blessings: A Primer in Creation Spirituality.* Bear & Company, 1983.

Griffin, Susan. *Woman and Nature: The Roaring Inside Her.* Sierra Club, 2000.

Gottlieb, Roger S., ed. *This Sacred Earth: Religion, Nature, Environment.* Routledge, 1996.

Kaza, Stephanie. *Mindfully Green: A Personal and Spiritual Guide to Whole Earth Thinking.* Shambhala, 2008.

Kaza, Stephanie and Kenneth Kraft, eds. *Dharma Rain: Sources of Buddhist Environmentalism.* Shambhala, 2000.

Kaza, Stephanie, ed. *Hooked: Buddhist Writings on Greed, Desire, and the Urge to Consume.* Shambhala, 2005.

Lappe, Frances Moore. *EcoMind: Changing the Way We Think, to Create the World We Want.* Nation, 2011.

LaDuke, Winona. *All Our Relations: Native Struggles for Land and Life.* South End, 1999.

LaDuke, Winona. *Recovering the Sacred: The Power of Naming and Claiming.* South End, 2005.

Le Guin, Ursula K. *Always Coming Home.* Bantam, 1985.

Leighton, Taigen Daniel. *Bodhisattva Archetypes: Classic Buddhist Guides to Awakening and their Modern Expression.* Penguin, 1998.

Loy, David R. *Money, Sex, War, Karma: Notes for a Buddhist Revolution.* Wisdom, 2008.

Loy, David R. *The Great Awakening: A Buddhist Social Theory.* Wisdom, 2003.

Macy, Joanna. *World as Lover, World as Self: Courage for Global Justice and Ecological Renewal.* Parallax, 2007.

Macy, Joanna. *Dharma and Development: Religion as Resource in the Sarvodaya Self-help Movement.* Kumarian, 1985.

Neihardt, John G. *Black Elk Speaks.* University of Nebraska, 1961.

Nhat Hanh, Thich. *Interbeing: 14 Guidelines for Engaged Buddhism.* Parallax, 1993.

Nhat Hanh, Thich. *The Sun My Heart.* Parallax, 1988.

Nisker, Wes. *Buddha's Nature: A Practical Guide to Discovering Your Place in the Cosmos.* Bantam, 1998.

Plotkin, Bill. *Nature and the Human Soul: Cultivating Wholeness and Community in a Fragmented World.* New World Library, 2007.

Porter, Tom (Sakokwenionkwas). *And Grandma Said... — Iroquois Teachings as passed down through the oral tradition.* ExLibris, 2008.

Roszak, Theodore. *The Voice of the Earth.* Simon & Schuster, 1992.

Roszak, Theodore, Mary Gomes and Allen D. Kanner, eds. *Ecopsychology: Restoring the Earth, Healing the Mind.* Sierra Club, 1995.

Sartor, Linda. *Turning Fear into Power: One Woman's Journey Confronting the War on Terror.* Psychosynthesis Press, 2014.

Shepard, Paul. *Nature and Madness.* Sierra Club, 1982.

Snyder, Gary. *The Practice of the Wild.* North Point, 1990.

Stamets, Paul. *Mycelium Running: How Mushrooms Can Help Save the World.* Ten Speed, 2005.

Swimme, Brian and Thomas Berry. *The Universe Story: From the Primordial Flaring Forth to the Ecozoic Era — A Celebration of the Unfolding of the Cosmos.* Harper, 1992.

Vaughan-Lee, Llewellyn, ed. *Spiritual Ecology: The Cry of the Earth.* Golden Sufi Center, 2013.

## JOURNALS, ORGANIZATIONS AND WEBSITES

Buddhist Peace Fellowship: buddhistpeacefellowship.org

Clear View Project (Buddhist-based resources for social change): clearviewproject.org

Ecological Buddhism: ecobuddhism.org

Eco-Chaplaincy Initiative: ecochaplaincy.net

Genesis Farm (fostering Earth literacy): genesisfarm.org

Global Alliance for the Rights of Nature: TheRightsofNature.org; RightsofMotherEarth.com

Metta Center for Nonviolence: mettacenter.org

The Pachamama Alliance (Awakening the Dreamer): pachamama. org

Radical Joy for Hard Times: radicaljoyforhardtimes.org

Sarvodaya Sharmadana Movement: sarvodaya.org

Shalom Center with Rabbi Arthur Waskow: theshalomcenter.org

What's Your Tree? with Julia Butterfly Hill: whatsyourtree.org

White Awake: whiteawake.org

Women's Congress for the Rights of Future Generations: FutureFirst. us; wcffg.org

## SYSTEMS THINKING

Bateson, Gregory. *Steps to an Ecology of Mind: Collected Essays in Anthropology, Psychiatry, Evolution, and Epistemology.* 1987, reprint University of Chicago Press, 1999.

Charlton, Noel G. *Understanding Gregory Bateson: Mind, Beauty, and the Sacred Earth*. SUNY, 2008.

Laszlo, Ervin. *Introduction to Systems Philosophy. Toward a New Paradigm of Contemporary Thought*. Gordon & Breach, 1972.

Laszlo, Ervin. *The Connectivity Hypothesis: Foundations of an Integral Science of Quantum, Cosmos, Life, and Consciousness*. SUNY, 2003.

LaConte, Ellen. *Life Rules: Nature's Blueprint for Surviving Economic and Environmental Collapse*. New Society, 2012.

Macy, Joanna. *Mutual Causality in Buddhism and General Systems Theory: The Dharma of Natural Systems*. SUNY, 1991.

Meadows, Donella, Jorgen Randers and Dennis Meadows. *Limits to Growth: The 30-Year Update*. Chelsea Green, 2004.

Rivers, Dennis. "Nine important implications of systems/chaos/complexity theory for our lives." April 29, 2014 — univ-great-turning.org/library/nine-important-implications.pdf

Sahtouris, Elizabet. *EarthDance: Living Systems in Evolution*. iUniverse, 2000

Sweeny, Linda Booth. *Connected Wisdom: Living Stories About Living Systems*. Chelsea Green, 2008.

## POETRY, STORY AND RESOURCES FOR RITUAL

*Along with vast numbers of poets and all spiritual traditions:*

Brown, Molly, ed. *Lighting a Candle: Collected Reflections on a Spiritual Life*. Psychosynthesis Press, 2010.

Brown, Molly Y. and Carolyn W. Treadway, eds. *Held in Love: Life Stories to Inspire Us through Times of Change*. Psychosynthesis Press, 2009.

Dellenger, Drew. *Love Letter to the Milky Way: A Book of Poems*. White Cloud, 2011.

Flynn, Carolyn Brigit, ed. *Sisters Singing: Blessings, Prayers, Art, Songs, Poetry & Sacred Stories by Women*. Wild Girl, 2009.

Musawa, ed. *In the Spirit of We'Moon: Celebrating 30 Years*. MotherTongue, 2011.

Rilke, Ranier Maria, trans. Joanna Macy and Anita Barrows. *Rilke's Book of Hours: Love Poems to God*. Riverhead, 1996.

Rilke, Ranier Maria, trans. Joanna Macy and Anita Barrows. *In Praise of Mortality: Selections from Rainer Maria Rilke's Duino Elegies and Sonnets to Orpheus.* Riverhead, 2005.

Roberts, Elizabeth and Elias Amidon, eds. *Earth Prayers from around the World: 365 Prayers, Poems, and Invocations for Honoring the Earth.* Harper, 1991.

Roberts, Elizabeth and Elias Amidon, eds. *Prayers for a Thousand Years.* Harper, 1999.

Rumi, Jalal al-Din, trans. Coleman Barks with John Moyne. *The Essential Rumi.* Harper, 1995.

## Facilitating Groups and Workshops

Lakey, George. *Facilitating Group Learning: Strategies for Success with Adult Learners.* Jossey-Bass, 2010.

Stanfield, R. Brian. *The Workshop Book: From Individual Creativity to Group Action.* New Society, 2002.

Starhawk. *The Empowerment Manual: A Guide for Collaborative Groups.* New Society, 2011.

Taylor, Peggy and Charlie Murphy. *Catch the Fire: An Art-full Guide to Unleashing the Creative Power of Youth, Adults and Communities.* New Society, 2014.

Weston, Anthony. *How to Re-Imagine the World: A Pocket Guide for Practical Visionaries.* New Society, 2007.

## Working with Children, Teens and Young People

Cornell, Joseph. *Sharing Nature with Children II.* Dawn, 1999.

Faber, Adele and Elaine Mazlish. *How to Talk So Kids Will Listen and Listen So Kids Will Talk.* 1980, reprint Avon, 1999.

Sartor, Linda and Molly Brown. *Consensus in the Classroom: Creating a Lively, Learning Community.* Psychosynthesis Press, 2004.

Sobel, David. *Beyond Ecophobia: Reclaiming the Heart in Nature Education.* Orion Society, 1999.

Sobel, David. "Beyond Ecophobia." YES! Magazine, November 2, 1998. [online]. [cited July 6, 2014]. yesmagazine.org/issues/education-for-life/803.

Sullivan, Kathleen and Peter Lucas. *Action for Disarmament: 10*

*Things You Can Do!* United Nations, 2014.

Young, Jon, Evan McGown and Ellen Haas. *Coyote's Guide to Connecting with Nature*, 2nd ed. Owlink Media, 2010.

## WEBSITES

Be the Change Earth Alliance, Student Leadership: bethechangeearthalliance.org

Climate Classroom, National Wildlife Federation: Climateclassroom.org

Generation Waking Up "Igniting a generation of young people to bring forth a thriving, just, sustainable world": generationwakingup.org

United Nations Cyber School Bus, with classroom toolkit: cyberschoolbus.un.org

## CURRICULA FOR STUDY ACTION GROUPS

Be the Change Earth Alliance, Community Movement, Action Circles: bethechangeearthalliance.org

Ethics for a New Millennium Study Circle: dalailamafoundation.org/programs/study-circles

Local Futures — International Society for Ecology and Culture, Roots of Change Study Circle Program: localfutures.org/study-circle-program

Northwest Earth Institute, eight discussion courses: nwei.org

Resilience Circles: localcircles.org

Women's International League for Peace and Freedom (WILPF), "Challenging Corporate Power, Asserting the People's Rights" study course: wilpf.org/CPOWER_10sessions

# Index

# Acknowledgments

The Work That Reconnects is by nature a collaborative effort; each occasion to teach and lead a practice brings a companionable sense of all who shaped it and lets themselves be shaped by it. This stems in large part from the initial decision to offer it as an open-source body of work. Some faces and names are blurred by the years, yet there's ever that sense of resonance with other lives — like entering a river with many tributaries or joining a pilgrim's path made by many walkers with their own songs and burdens.

Across the 16 years since the first edition of *Coming Back to Life*, we coauthors have received continual and vital support in our efforts to describe and document the Work That Reconnects.

For their inspiring and supportive presence in our lives, we thank our husbands: Jim Brown and, until his death in 2009, Fran Macy. For essential and steady assistance to Joanna we thank Doug Mosel (seven years of service) and Anne Symens-Bucher, who succeeded him (nine years and counting). Anne brings the added blessing of Canticle Farm, cofounded with her husband Terry, as a demonstration of Franciscan generosity and a base for the Work That Reconnects. Endless thanks as well to America Worden for her diligent support in fielding and responding to emails.

For their agreement to serve as Stewards and give counsel on continuing the Work That Reconnects in the period after Fran Macy's passing, we are grateful to Barbara Ford, Kurt Kuhwald, Randy Morris, Chad Morse, Coleen O'Connell, Kathleen Rude and Kari Stettler.

We are grateful to Werner Brandt for creating and managing the WorkThatReconnects.org website and to Dennis Rivers for his wisdom and assistance in the use of open-source technology.

Ongoing inspiration and stimulation have been coming across the planet from countries where the Work That Reconnects took root 30 years ago. We owe a lot to the energy and creativity of our friends of the Gesellschaft für Angewandte Teifen Ökologie in Germany, including Gunter and Barbara Hamburger, Gabi Bott, Norbert Gahbler, Marliese Keppler, Helmut Czekalla, Geseko von Lüpke, Sarah Metzger and their offspring who grew up with this work.

A generation of colleagues in the UK have tested and grown this work as well as modeled new ways of outreach and training. We owe special thanks to Chris Johnstone for his enormous contributions as trainer, networker and editor of the online newsletter, *Great Turning Times*. *Active Hope*, which he coauthored with Joanna, generated insights important to this book. We thank Hanna Morjan, Gill Emslie and Jane Hera for their support and facilitation of the work at Findhorn Foundation in Scotland.

Immeasurable thanks to our colleagues in Australia and New Zealand for their rare contributions to the spirit of this work. Much has flowed from the groundbreaking 30-day Seeds for the Future retreat in 2005; John Croft, Bobby Allan and Jo Vallentine are among the many whom we thank for that generative journey. And for creative adventures with John Seed across 30 years, especially evident in Chapters 3, 8 and 13, we are grateful beyond words.

To Claire Carré we offer thanks for bringing the Work That Reconnects into France and initially Belgium, for the genesis of the Roseaux Dansants network and for her remarkable capacity to enrich the work with dance, drama and movement.

For their written contributions to Chapter 12: Learning with Communities of Color, we are grateful to Patricia St. Onge, Adelaja

Simon, Adrián Villaseñor Galarza, Andrés Thomas Conteris and Andrea Avila.

For the ideas and practices they contributed to Chapter 11: The Work That Reconnects with Children and Teens, we want to thank Pam Wood, America Worden, Megan Toben, Ruth Burnett, Anna Mae Grimm, Kathleen Rude, Dianne Monroe, Emily Ryan, Salina Espinoza-Setchko, Dave Spitzer, Gretchen Sleicher, Simone Lipscomb, Eva Schilcher, Elizabeth Koelsch-Inderst and Sheri Prud'homme.

Heartfelt thanks to Barbara Hundshammer and Louise Dunlap for describing their distinctive uses of the Work That Reconnects in Appendix D.

Thanks to Paul Cienfuegos for the clarity he brought to understanding the role of the community rights movement in the Great Turning. Thanks to Kim Bizzarri for urging us to explore more deeply the challenges of bringing the work into corporate settings. Thanks as well to Dahr Jamail for helping us to see the fragmenting effects of electronic media on people's thinking and concentration, in what we call "hijacked attention."

Gratitude to all who helped us draw out the contemporary political relevance of the Buddha's teachings. These include the Sarvodaya Movement in Sri Lanka — with its strong counsel to "trust the intelligence of the people" and to "start with the children" — and the "Think Sangha" of the International Network of Engaged Buddhists, along with David Loy's excellent articulation of the institutionalized forms of greed, hatred and delusion.

Thanks to our colleagues who draw on the Work That Reconnects to help people see and respond to the suicidal import of nuclear weapons and nuclear power. They include, among many others, Kathleen Sullivan, Linda Seeley, Johannes Philpp, Jonathan Watts, Mary Olson, Marylia Kelley, Mary Beth Brangan and Arnie Gunderson, along with LeRoy Moore, Judith Mohling and Christopher Hormel of the Rocky Flats Guardians.

We are grateful to the Interhelp network for the faithful and creative ways they are carrying the work forward on the East Coast. We coauthors first met at an Interhelp gathering in California in 1987.

We thank Dori Midnight for her exquisite dandelion drawing of the Spiral, which she made in minutes at a workshop in Guelph, Ontario. Gratitude for Anita Barrows for her poem concluding Chapter 2 as well as the many passages from Rainer Marie Rilke that she translated with Joanna.

We thank Carolyn Raffensperger of the Science and Environmental Health Network for her leadership in bringing forth the Precautionary Principle and the Women's Congress for Future Generations. We have also been inspired by the movement for the Rights of Nature and of Mother Earth.

We are grateful for filmmakers who bring the Work That Reconnects to a broader audience, including Leo Daedalus for the training DVDs, Chris Landry for *Joanna Macy and the Great Turning*, and Jörg Röttger and Leander von Kraft of Neue-Weltsight, Potsdam for their 7 DVD set in German and English made at a 2013 intensive. We thank Paloma Pavel and Richard Page for generously and faithfully recording numerous workshops and presentations through the years.

Last but not least, we thank the good people of New Society Publishers who believe in this work and have published the three defining books about it, as well as Joanna's autobiography, *Widening Circles: A Memoir*.

# About the Authors

## Joanna Macy

*Joanna Macy*
ADAM SHEMPER

JOANNA MACY, eco-philosopher, activist and scholar of Buddhism and systems theory, has an international following thanks to 50 years in movements for civil rights, global justice and ecological sanity. Her 12 books include *Coming Back to Life, Widening Circles: A Memoir* and translations of the poetry of Rainer Marie Rilke. Her two-DVD set, titled *The Work That Reconnects*, demonstrates the group work featured in this book. She lives in Berkeley, California close to her children and grandchildren.

## Molly Young Brown

MOLLY YOUNG BROWN combines the Work That Reconnects, ecopsychology and psychosynthesis in her work: teaching online courses, writing and publishing books and essays, coaching and mentoring and giving talks and workshops internationally. Her five books include *Coming Back to Life* and *Growing Whole: Self-realization for the Great Turning*. She lives in Mount Shasta, California with her life partner Jim Brown.

*Molly Young Brown*
JILL GARDNER

If you have enjoyed *Coming Back to Life* you might also enjoy other

# BOOKS TO BUILD A NEW SOCIETY

Our books provide positive solutions for people who want to
make a difference. We specialize in:

**Sustainable Living • Green Building • Peak Oil
Renewable Energy • Environment & Economy
Natural Building & Appropriate Technology
Progressive Leadership • Resistance and Community
Educational & Parenting Resources**

---

## New Society Publishers

### ENVIRONMENTAL BENEFITS STATEMENT

New Society Publishers has chosen to produce this book on recycled paper made
with **100% post consumer waste**, processed chlorine free, and old growth free.

For every 5,000 books printed, New Society saves the following resources:[1]

| | |
|---:|---|
| 37 | Trees |
| 3,366 | Pounds of Solid Waste |
| 3,704 | Gallons of Water |
| 4,831 | Kilowatt Hours of Electricity |
| 6,120 | Pounds of Greenhouse Gases |
| 26 | Pounds of HAPs, VOCs, and AOX Combined |
| 9 | Cubic Yards of Landfill Space |

---

[1]Environmental benefits are calculated based on research done by the Environmental Defense Fund
and other members of the Paper Task Force who study the environmental impacts of the paper
industry.

---

*For a full list of NSP's titles, please call* 1-800-567-6772 *or check out our website at:*

**www.newsociety.com**

new society
PUBLISHERS